The Fundamentals of Animation

Paul Wells

This book is dedicated to my wife Jo and my children, Freddie and Lola, to the memory of John Grace and to all the animators and artists who have brought the world to life.

How to Get the Most from this Book

Main Text
The main text of this book is written in a way that is divided up into relevant headings indicating the key points and ideas throughout. The author's own writing seeks to add continuity and perspective, and provide a main authorial 'voice', but the main intention is that the book is 'multi-voiced'. It draws upon the views of professional practitioners, artists, students and scholars, who all contribute particular kinds of relevant expertise and experience. This means that you can learn from the most established and renowned figures, as well as industry stalwarts, your peers, and up-and-coming individuals working in the field, just like you. Largely, the main text discusses general issues and concepts, while the captioned images and various kinds of box outs throughout the book address specific points or engage with particular skills and knowledge. You can 'dip' into various sections, or read continuously – it is up to you.

Captions
Captions will provide you with information on the image you are seeing, its source and its creator. Further, additional observational, critical or analytical material will be added so the image does not just serve as a piece of illustration, but makes a point or suggests an idea that might be significant. While having many images, this is not a picture book. Learn from images – don't merely view them.

Core Skills Box Outs
Where the 'Core Skills' boxes appear, there is a summation of practical hints and techniques, and some suggestions about further study or investment. These box outs normally indicate the key elements of what you need to be good at if you are to succeed in a particular aspect of animation practice.

Tutorial Box Outs
These more extended box outs usually concern particular techniques and approaches as an exemplar of practice, or as an idea of what a student can expect in certain contexts and situations. They are sometimes written by other experts in the field, consulted for their particular insights and advice about an area of work.

Historical Context and Box Outs
In Section Two, brief histories of Drawn and Cel Animation, 3D Stop-motion Animation, Digital Animation and Alternative Methods are provided in order that you can gain an understanding of the history and context of working techniques. Also included are box outs taking up some key concepts and ideas that arise from the histories, and are worth considering as issues for debate, or as aspects to enhance your thinking about practice.

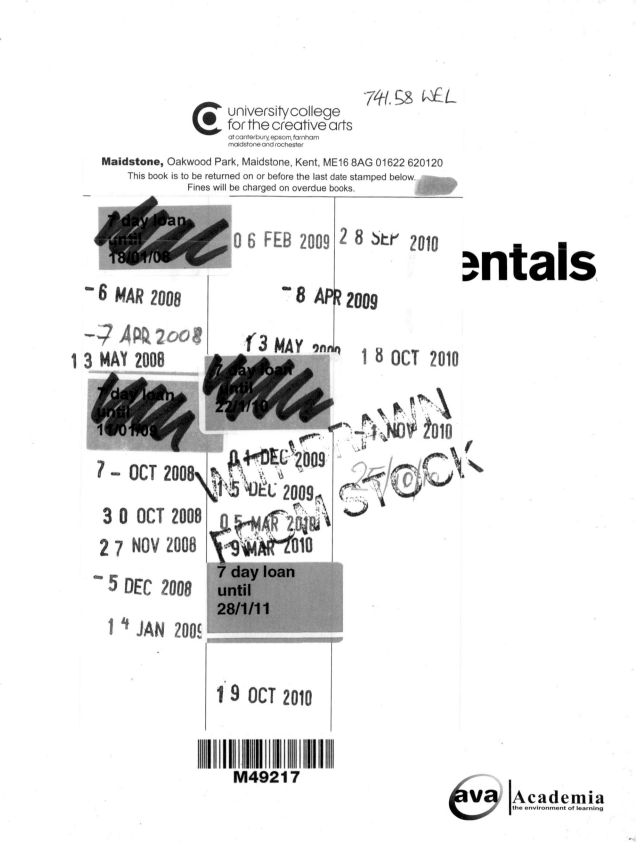

entals

ava | **Academia**
the environment of learning

777.7
WEL

An AVA Book
Published by AVA Publishing SA
Rue des Fontenailles 16
Case Postale
1000 Lausanne 6
Switzerland
Tel: +41 786 005 109
Email: enquiries@avabooks.ch

Distributed by Thames & Hudson (ex-North America)
181a High Holborn
London WC1V 7QX
United Kingdom
Tel: +44 20 7845 5000
Fax: +44 20 7845 5055
Email: sales@thameshudson.co.uk
www.thamesandhudson.com

Distributed in the USA & Canada by:
Watson-Guptill Publications
770 Broadway
New York, New York 10003
Fax: +1 646 654 5487
Email: info@watsonguptill.com
www.watsonguptill.com

English Language Support Office
AVA Publishing (UK) Ltd.
Tel: +44 1903 204 455
Email: enquiries@avabooks.co.uk

ISBN 13: 978-2-940373-02-4
ISBN 10: 2-940373-02-7

10 9 8 7 6 5 4 3 2

Designed by Them
Index by Indexing Specialists (UK) Ltd.

Production by AVA Book Production Pte. Ltd., Singapore
Tel: +65 6334 8173
Fax: +65 6259 9830
Email: production@avabooks.com.sg

Contents

Introduction

↑ **Still from The Incredibles – Brad Bird**
Brad Bird's engaging Bond-cum-Superhero
spoof with Bergmanesque touches is both
mainstream and experimental; at once a CGI
'cartoon' with credible human characters yet
progressive in its use of the technology and the
variousness of its storytelling devices.

Animation and Popular Culture

'The art challenges the technology and the technology inspires the art. Technical artists are coming from computer graphic schools, and learning sculpture, drawing and painting, and traditional artists are learning more about technology. The more we get their cross-pollination the more we will stretch the boundaries of this medium.'
John Lasseter: PIXAR Animation[1]

Animation is one of the most prominent aspects of popular culture worldwide. It informs every aspect of the visual terrain that surrounds us everyday. It is present in its traditional form in the films produced by Disney, PIXAR, Dreamworks and Ghibli, and in television sit-coms like The Simpsons and South Park. Equally, it exhibits its versatility in every ad break, as anything from washing machines to cereal packets take on the characteristics of human beings and persuade us to buy them. Computer-generated animation finds close affiliation with the computer games industry. On the world wide web, most sites have some form of animated figure or banner, as well as housing new forms of cartoon. And on mobile phones, too, animated characters and games proliferate. As well as all this, independent animated film survives in the face of economic adversities, providing festivals with inventive and affecting shorts, while the 'invisible art' of animation within the special effects tradition carries on transforming, and in some aspects eradicating 'live action' in blockbuster features. Animation also continues to embrace new applications in science, architecture, healthcare and broadcast journalism, to name but a few. Animation is simply everywhere.

This is no surprise. Animation is the most dynamic form of expression available to creative people. Animation is a cross-disciplinary

and inter-disciplinary art and craft, embracing drawing, sculpture, model-making, performance, dance, computer science, social science and much more. It has a distinctive language that enables it to create the art of the impossible. Whatever can be imagined can be achieved. This unique vocabulary can be used in a variety of different ways – for example, traditional drawn or cel animation, computer-generated animation, or stop-motion animation – but crucially, whatever technique is used (and there are many more) it can service works from the most outlandish of cartoons to the most abstract of avant-garde films, and all else in between. This is why animation has remained the most consistently experimental art form even as it has entered the mass popularity of mainstream visual culture.

Animation continually offers new possibilities narratively, aesthetically and technically, encouraging new animators, artists and practitioners to explore new kinds of storytelling,

to create new graphic and illustrative styles, and to use both traditional and new tools in the execution of their work. This book will address all of these aspects, seeking to be a useful primer in the 'how to' of animation across a number of disciplines, but also considering a range of critical ideas and historical perspectives that are pertinent to creative work of this kind.

Liz Faber and Helen Walters suggest that animation may be found 'occupying a space between film-making, art and graphic design'[2], while veteran animator, Gene Dietch offers a more technically determined view, suggesting frame-by-frame cinematic animation is 'the recording of individually created phases of imagined action in such a way as to achieve the illusion of motion when shown at a constant, predetermined rate, exceeding that of human persistence of vision'.[3] Much of the 'particularity' of animation, though, is in all the work that must be done before it becomes a film or digital presentation. Animated 'movement' is artificially

created and not recorded from the real world. Consequently, animation almost intrinsically hides its process, and the 'art' that characterises that process. Only the outcome is important in the public imagination, but for the prospective animator, the core work is in the process, and it is that which is reflected throughout the rest of this book.

In many ways, when animation is made in the traditional frame-by-frame form, it is comparatively easy to define, but this is significantly problematised in the digital era. Comics artist and theorist, Scott McCloud, has suggested that 'as the technological distinctions between media fall away, their conceptual distinctions will become more important than ever'.[4] This book, then, seeks to combine the traditional and orthodox ideas at the heart of animation with the 'bright new dawn' of the impact of the digital era, offering case studies and advice from artists, scholars and practitioners. In this book there is no difference between theory and practice – they are one →

← **Animex 2005 Sting – Morgan Powell**
Contemporary animation often reflects its relationship to popular culture and uses a number of sources. Here Morgan Powell of Seed Animation references Batman, Manga comics and animé.

→ **Combining traditional and new approaches**
Preparatory drawing and final computer images – Paul Wollenzien
Paul Wollenzien is a former student of Sheridan College in Canada, a college that stresses the vital interface between traditional drawing skills, creative character development and the inventive use of computer software.

→ and the same, as actually, they always have been. You cannot be a good animator, or indeed, an artist of any sort, without embracing historical perspectives and critical insight, all of which are embedded in any forward-thinking and original practical work.

It is likely that the 21st century animation practitioner – you – is interested in and engaged with the visual dynamics of popular culture – comics; graphic novels; animé; pop promos; advertising; websites dedicated to left-field interests; cult tv and movies; and fan cultures; contemporary modern art; and any aspect of visual culture that has entered into the mainstream of the popular imagination by the time this book has been published. For the most part, all creative people start off as 'fans' of something and want to make something like the art they admire. These are the catalysts for animators wanting to emulate a particular style or approach, while at the same time trying to find an individual 'voice'.

It is likely, too, that many contemporary animators have found access to the medium through increasingly affordable software packages, and the trial and error of making animation in back-bedroom 'studios'. Animators with no formal training have been able to use Flash animation, for example, to create quality work without a colossal budget or using the extensive film crews present in the credits of major movies. Further, college and university courses have proliferated to accommodate the increasing interest in animation, and there is training available in traditional 2D and 3D animation, and digital 3D graphics and animation.

Inevitably, in a global culture so aware of the works of PIXAR or Dreamworks studios, and so invested in computer games, there is high creative aspiration among fledgling practitioners, but a note of caution also needs to be added. As Bill Fleming has noted: 'The problem with technology is it can greatly simplify some tasks while greatly complicating others…In 2D, the

animator simply draws the body perfectly and doesn't have to worry about the technology getting in the way or falling short. Being a digital animator means also being a technical engineer and in many cases a programmer'.[5] So making choices is crucial – what is the best approach for you, your ideas, your abilities and your ambitions? This book will try and help you make those choices.

Animation offers extraordinary versatility and range in its style and techniques, but there are some fundamental principles at its heart that distinguish it as an art form, a practical craft, and a distinctive means of expression. It is hoped that the following discussion will highlight those principles by engaging with the process in developing an animated film; defining the multiple roles and perspectives in thinking about the use and execution of animation; and through the advice and support offered by a range of case studies in which students and professionals making animated films in a variety

of contexts speak critically about their projects, and share 'best practice'. At a time when there is an increasing number of books about animation – and any number of 'making of' documentaries on DVD, concerned with technical considerations, historical perspective, creative outcomes and critical analysis – it is crucial that these aspects are not seen as separate, but part of the same approach. The whole point of this discussion, therefore, is to keep these perspectives working together in a book that I hope will be thought provoking and practical, and ultimately, fundamentally useful to the critically engaged, creative practitioner.

REFERENCES
1) Quoted in the PIXAR Animation Masterclass, London Film Festival, National Film Theatre, November 2001
2) Faber, L & Walters, H. Animation Unlimited: Innovative Short Films Since 1940, London: Laurence King Publishing, 2004, p6
3) Cited in Withrow, S. Toon Art: The Graphic Art of Digital Cartooning, Lewes: Ilex, 2003, p11
4) McCloud, S. Reinventing Comics, New York: Paradox Books, 2000, p205
5) Quoted in Withrow, S. Ibid, 2003, p54

Why Animation?

Why choose animation instead of live action? There are many possible answers to this question, but the following points may serve to summarise some of the key perspectives:

– Animation offers a different vocabulary of expression to live action and enables greater creative freedoms.
– Animation gives a greater degree of control over the construction and outcome of the work.
– Animation may be usefully related to and operate within the physical and material world of live action.
– Animation can offer a different representation of 'reality' or create worlds governed by their own codes and conventions that radically differ from the 'real world'.
– Animation can achieve anything that can be imagined and create an 'art of the impossible'.

All these perspectives acknowledge a distinctiveness in the form, which may be recognised in all its approaches and disciplines. The process by which an animated film might be made, though, is variable. It has some generic consistencies, but often varies with the technique employed, the purpose of the project and its outcome, and crucially, as a result of the working methods employed by an individual or a collaborative team. The following 'process' guide, therefore, is only one model of an

The Animation Process

– **Concept: The Inciting Idea**
 Independent Project/Studio
 Project/Commercial Commission
– **Creating Schedule of Work**
 Budget/Planning/Timeframe
– **Reviewing Resources**
 Technique/Technical Needs/Team Involved
– **Research**
 Facilitating the Idea
– **Story**
 Narrative/Dramatic Scenarios/Comic Events
– **Preparatory Visualisation**
 Sketches/Models
– **Formal Design**
 Characters/Costume/Contexts/Conditions
– **Storyboard**
 Thumbnail Version/Reference Version/
 Fixed Version
– **Script**
 Descriptions/Dialogue
– **Vocal Performance/Initial Soundtrack**
– **Animatic**

– **Shooting Script**
– **Animation Analysis**
 Executing Action/Performance/Effects
– **Aesthetic Analysis**
 Colour/Style/Materials
– **Layout**
 Cinematic Considerations
– **Dope Sheet**
 Construction and Execution
– **Development Soundtrack**
– **Backgrounds/Sets/Virtual Contexts**
– **Animation Sequences**
 Movement Tests/Blocking Decisions
– **Creating Sequences**
 Using Film Language
– **Construction**
 Combining Elements
– **Post-production Analysis**
– **Final Mix/Edit**
– **Output to Chosen Format**
– **Exhibition**

The Animator's Desk
→ Here constructed for the Animation at the Ark Exhibition at the Children's Cultural Centre in Dublin, Ireland.

approach to practice, but it encompasses many of the core aspects required.

It's important to recognise that this is not a strict linear process. Many aspects of the production process overlap and become subject to the ups and downs of creative practice. Things do go wrong and need to be recovered; aspects of any production are constantly reviewed and revised as they go along; and things that seem hard and fast can quickly be jettisoned in preference to another idea or in response to a pragmatic concern. One key point remains though, and that is the importance of pre-production, the first concern of this discussion.

Key Principles and Processes
Introduction

Being pragmatic and practical at the pre-production stage will enable the project to succeed because there is the opportunity to prepare for its demands. While it is vital that the animator is imaginative, it is equally vital to know how that which is imagined can be realised.

Pre-production – the preparation of the essential resources and materials to make and complete a project – is an often undervalued part of making animated films. Pre-production begins right from the initial idea and must always be informed by a clear understanding of where the budget will come from; how much time there is; how the work will be conducted; and how the idea itself will translate into a high-quality animation, with, hopefully, some originality.

In every pre-production process there is challenge and difficulty, but if mistakes are to be made and learned from, it is best that they take place during this period of preparation. Refining the idea through the initial script development and visualisation process is crucial, and getting a real sense of how the story, whatever its terms and conditions, will be actually executed in relation to its technique is fundamental.

Concept

Often one of the most difficult aspects of doing any piece of creative work is finding an idea that has genuine potential for an original film, and the worst thing that anyone can do is place a piece of blank paper in front of someone and say 'write' or 'draw'. Some techniques for generating initial ideas follow.

→ Storyboard for The Old Box – Paul Driessen
Driessen drew from personal memories to find a narrative that would also be suitable to try out new aspects of working in the animated form.

Paul Driessen is one of the acknowledged masters of animation and one of the most distinctive film-makers in the field. Aside from his signature visual style, the key strength of Driessen's films is their conceptual focus – the inciting idea that informs the making of the film.

What follows, then, is a range of starting points for ideas, supported by some individual examples and comments by Driessen himself. While clearly geared to a personal film-making agenda, these approaches are also suitable in response to a commercial brief, or as a story development process within the body of a bigger narrative process.

Methods of recording

The context in which an animator may try to generate ideas may be important, and the method by which these initial musings are stirred and recorded is crucial in the beginning of the process. Some artists prefer to write stories in prose; others to generate any number of stimulus sketches; some work from bullet-pointed conceptual thoughts or odd notes made over a period of time. The 'starting place' is rarely a mystical moment of the muse descending, but an accumulation of developing thought and trial and error until an inciting idea – which must also be 'an exciting idea' – emerges, which has the substance that can be pursued further.

Driessen: 'I do not draw my stories at this stage, but I write them down. I can vaguely picture in my head what it will look like, but there is no definite image yet. Writing is abstract. I'm not hampered by design. Writing also goes much faster than drawing and one can insert afterthoughts and correct flaws, without spending time on draughtsmanship, however sketchy. But it does depend on how your mind works, the kind of stories you write, your style and experience within that approach. Some people need doodling, need to see images to find clues and directions. Eventually, I do make a storyboard. It suggests the look of the film and defines, more or less, the various shots, the progress and order of the action.'

Using personal backgrounds

Our biggest resource in the first instance is ourselves, and thinking about our backgrounds and the characters and possible narratives that inform them is a ready place to generate possible material. Many creative works have a strong autobiographical tendency because the artist has such in-depth knowledge on the subject and can transform it into a set of aesthetic and social, as well as personal outcomes.

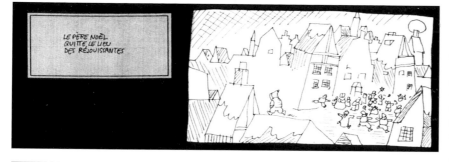

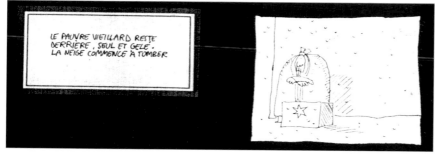

Using personal experiences and memory

Using personal experience and memory is, of course, intrinsically related to drawing upon background, but it needs to be subjected to a rigorous process of interrogation. It is important to observe more objectively; analyse incident and experience structurally; and treat the things that happen as possibilities for narrative and other forms of expression.

Sense Memories

Everyone has an 'emotional' memory that is built on our five senses – seeing, hearing, smelling, touching and tasting. Recalling when we saw something beautiful or tragic; heard a particular piece of music; smelt a potent odour or fragrance; touched something or someone; or tasted something delicious, may be the key catalyst to a prospective story idea. Using the senses is fundamental to the animator's craft, as these have to be projected through the medium in highly specific and connective ways.

The formative years

Many artists of all kinds are influenced by the creative work of their youth. Long-term personal likes and dislikes are often the first things that are emulated or aspired to in creative work before a clear and original 'voice' develops. These influences can be conscious or unconscious.

Using iconic images

Contemporary culture is a visual one. We are surrounded by visual stimulus in images, signs and pictorial information, as well as the physical environment itself. Sometimes particular images and signs take on an 'iconic' value and pass into popular culture as situations and scenarios that are known to a mass population, and these can be used as the foundation of further interpretation or development.

Driessen: 'Just imagine a cabin sitting on a railway track in the middle of nowhere. Then make a list of everything that has to do with the railways, the era of locomotives, whatever comes to mind, and stories and gags start to emerge from that imagery.'

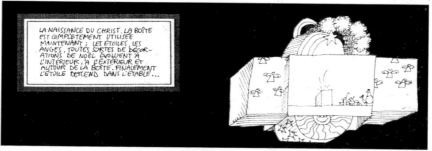

Fantasy versus reality: observation and imagination

Everyone is blessed with the ability to fantasise –
to re-imagine the world on our own terms and
conditions, fulfilling our inner most passions and
desires. Most people realise their fantasies are
often in stark contrast to the real world in which
they live. This very juxtaposition can be very
fruitful for the artist, as acute observation of the
patterns of the real world set against a free
imagination unfettered by rules, regulation and
convention, can produce interesting points of
comparison. This can set off potent ideas for
personal expression.

Using oppositions and comparisons

In a similar way to using the tensions between
reality and fantasy, the self-evident points of
comparison and opposition between people,
other creatures, the environment etc., can enable
a particular kind of 'dramatic conflict' that can
generate ideas. Creating a particular tension or
problem that must be resolved in some way is a
fundamental aspect of many narratives and often
emerges from the dramatic conflict of opposition
or difference.

Driessen: '[For On Land, At Sea and In the Air]
I had made a lot of notes about comparable
situations. Like hills and valleys, fire, water and
soil; aggression versus peace; complementary
colours etc. The moment I had established the
land, sea and air environments, I added the
themes influencing each segment, like rain,
hunger, love, up and down, and the stories

→ **Sketch (right) and storyboards (below)**
↘ **from Three Misses – Paul Driessen**

Much later in his career, looking for a fun cartoon idea for a new film, Driessen used the very story exercises he had done with his students to combine three popular narratives: 'I designed the film as a series of cliffhangers; at the moment of tension I would cut to the next story and so on. I also inserted some reminders of previous action into the subsequent stories: the apartment man closes a door behind which Little Red Riding Hood, the wolf and the unfortunate dwarf are seen; and the falling-off-the-roof lady is passed by the cowboy jumping off the cliff'.

almost evolved from there by themselves. I learned that whenever I hit upon a good premise for a film, the stories would follow without much effort'.

Using and revising traditional story premises

Most people are brought up hearing stories, reading stories and creating stories about their own lives and experiences. People are highly attuned to the capacity for narrative, and everyday they express their inner life, the things that happen to them and to others as 'stories', built on an instinctive structure of a beginning, a middle and an end. There are some key story ideas that we retain from popular narratives and their innate structures – these can work as very effective stimuli for developing the stories further.

Driessen: 'Another film I tried out on my students was a story exercise (after I'd done it myself) – Oh, What A Knight. It has a typical cartoon premise. As a start I used a traditional tale – the knight rescuing a damsel in distress. We all know the outcome, the knight will overcome all obstacles and eventually free her. But then what? What will make the end funny? Using the same structure, I gave the students exercises with traditional story ideas like "a woman being tied to the railway track and a cowboy coming to the rescue", "someone falling off the roof and her neighbour trying to catch her in time", "Snow White threatened by her stepmother and the dwarves coming to the rescue"'.

Research

Research is an important yet undervalued component of animation. It may require visits to the library, real locations and places of visual stimulus; it might need working online, primary material, tracing people to interview or access to documents or images not in the public domain. Research is the next step in developing the initial concept.

Pre-production research must also include technical planning – can the software used facilitate what is required? Is the resource available appropriate, useful and able to achieve the outcomes imagined? Research is necessary in any number of ways, because it properly informs the project both in relation to form and content.

Jurassic Park research and development

Here Ellen Poon, one of the senior animators at Industrial Light and Magic talks about the ongoing research process in the development of Jurassic Park:

Poon: 'I do not think that there is a limit to what our imagination can create, and the classic cartoons proved that. What we are trying to do at ILM is to push the boundaries and create something that we have not seen before. With Jurassic Park we tried to use models to do the animation at the start, but the movement turned out to be insufficiently fluid to be persuasive, so we did a test and built some dinosaurs that we could scan into the computer.

'We did some animation of T-Rex, and there was a strong sense that these were real animals moving around. You can combine these computer-generated elements with live action in the computer environment so they seem wholly realistic and indistinguishable. First, we had to consider the movement of the creature; second, we had to consider the look and texture of those creatures because they have to look and act like animals – they have to breathe and sweat like real animals; and third, they must be as persuasive as the live-action environment.

'The animators studied a lot of live-action footage of animals running around – maybe feeding or hunting – just studying the movement to get some idea of the spirit and character of the animal. Also, they did some mime classes when they actually had to become a dinosaur and actually establish a character. By trying to understand the spirit of the creature they can try and put that into the animation.

'Like the character development in any movie, you can see the progression from when the creature is introduced, to how it interacts with the live-action actors and actresses, and how it behaves. This helps with making sure that the animation of the creature matches the stage of development they should be at, at the particular moment within the story. This has to work alongside the technical issues like lighting, or creating skin tone, or authenticating the texture of the creature.

'We did a lot of research on skin movement in animals. We shot a lot of the live-action scenes with objects moving around in the environment, so we could create lighting diagrams, which helped us to make sure that everything looked right when the dinosaurs moved in and out of shade; basically that they were never anything but part of the environment.'

When accuracy is important

Independent Japanese animator, Minoru Maeda, had a different research issue for his film, The Sun Was Lost, concerning the bombing of Hiroshima, because he wanted to depict the city before the bombing:

Maeda: 'There was no way of knowing what the scenery in the city was like. The main problem was the colour issue. Even if I discovered a photograph, it was a black-and-white photograph. However, I wanted to depict the scenery before it was destroyed respectfully and realistically, because it later disappears. I listened to the story of one senior citizen and gathered information on the old city.

'I also collected historic material on a similar city in the same period and took a photograph of a remaining building for reference material on colour and size. Even if I am not familiar with the past, there will be someone in the audience who is; that's why I discussed everything with senior citizens before I began drawing.'

For any project, identify a range of research questions at the outset – this 'problematises' the process, but ensures all the key issues are taken into account at the outset.

↑ ↑ ↗ **Photographs of the temple building as inspiration for The Sun Was Lost – Minoru Maeda**

The traditional temples in Hiroshima were made of wood, but when rebuilt after the war, were constructed in concrete. This required that Maeda use the contemporary design of the temple – which sought to echo the traditional design – but re-imagine it in its original form, taking into account the different aesthetic. In any form of art based on a real past experience there is the responsibility to represent the event and its context as respectfully as possible, but some compromises may be necessary, either because the artist wants to express a particular point of view, or because it is necessary to take educated guesses. At one and the same time, then, Maeda's Hiroshima is both a real and partially imagined place. It is the research, however, which authenticates the imaginative aspects.

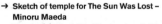

→ **Sketch of temple for The Sun Was Lost – Minoru Maeda**

Here is Maeda's sketch of the temple, which is still, however, only indicative of the final design, and the fully conceived and coloured rendering in the film. The temple is important because it was being used as a classroom instead of a school in 1945, and of course, carries with it significant symbolic implications.

→ **Photographic records of Hiroshima**
→ **for The Sun Was Lost – Minoru Maeda**
   Having a photographic record of something is
   often extremely important. The older buildings,
   pictured here, still exist, but are rapidly being
   pulled down in the creation of new estates. The
   images clearly inspire many of the designs in
   the film. Such older buildings now figure in the
   suburbs, but in the pre-war era were present
   across the whole city.

→ **Final designs (right) and their**
↘ **photographic source material**
↓ **for The Sun Was Lost – Minoru Maeda**
   Final designs from Maeda's film show how he
   has created not merely the 'old' Hiroshima, but
   an innocent place, which almost prefigures the
   'modern' era, epitomised by the atomic bomb.
   Children play in the street yet there is little that
   seems 'urban' in the modern sense. This is a
   pre-war idyll.

← Storyboard and shooting script, and
↓ character cut-outs for The Sun Was Lost –
Minoru Maeda
Maeda's storyboard also functions as a
shooting script in this instance, delineating the
relationship between the original design, the
intended action, and the possible ways in which
the sequences will be shot. The characters
were drawn on paper and coloured in, before
being cut-out and pasted on to a cel. The film
was shot on 35mm stock.

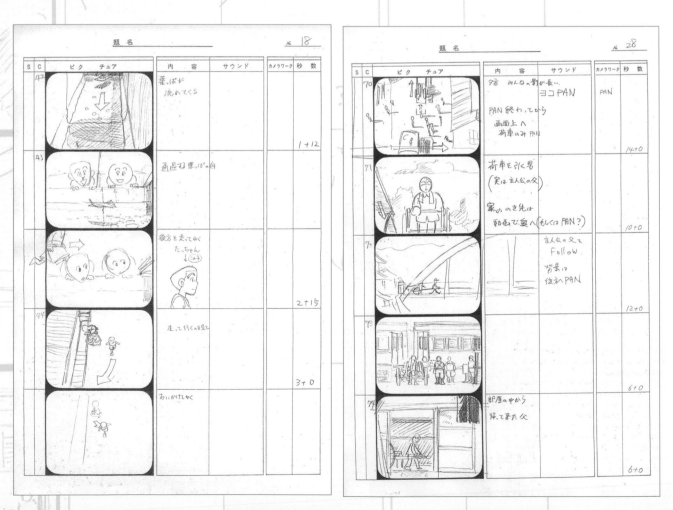

→ Mapping The Sun Was Lost using
photographic evidence – Minoru Maeda
Maeda's research was aided by a conversation
he had with a senior citizen who remembered
the period, gave him maps of Hiroshima before
the bombing, helped him draw sketches of
places and took him to the temple (right) where
he recollected stories and incidents. These
techniques significantly aided the preparation
of the film.

↗ Sketch showing characters' heights and
→ model sheets for The Sun Was Lost –
Minoru Maeda
The designs shown here indicate some of the
process work involved in preparing the film.
Based on a combination of archive photos and
the aesthetic conventions of contemporary
children's manga, the drawing above shows the
variations in height of the characters, while the
designs on the right show the model sheets for
a period bus and truck, and a boy and a girl
who feature in the narrative.

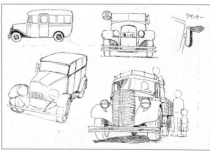

Preparation

The visualisation of an animated film is the key component in thinking about how a story might be told, how a visual 'gag' might be constructed, how a technique might be applied, and how the animation will work as a piece of film. Underpinning the process of visualisation is drawing.

↓ **Doctor's surgery study sketch – Joanna Quinn**
Drawing from life often discovers more exaggerations in postures than those imagined, as this hunched man seen in a doctor's surgery shows.

Drawing, however primitive or sophisticated, and for whatever technique, is a necessary process. Drawing can work in a number of ways and is an intrinsic skill everyone possesses. All children draw and are totally unself-conscious about it. As the years pass, though, the belief that we all can draw is somehow socialised out of us and is merely understood as an 'artistic' skill.

Simply, any act of sketching offers up a perception of the world, and a model by which to communicate thoughts and feelings, and a range of sensory experience. It can enable the invention of a world by asking questions of the one we all live in. Primarily, though, drawing records the act of observation – a key skill in the animator's armoury – and sometimes as an act of memory, in the recollection of times and places of significance.

All drawing affords the possibility, though, of experimentation and interpretation, and works as core research in developing a vocabulary of human movements and gestures; an understanding of environments; the invention of fantastical figures and places; or simply, the expression of line, form, shape and colour, for its own sake.

St Davids Court Surgery 22/11/04 10.45

→ **Preparatory anatomical sketches –**
← **Joanna Quinn**

↓ Joanna Quinn makes an important distinction when she suggests: 'my drawings are purely interpretations of what I am looking at, rather than being aesthetically good drawings'. Inexperienced artists can often be inhibited in their expression and vision by thinking that their drawings are insufficiently 'artistic' or of a certain standard.

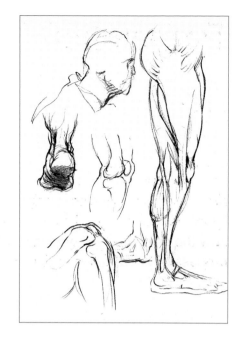

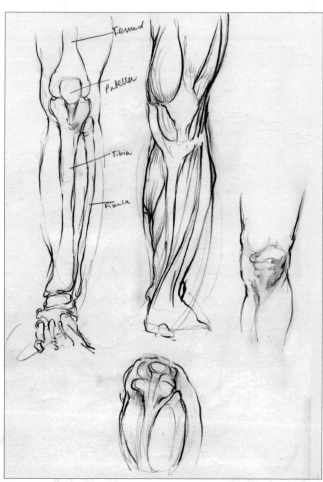

Life drawing

Master animator, Joanna Quinn, creator of Girls' Night Out and Body Beautiful discusses how she works as an example of good practice:

Quinn: 'Life drawing and drawing from life is an essential part of my animation. Even though people say I'm a good "drawer" and have a good understanding of three-dimensional movement, I still need to draw from life. If I don't, my drawings become flat and timid. When I'm doing a lot of observational drawing outside of my animation, my line becomes a lot more confident and I think three-dimensionally.

'I carry a sketchbook around with me and draw at every opportunity. I use my sketchbook as a visual notebook and the drawings are interpretations of what I'm looking at.

'Yesterday I sketched a man reading his newspaper in the doctor's surgery. The pose looked a familiar one i.e. slumped over, leaning forward with the paper, arms resting on legs. When I looked closer, I couldn't believe how hunched over he was and his head hung so low his torso was almost doubled up. His feet were interesting too, one foot forward and the other pulled back under his chair. If I'd drawn this pose from my imagination I would never have exaggerated it as much, which is exactly why it is so important to draw from life. We may think our imaginations are far more adventurous than real life, but for me truth is always stranger than fiction.'

Narrative Drawing

Mario Minichiello is a politically engaged artist, illustrator, and champion of the 'slow art' of narrative drawing in the multimedia age. He has regularly worked within the context of broadcast and broadsheet media. Such work can help delineate narrative structure while simultaneously suggesting the symbolic or metaphoric resonance of the imagery that may finally feature in a film.

Minichiello: 'The act of drawing empowers the artist to look at the world, to deconstruct and rebuild it. Drawing as a discipline will enable the maker to develop a visual memory, meaning that past experiences and observations can be used in informed, insightful ways that, in turn, change the nature of what is created and communicated. In truth drawing has much in common with text in that it has rules and these rules can be broken. The basic rules of construction to drawing are: grammar (mark making), syntax (composition) and meaning (content, subject). In drawing we use media, process, techniques, craft, methods, mark making, compositions, juxtaposition, context, gesture, atmosphere, character development and description.'

The influence of the camera
'But all this relies on ideas, which themselves rely on observation, memory, experience and critical judgement. It is apparent that with each group of new students I have taught, the

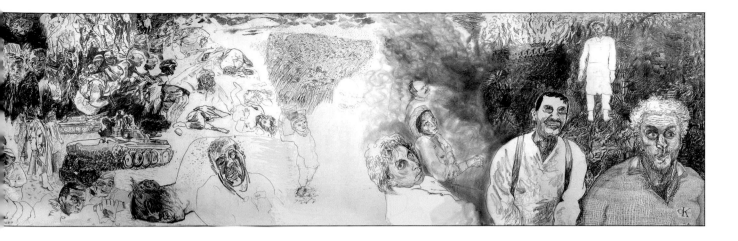

**↑ Sketch entitled Afghanistan –
Mario Minichiello**

This piece is a 28 x 5ft, horizontal drawing concerning the Afghanistan war. It is in the tradition of narrative animatic work like Egyptian hieroglyphics, friezes on Greek vases, Japanese scrolls, the Bayeux Tapestry, and the later sequential art of William Hogarth and Rudolph Topher. The viewer animates the narrative by moving physically along the drawing reading left to right. At the start Bush is made up of the shadows of war – literally the shadows that bombers and helicopters make on the ground against the sun. This was to reflect his remark that he was a 'war president'. The background tonal work seeks to capture in handmade drawing the noise of war – the sound of engines, bombs, bullets, and radio prattle, as well as TV hum and hiss. The end of the war descends into insanity and gang war.

**← Sketch entitled Raining Death from
the Sky (detail) – Mario Minichiello**

Drawing 'action' sequences involving machines and vehicles can be demanding, but it offers the opportunity to think about the choreography of possible motion, direction and outcome in animation.

**← Sketch entitled Prepare and Wait (detail)
– Mario Minichiello**

Capturing the variousness of human expression and attitude is also a key part of constructing performances in animated sequences. Narrative drawing can act as an important preparation in this respect.

influence of the camera on their visual thinking has been a profound one, not the camera craft of directors like Hitchcock, but the more mundane experience of the 'snap shot'. Drawing goes beyond what a camera or any mechanical process can do, it has the limitless freedom of the mind and as such enables the artist, animator and illustrator to transport the viewer to any space, through any experience, telling stories often without words, creating empathic characters that have complexity and connections to the viewer, and above all that entertain and inform.'

The overlooked importance

'Perhaps because of this, drawings have retained an almost magical or indefinable relationship with us – the subject has been taken for granted, not seen as particularly important. Many art schools have stopped teaching drawing, replacing their life room studios with computer suites. Drawing, particularly narrative image-making, has become associated with the past or with play, and is somehow not seen as intellectually challenging or culturally significant.

'The truth is that artists who make narrative drawings have never done so in a "dumb" way. For years in my own university department the assumption seemed to be that illustrators drew fluffy sweet teddy bears and animators made them move. An illustrator's or animator's ability to draw a bear accurately is simply a given thing. Beyond that the issues become more complex and personalised. None of us ever just

draws a bear, without asking questions or thinking about what we have to communicate. What kind of bear? What is he or she like? The character has to work without, as well as with words. These are the ideas that breathe life into a character, dictating how it looks, moves, stands, its texture, colour, temperament, where it lives, and how it reacts to its environment. This level of consideration has to be applied to everything we draw. The methods of drawing education go beyond simple training in terms of craft or skill. Michelangelo in the 15th century said: "I paint with my brains". As makers of animation or illustration this is custom and practice for us.'

The power of narrative drawing

'To undervalue the power of narrative drawing is to overlook potentially the most multifunctional weapon in our armoury. For artists, designers and many academics over a range of art disciplines, the practice encompasses a multitude of possibilities and may be applicable to any part of the creative process, allowing artists to explore their subject, to "actively look" in original and diverse ways. From simple sketchbook notes that can be little more than notation, only used as a memory aid, to highly finished works produced specifically for the public arena, drawing enables one to try out ideas and plan compositions irrespective of what media is used to finally complete the work with. Most of all, it allows animators to "visually think out loud" gaining them entry into a dialogue with their imagination.'

Technique and Approach

Gerald Scarfe is an internationally renowned political cartoonist, illustrator, designer and animator and his work is an excellent example of the way form and content find a particular synthesis in technique. Scarfe's drawing embodies the mood, attitude and intention of his thematic expression, intensifying the symbolic or metaphoric weight of his ideas. This kind of 'condensation' – the maximum of suggestion in the minimum of imagery – is intrinsic to successful animation, particularly in the short form.

Scarfe: 'The most important thing is to build up a mood, which is productive in liberating your imagination further. I fully believe in "attacking" the paper so that you can bring out what you are visualising in your mind. I liken it to a dream – even as you are recalling it and attempting to tell someone about it, it starts to evaporate – and you cannot remember the end, so getting the "bare bones" down is crucial. Even three or four lines can work as a stimulus to develop the piece. Sometimes I am knee deep in paper trying to work an idea through, but it comes eventually.'

Impulse and spontaneity

'I like to work "big". I use paper that is a metre high, and I work from the shoulder, not the arm or wrist, so I can get the muscle into the drawing. I like the size and the vigour of the initial drawing, and certainly using pen and ink straight on to the paper. I have needed strong nibs to accommodate the enthusiasm of the approach. You have to draw "in the moment" to capture the impulsiveness of the invention, and to capture

what you can. You can add the detail later, but that becomes clearer when you have got the essence of the image.'

The line

'I have concentrated on and developed a clearer "line" over the years. I used to put in a great deal of detail – from pubic hair to warts – but now I simplify for a clearer message. My style has been described as serpentine and flowing, but I see it as like handwriting – you somehow develop your own technique through practice, and this becomes an individual signature style.'

Drawing as recall

'Drawing with clarity helps me to recall things, though. I had to do a caricature of Arnold Schwarzenegger, and so I observed him, making lots of brief sketches to get an immediate sense of him. Those, coupled with some photographs I had, enabled me to do the work. The sketches are like brief words in a diary – everything comes back to you because of those few jottings, and you are able to proceed with the final drawings knowing that you have got a sense of the individual as they are and the creative way in which you want to depict them.

'When I was younger there were two important aspects that led to my investment in drawing. First was the fact that I was an asthmatic and drawing proved to be my only real method of communication and the way in which I exorcised my fears. Second was my work at a commercial studio where I drew everything from bicycles to lamps to alarm clocks, and learned to draw representationally, and to make that effective and persuasive. But that had its problems. For example, I would take what was really a ropey old piece of flannel and draw it as a beautiful soft blanket – it was all lies! When I began drawing in a more ferocious and grotesque way, it was →

→ **A concept painting of marching hammers for Pink Floyd's film The Wall – Gerald Scarfe**
Another visual metaphor from Pink Floyd's The Wall – the marching hammers represent a fascist oppressiveness and conformity, literally reducing 'Pink' to a tiny, insignificant figure in the social order. These are animated in a way that foregrounds the associations with the 'goose-step' of the Nazi military during the Second World War – an effective physical movement 'short cut' to point out the fascist aspect of the metaphor. Animators need to be aware of specific kinds of movement that already have social, cultural and political meanings attached to them to use as an immediate visual cue in their narratives.

→ probably a reaction to this, and a desire to be more truthful through drawing. Even then, though, having schooled myself through doctors' books on anatomy and learned about muscles and bones, I was then accused of having a Swiftian style "disgust of human flesh". Really, I just enjoyed the flexibility and malleability in drawing grotesque bodies.'

The dynamic quality of drawing for animation

Scarfe (cont.): 'Drawing for animation is very different and I began to realise what novelists mean when they say that characters take on a life of their own and almost tell you what they want to do. I would create a character and knew that they needed to cartwheel or dive off a swimming board or something, essentially because I knew they must move. So, you give them an action that makes that happen, and just as in the same way as the political cartoon works, you must always be asking what might happen in the next frame, so the character and the audience are always anticipating what happens next.'

The Wall

'I learned a lot about animation on The Wall working with people like Geoff Dunbar, Jill Brooks and Mike Stuart. My role as director ironically meant that I did less drawing, but I designed the characters and corrected the pencil drawings. What I learned though was that it was very difficult to try and get animators to think differently and move away from the Disney house style, or the Tom and Jerry house style – the whole "squash 'n' stretch" orthodoxy in animation. I wanted them to realise that these are moving drawings, not cute characters running around. I wanted them to think differently.

'I was reassured when I went to the Zagreb Festival, that there was a whole Eastern European tradition that worked from a completely different point of view technically and aesthetically.

'When I worked on Hercules, some of the Disney animators had real trouble adapting to my designs and intentions and fell back on what they knew, but others really responded well and elements like Hades and the Fates work well and just about retain my style! I always wanted to present a sense of movement even in the preliminary drawings. This sense of anticipation is very important in the development both of the character and the movement.'

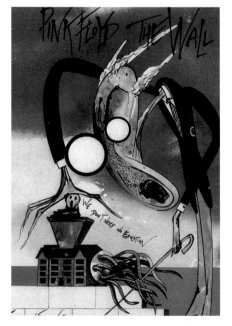

← ↑ **Concept paintings for Pink Floyd's film The Wall – Gerard Scarfe**
Scarfe's inspirational artwork for the character 'Pink' enables the animator to understand how emotion is played out through the face and body. The vulnerable posture and the gaping, screaming mouth, demonstrate a horrific solitude and pain.

Animation can encompass the 'grotesque' and literally depict metaphoric ideas. Here, Scarfe's teacher is a manic and cruel figure, viciously and apparently literally 'mincing' his pupils. This is a vivid and bitterly critical visual metaphor for the ways in which children are processed through the education system, with little thought for their individual sensibilities and talents. This kind of social comment finds its roots in political cartooning, and further back, in the British caricaturial tradition, embodied by Hogarth, Gilray, Cruickshank and Leech.

↑ ↑ **Still from Cow on the Frontier – Dragutin Vunak and still from The Fly – Aleksandar Marks and Vladimir Jutrisa**
Two examples of the alternative tradition in Eastern Europe, so admired by Gerald Scarfe. Minimalistic, yet highly suggestive in their meanings, the films demonstrate a 'reduced' or 'limited' animation technique, using the flat planes of modern art and very basic movement sequences for the characters. These films were often made in a spirit of resisting repressive authoritarian regimes and were therefore sometimes surreal, abstract and symbolic in their approach, vastly different from the dominant Disney style.

← **Preparatory sketches for Carmen – Peter Parr**
Peter Parr, working at the Arts Institute at Bournemouth, is one of the most renowned teachers of animation in Britain. He stresses the core skills of drawing and visualisation in his work with students, pointing out the relationships between character, emotion and 'dramatic' movement. Here is a sequence from his preparatory work on the S4C Operavox animation, Carmen. Note the fluid dynamics of the sword fight and the sense of the 'cinematic' in the initial compositions.

A selection of observational drawings and sketches – Peter Parr

Drawing particular figures, objects and environments can be a stimulus for narrative ideas, potential dramatic contexts, comic scenarios, backgrounds and layouts in an animated story. The value of the animator's sketchbook therefore cannot be underestimated. As well as facilitating a possible story, such a variety of styles may help to identify a signature style or technique that the animator is most comfortable working in.

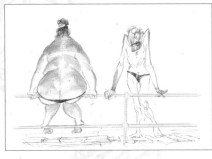

Still from Gilbert and Sullivan: The Very Models animation – Barry Purves

Note here the use of total artifice in creating a deliberately 'theatrical' piece. Theatre cannot create the realism and literalism of a great deal of live-action cinema and digital imagery, and prefers to foreground its illusionism. Purves' Gilbert and Sullivan: The Very Models shows Gilbert and Sullivan playing out the characters and scenarios of their light operas, with their manager, Richard D'Oyly Carte. The ship and sea are created purely through use of backdrops and two-dimensional props, and character through costume, which also implies gender, status and role. Thus the design is fundamental to the storytelling process.

Story and Design

Here on the right are some points from Barry Purves to consider when designing animation. Purves is a master stop-motion animator with over 50 international awards for his films, which include Screenplay, Rigoletto and Gilbert and Sullivan: The Very Models.

When you design animation…

– Animators should try and engage with other art forms, particularly those that privilege movement – for example, dance; and those that tell stories by other means – for example, opera, through music.

– Animation is basically an art of 'metaphor' and is perfect for all kinds of role-play to show different perspectives and ideas about the culture we live in.

– 'Acting' is at the core of affecting animation, and it is particularly important to concentrate on body language and physical gesture as the tools of expression.

– Make sure that your 'acting' through the figure is simple and clear – one simple gesture is better than five noisy ones.

– Try not to move everything in every frame – pauses are beneficial and silences can be dramatically effective.

– Not all animation should aspire to be 'realistic', but it should be credible. Establish the 'illogical logic' of the world you create and give it credibility.

– Try to make sure that all the elements of your animated world are used to tell your story – for example, colour, design, lighting etc. – and that these elements are integrated in a coherent way.

– Animation is a form of choreography, so don't just concentrate on the face and don't be afraid of showing your whole figure in the frame. Hold poses, stretch movement and change the rhythm – 25 frames do not have to be divided equally. Animation is not mathematics and there are no set laws.

– Try to capture the 'essence' of your character's figure in the design, and build a specific vocabulary of movement for it, so that the 'meaning' in the acting will be clear and distinctive.

– Embrace the artifice and illusionism of animation, so that you are able to create 'plays within plays' or 'films within films' to condense your plot, but more importantly, to 'illuminate' a supposedly-known or taken-for-granted world, from a different perspective.

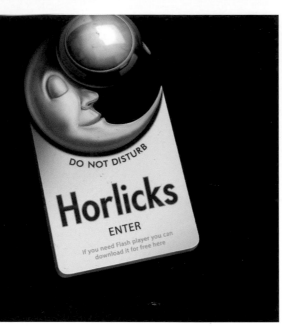

Design as Concept

The website for the night-time beverage Horlicks was created by Williams Murray Hamm, an advertising agency, and Sennep, a creative design partnership. The design was absolutely intrinsic to both communicating a concept and facilitating the ways in which the website could use animation to further consolidate ideas about the brand, the product, its function, and its distinctive appeal. Williams Murray Hamm's designer and creative director on the brief, Gareth Beeson comments on the project:

The concept of night-time

Beeson: 'One of the key design concerns was revealing information out of a dark background, because we were essentially setting our text and images within a night environment. We worked with Sennep looking at film credits, especially Sergio Leone's Once Upon a Time in the West, for inspiration about the cinematic revelation of accessible information, and that really helped.'

Matt Rice and Hege Aaby (Sennep) both studied graphic design at Brighton University and Central St Martins respectively. Their college work veered towards moving image, stemming from an interest in title sequences.

They met while working for Digit, an interactive design company, where they worked on Flash animation for websites and interactive installations. Animation is an integral part of their work, which is mainly web-based, as Flash allows them to create movement by using a combination of frame by frame animation, tweening and programming.

Rice: 'The information on the website was divided into three categories; "Can't Sleep", "Understanding Sleep" and product information. Based around these categories the following, loose narrative was built:

"You are in the bedroom, the 'Can't Sleep' area, where the ticking of the alarm clock, car lights, moving curtains etc. keep you awake. In the bedroom you find tips about how to sleep better, brought to you by the firefly – your guide through the website. From the bedroom you can drift off to semi-conscious sleep, to the 'Understanding Sleep' area where objects from 'Your Day' float around in a surreal, dreamy landscape. From there you can fall into deeper sleep – the cloud area, where you find the product information.'"

Creating the atmosphere

Rice (cont.): 'You drift in and out of sleep depending on how you choose to navigate, and our aim was to make the transition between the areas as seamless as possible. We wanted the website aesthetics to appeal to people of all ages and to have a dreamy, fairytale-like feel to it.'

← **The door hanger detail from the Horlicks website – Sennep**
A single image here condenses the ideas of night-time, Horlicks and sleep with the 'Do Not Disturb' sign often hung from bedroom doors. This ready confluence of ideas intensifies the meaning of the design yet gives it clarity and purpose.

↑ **Initial Photoshop ideas for the Horlicks website – Sennep**
The initial design had a more 'photographic' approach and a less dream-like ambience. It was created in Photoshop.

↑ **The Horlicks bedroom at night – Sennep**
The bedroom at night at the beginning of the implied narrative: 'Can't Sleep' leads on to 'Understanding Sleep', and ultimately, to 'Horlicks' as the resolution to difficulties with sleeping.

→ **The site entry page for www.Horlicks.co.uk**
The sense of calm is all-pervading on this site, and is created by the refined design and well chosen minimal wording.

↘ **An early perspective sketch of the Horlicks bedroom**

↓ **Early designs for the moving objects in each of the sections**

The technical problems arising from the approach

Rice (cont.): 'To create animated websites we use Flash. This project was executed by using pencil and paper, Photoshop, Freehand, Illustrator and Flash. In this case we worked up initial layouts in Photoshop from thumbnail sketches produced while brainstorming. We drew outlines and traced objects in Freehand and Illustrator. The outlines were brought into Flash where the objects were coloured in and animated. Individual objects were animated frame by frame, while the overall movement and interactivity of the website was programmed using Action Scripting.

'A website always has to load, so to avoid too much waiting time at the start we split the website into three parts to make the loading as seamless as possible. The facts about sleep are meant to keep the user occupied while the website is loading behind the scenes.

'We wanted the user to be able to explore the website and discover content in an almost "accidental" way. At the same time it had to be easy for the user to go straight to the content he/she was looking for. This was resolved by creating two ways of navigating – a quick way to navigate by using the ever-present moon or by finding and clicking on objects throughout the website.

'Another challenge was to integrate the content in a way where we would avoid long scrollable text areas. By using animated, interactive elements such as fairy lights in the bedroom, and the stars and bubbles in "Understanding Sleep", we were able to break the text down to short sentences and digestible paragraphs.

'We feel that we have managed to create an atmospheric, online space for Horlicks and there is not much we would want to change. However, we wish we had time to add more incidental animation. During the brainstorming we had lots of animation ideas, particularly involving the moon. Although a lot of character comes from the moon and his lazy eyelid, we would liked to have played more with his facial expressions – given him even more personality with a little sniff of the nose or a sleepy yawn now and then.'

In this example, Sennep has worked hard to exploit the specific limitations of the design strategy for maximum effect in regard to the necessary appeal of the product and the information that needed to be provided. The animation effectively facilitates the interactive participant's involvement and engagement with the material. In the initial design stage, the avoidance of visual cliché in preference to the reworking of familiar visual elements has enabled the 'message' to be accessible and freshly realised.

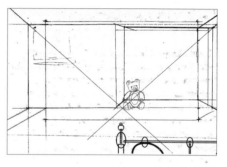

Skills

Sennep recommends:
- When you get started set yourself a simple task.
- Make sure you have a good story or a strong idea before you get started.
- Take inspiration from movement around you.
- Play around and experiment.
- Create your own style.
- Always keep a sketchbook and/or a camera close to hand.
- Animation is time consuming and you might want to team up with someone to make the process quicker and more enjoyable.
- Patience is a virtue.
- Have fun! It will show in your work.

Storyboards and Narrative

The key aspect of the visualisation process is storyboarding. Though this is intrinsically related to the script and soundtrack – considered later in this pre-production section – it is addressed here as a logical continuity of the drawing and design process. It is in the storyboard stage that visualisation is intrinsically linked to narrative – literally telling the story in pictures.

There can be three stages to the storyboarding process: a thumbnail version, either created by one or more animators developing sequences; the reference version, which has a provisional, but agreed structure, with more detailed and larger drawings; and a fixed version, the final structured storyboard that is used in the 'animatic' or 'story reel', is correspondent

to the provisional soundtrack and informs the finalisation of a shooting script. Depending upon the approach of individuals or studios this may vary, and as it is continually important to stress, aspects of the process overlap and have different time frames.

PIXAR Animation Studios has a rigorous preparation process for its pictorial story development. Director, Pete Doctor, and Editor, Lee Unkrich explain aspects of storyboarding:

Doctor: 'We work off a "beat board". As we are developing the story, we pin a number of story "beats" – basic scene ideas, images, exchanges – on to a board and shuffle them around until we really get the essence of the story, what is the basic "plot". Sometimes we use blue cards to signal various character points – character attributes that we want to nail down. As we are doing this we are writing things down – developing a treatment, and beginning a script, just like you would in live action. This is just the

↑ **Stills from Monsters Inc. –**
↗ **Pete Doctor for PIXAR**

Monsters Inc. went through a rigorous process of story development to ensure that all aspects of the narrative were essentially fixed before animation took place. Storyboarding becomes an invaluable tool in this process, not merely helping story development, but key aspects in the progress of characters, their relationships and important emotional turning points.

Storyboarding also offers the possibility of creating provisional camera positions, suggesting elements of the art direction and design, and composition in the achievement of specific effects i.e. a visual 'gag', an emotive close-up etc.

    Key Principles and Processes   The Fundamentals of Animation

starting point. But the key thing is fixing the storyboards, and then a story reel. Our Head of Story will "pitch" various sequences from this material to the staff, and if we think it is entertaining, we will film it on video, using the images, our own voices and special effects'.

Unkrich: 'We have a lot of fun getting a "pitch" like this to a live audience, but we are also deluding ourselves sometimes; some of the things we found funny were not so funny after a while, and maybe were not so funny in the story reel. A story reel is effectively a "rough draft" of the movie. We take all the storyboards and combine them with temporary dialogue that we record with employees at PIXAR, and we put in sound effects and music, and edit things together so that we create our "movie", and try and make it as watchable as the finished film that you go and see in the theatre. We spend a huge amount of time on this. A movie can take about five years to make, and only about a year and half of that is the actual animation. Our

attitude is that if it is not working in the story reel then it is not suddenly going to magically get better because it has got pretty animation in it. If you get the story right, and the scenes are working well, then the animation will take it up to a whole other level.

'It is one of the real luxuries that we have over live action in that the story reel gives us the opportunity to see that "in-between state" between the script page and the finished film. Normally, you have your script – that's your bible; you go out and shoot it, and that's what you get. But we get to see if something is not working in advance.'[1]

REFERENCES
1) Quoted in the PIXAR Animation Masterclass, London Film Festival, National Film Theatre, November 2001

Preparation: Storyboards and Narrative

Storyboards and Composition

Nelson Diplexcito is a film-maker and lecturer at Loughborough University, UK. He defines his film-making practice by its difference to traditional 'classical' narrative and also the expectations of 'abstraction' in avant-garde films. He insists that this is closely related to knowing the rules of composition and uses of space in the image frame, and breaking them for particular effects. Animators need to address this aspect of their work very consciously.

Diplexcito: 'Setting out to design pictures, animate images or direct movement will involve an understanding of compositional and spatial devices. The organisation of elements within the picture field, screen space or space within the frame is central in communicating the intention of the maker and the meaning of the work to the viewer.

'How do we begin to organise the space within the frame and what is, and how do we achieve, effective composition? An effective composition is one that can be seen to communicate visual sense and directs the viewer's eye towards those aspects that the maker wants them to see. Visual sense is central in articulating the space within the frame and in communicating and directing the viewer to the meaning and reading of the work. I have outlined below considerations that may be helpful in attaining effective pictorial and visual sense in your storyboards. Some of these you will be familiar with, others will come to you intuitively and some you will begin to recognise through experimentation and visual practice.'

A concept and the appearance of reality

'The concept and the appearance of "reality" establish the framework for the compositional and spatial indicators within the picture field. The establishment of "the look" or the "texture of reality" can in turn communicate and underpin the concept. The concept and the appearance of reality can bind even the most non-linear set of drawings and unconventional narratives together. What is ultimately important is that the storyboard depicts the direction of movement and that it frames and communicates key events in the film clearly.'

Off-screen space and the illusion of depth

'Connected with the concept and the appearance of reality is the establishment of "off-screen space". Off-screen space is what the viewer physically cannot see, but believes exists beyond the limits of the visible frame. An object that is partially seen, for example, extends beyond the parameters of the frame. This can also be achieved through off-screen dialogue between characters, off-screen sound, character reaction and subjects entering and exiting the screen space. The illusion of depth is another space that has to be created and given consideration. The set, scene or background is an integral part of the composition and has to be arranged in a way that will support the theme, main character or subject. The arrangement of materials and "props" can be used to frame the main character, focus attention and indicate both a relationship to the drawn and described environment. It also communicates to the viewer the space has a "textural" depth and is not merely a backdrop for action to take place in.'

→ **A narrative premise**
Storyboard for The First Snow of Winter – Hibbert Ralph
Here there is a simple example of a 'narrative premise' or the prompt to a 'story event'. Puffy suggests to Sean that they should scatter a flock of gulls. Such prompts introduce and stimulate pictorial action.

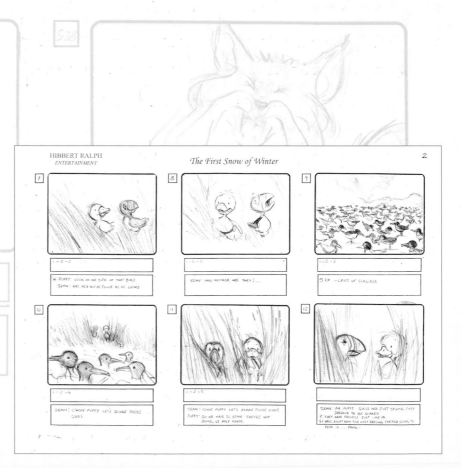

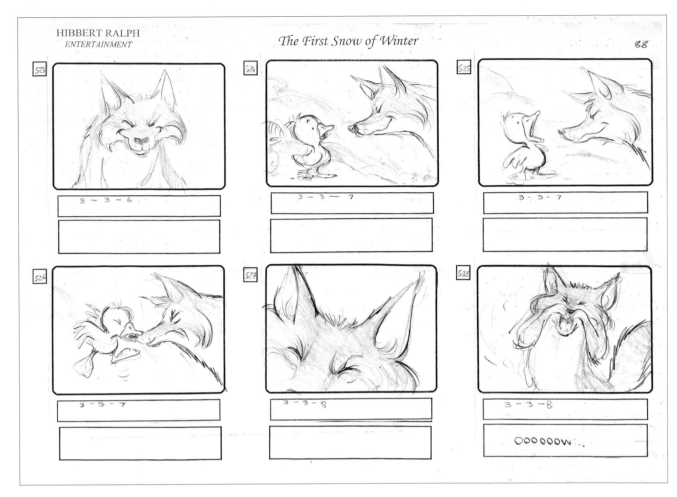

Drawing within the space frame

'In most cases the picture field will have four "borders" and these act as the parameters of the space frame. Images that are introduced should be essential to the scripted material and content explored, and be located in response to the limits of the space within the frame. It is important to recognise that elements introduced into this "field" will create, alter and affect the space. If elements already exist in this space the introduction of new elements and their subsequent occupancy will affect the overall composition and they will begin to assume a spatial relationship. Their occupancy may create spatial significance and images depicted may appear to recede or approach pictorially depending on the overall design. These decisions must be made in relation to the content of the material and the purpose of the shot, as these will directly influence decisions regarding location and prominence of these elements. The nature of storyboarding allows for continual revision and this is central to reaching effective composition.'

Visual difference in sequential drawing

'One of the functions of storyboarding is that it can indicate potential problems in pictorial design and sequence order before the project reaches the production stages of the animation. The storyboard may indicate that the drawings do not contain the range of shots necessary to create visual interest. The framing of individual shots may suggest an over reliance on one fixed viewpoint or that the action depicted takes place principally in the foreground. One approach to discovering the range of images possible in storyboard drawings is to assume that your eye functions as a film/video camera. That it has the facility to track, pan, zoom, use high and low angles to record action and utilise a range of shots and lenses that include long, medium, close-up, extreme close-up and wide-angle camera techniques. Another technique is the use of tonality to direct attention to a given event or subject. Every picture has a range of tone →

↑ **Visual detail in action sequences Storyboard for The First Snow of Winter – Hibbert Ralph**
Storyboards can add a high degree of visual detail in action sequences – here Sean bites the fox's nose. The action and expressions become vital storytelling ingredients.

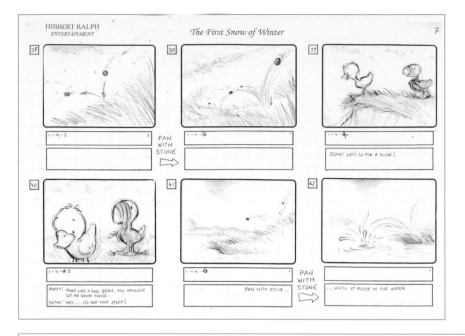

← Using objects to carry the narrative
Storyboard for The First Snow of Winter –
Hibbert Ralph

The action of a narrative is not always carried by characters, but by objects and environments. This falling stone – itself a version of the traditional 'bouncing ball' cycle most animators practice – drives the 'what happens next?' aspect of the story. Notice too, that the camera pans with the fall of the object, enhancing the movement of the stone and the distance it travels.

↓ Showing not telling
Storyboard for The First Snow of Winter –
Hibbert Ralph

Storyboards, for the most part, should be about 'showing not telling'. Sean slides down a bank and the images here take into account the various angles from which this might be seen, and the interaction between Sean's body and the physical landscape – both change as the slide progresses. The images also give a sense of the pace, rhythm and outcome of the slide.

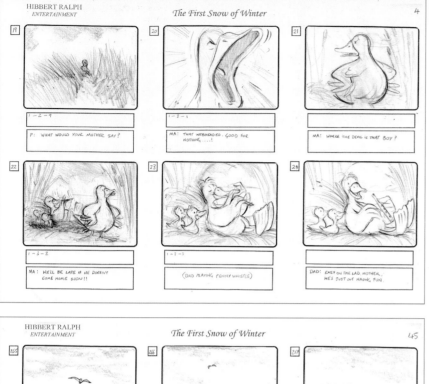

← **Character points**
**Storyboard for The First Snow of Winter –
Hibbert Ralph**

Storyboards must also indicate what Pete
Doctor earlier called 'character points' – these
are either key character traits or where a
character has a significant point of emotion or
revelation that is important in the story. Here
it is a mother's realisation that her son may be
absent or missing.

↙ **Contextualising narrative points**
The First Snow of Winter – Hibbert Ralph

This is sometimes significant in establishing a
specific mood. Here the bird flying, the two
figures staring out, the sense of stillness etc.,
all help to create an atmosphere and a suitable
context for Sean's feelings to be expressed.

→ contained within it, levels of brightness
alternating with areas of darkness. It is important
to constantly remind yourself how the scene is lit
and where and how the light falls on the various
elements within a shot.'

Diplexcito (cont.): 'It is worth noting that
effective pictorial design is not the quest for
a magical series of symmetrical compositions.
The nature of the frame is that it acts as a
locating device. If the figure or subject is
framed centrally, it may lead to problems with
the dynamic operation and symmetrical balance
of the image. The "rule of thirds" is a method
that may lead to more dynamic compositions,
as this involves sectioning the space frame
equally into thirds with an invisible grid of
horizontal and vertical lines. The intersection
of these lines is where the main activity of the
composition takes place. This practice allows
for the interplay of elements and can create a
more dynamic and balanced composition.

'Picture composition is about looking, it
is about experimentation, invention and
experience. Storyboards allow you to be both
experimental and creative in your compositions.
It is important to analyse films themselves; the
movement within the images, the movement of
the camera and how these individual shots are
assembled together in editing. It is important
that this research includes animation, but also
picture design from other disciplines – painting,
photography and graphics – to inform your
own work.'

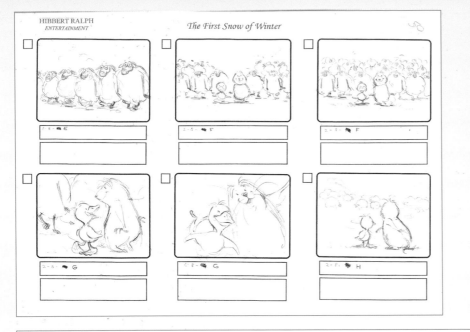

**Storyboard for The First Snow of Winter –
Hibbert Ralph**

Storyboards may also illustrate purely visual
sequences. One of the best visual jokes in the
film is the 'riverdance' sequence where the
main characters are joined by many others in a
dance routine, which works as a 'comic event'
because as the dance unfolds more and more
characters join in, seemingly from nowhere.
This is all achieved through the management of
the frame.

↓ **Action sequences**
**Storyboard for The First Snow of Winter –
Hibbert Ralph**

Related to purely visual sequences are
action sequences and the visual dynamics
that sometimes facilitate conflict and
confrontation – the example here is the fight
with the squirrels.

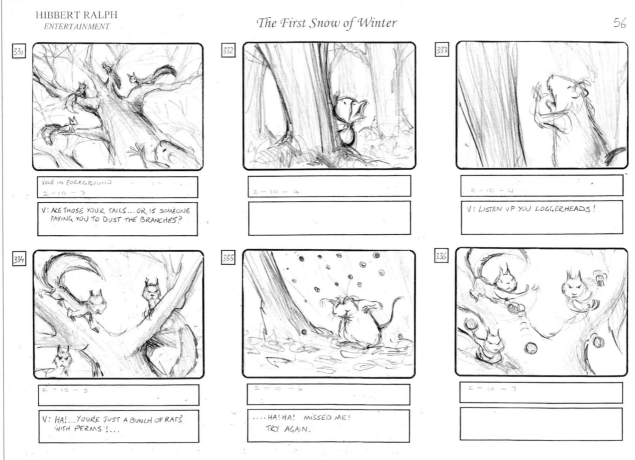

British Film Institute

↗ **Still from Creature Comforts – Nick Park**
Nick Park has become one of Britain's leading animators. Creature Comforts, his first Oscar-winning film, features animal characters with the voices of real people talking, offering their views on their own living accommodation and of animals in zoos. The successful combination of the 'right' animal to the voice – here a South American student talking about his experience of England speaking from a languid though highly gestural panther – creates both a winning character and achieves comic effect. This requires close observation and knowledge of human traits and attitudes, and is perhaps best represented in Park's most famous characters, Wallace and Gromit.

Character and Movement

Andrew Selby is an award-winning illustrator and a lecturer at Loughborough University, UK. He is committed to the view that character is central to inventive narrative, but equally, characters need to be developed as complex devices in their own right, and all their potential facets and nuances explored, using whatever approach – however unusual – as required.

A series of processes
Selby: 'Character development involves a series of processes. Whilst these processes have an order, it should be noted that there is not the perfect recipe to make a successful character. To generalise, a well-conceived character or series of characters will allow the

audience to believe and empathise with them. After all, if we as an audience cannot get excited about a character, or share in their joy or pain or fear, we will struggle to believe the story or series of events being portrayed.'

Acute observation
'Successful character development starts off with acute observation. It is widely believed that Nick Park's character Gromit the dog is a parody of his own mother. In this particular example, the feat is even more astounding because Gromit has no speech or dialogue with other characters in The Wrong Trousers (Aardman Animation, 1993), instead Park uses now famous facial expressions and subtle gestures to illustrate the pet's feelings to the audience.

'As a creatively visual student within a communication medium, being observant is a minimum requirement. You will need a great deal of visually observed material – an →

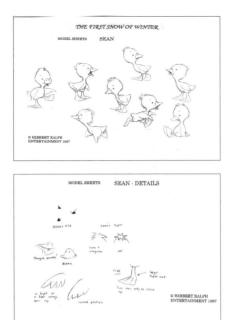

↑ **Model sheets for The First Snow of Winter**
↗ **– Hibbert Ralph**

These model sheets for the main character Sean indicate his facial expressions and head movement; his body posture from various angles; and the 'details' that distinguish his visual identity.

→ animator's sketchbook will typically contain a multitude of drawings, often of the same subject, from different positions. This allows the animator to understand their subject(s), not only in the way the figure moves, but also in its intricacies and individual subtleties. Animator's sketchbooks are an essential reference tool that are used over and over again, recycling imagery by changing features, profiles and adding weight to characters.'

Script analysis

Selby (cont): 'Once back in the studio, the animator will analyse the script closely to try and imagine the character as a real-life entity. This will typically involve the animator taking on the perceived persona of that character, human or otherwise, and observing this in a mirror. It will usually involve acting and probably making a fool of yourself in the process! But if you want the character to be truly believable, the first person you have got to convince is yourself.

'How will the character look? What kind of artistic treatment do you intend to visually describe your character? These decisions now need to be pondered. Making the first marks on the paper to try and work these questions out can be daunting. Some students find that working from an unusual starting point helps. Maybe random ink spots on a page create a shape or profile. Maybe a scribble over the sheet results in shapes appearing out of negative spaces, or perhaps standing on a chair dropping objects at random on to the floor. You might want to crop into areas, using a viewfinder, or maybe a digital camera and record your options. Sounds stupid? You've got permission to be stupid. Using your imagination and linking this creatively to your observation, is at the very core of your personal vision of the work you produce. It is the very essence of creating an individual, original character.

'As you "adopt" the persona of the character, you need to start recording this information through a series of drawings. Remember that these drawings will never make it to the final cut, they are merely a device to help the animator understand his character. So they can be created in any appropriate medium. Some animators will use graphite sticks to quickly deal with gesture and form of the figure, whilst others will draw with more of a pointed medium.

'Pin the drawings up in your studio. Surround yourself with what you have created. This is the point where the animator can begin to test his character out. For characters that have entirely believable human characteristics, the audience already buy into the character because they are used to seeing the human figure portrayed in this way through photography, television and film.

'The process of development is not a straightforward series of events leading to a memorable character. Repeats of certain stages might need to be covered to further

Key Principles and Processes

The Fundamentals of Animation

↗ **Still from The Hand – Jiri Trnka**
But what happens if you are trying to distort or exaggerate character? Jiri Trnka's puppet character Harlequin, from the 1965 animated film The Hand, manages to retain human characteristics despite being built of disproportionate bodily elements. The animator invests time and effort in a series of engaging observations of the way string puppets can mimic human conditions, drawing on his Eastern European cultural background.

↗ **Still from 25 Ways to Stop Smoking – Bill Plympton**
Plympton's signature-style 'average' guy, seen here trying to give up smoking in one of the extreme ways offered up in 25 Ways to Stop Smoking, demonstrates the juxtaposition between the plain, undemonstrative orthodoxies of the character and the excesses of the things he does, or that happen to him.

convince you (the animator) and your audience of certain key characteristics of your character. This can initially be frustrating for students who want to get on and shoot the film, but preparation at this stage is the key to success. Be patient! Once satisfied, the most important studies are committed to camera as a series of screen shots creating a basic animatic of the character. These will look like a series of freeze frames. From these still studies, the animator uses the knowledge gained from acute observation and continual drawing of the movement of his character to begin to create a walk cycle, where issues concerning movement of the character(s) will be experimented with and determined.

'Most college students of animation will not work as part of a team when they first encounter the subject of character development. Instead they will be required not only to be the director, but also the character development artist, the sound crew, the storyboard artist and a million things besides. However, it is important for you to see how the process works in a production company as you might be able to develop your skills further by joining and learning along with other creatively minded people.'

Bill Plympton, one of the world's most successful animators, offers a perspective from his time as a political cartoonist, stressing the relationship between the possible 'ordinariness' of a cartoon character and the 'exaggeration' of the events he participates in.

Plympton: 'Often character designers say because it is a cartoon, you have got to make a character "goofy"; you have got to give him a big nose and big ears and bulging eyeballs and buck teeth, and I go totally the opposite way; I think that the character should be extremely bland; really normal; sort of non-descript in his characteristics because when something weird happens to him, when he's excited, or when he gets eaten, or something like that, when he freaks out, there is a real contrast. And that's the secret of good animation – the movement between something that is sedate to something that is extreme, and that's what I play off, and that's what I think is important. I think that a good example is still Monty Python because these characters are very straight people – insurance salesmen, accountants, whatever – and then they want to hunt lions, and get drawn into Terry Gilliam's crazy animation.'

Character Development

Faisal and Friends[2] – a pre-school CGI animation series of 26 15-minute episodes – will be discussed later as an example of international collaboration, but it is also included here, as a pertinent example of the importance of two things. First, creating characters who serve the core conceptual premise of the programmes, and second, the creation of a simple character descriptor that sits alongside the key visualisations and model sheets.

The target audience

Faisal and Friends is made for an international audience including the Muslim world. Islamic motifs are reflected in the design of the characters and their natural environments, and the scripts promote ideas about responsible world citizenship through animated entertainment, as the friends help each other to deal with problems, laugh and play, seek assistance when in trouble, argue and make up again.

Aimed at a pre-school (2–5 year-old) audience, the loveable characters in Faisal and Friends have fun in their watery world, inventing new games through interaction with unfamiliar objects and creatures that they discover.

The series follows the adventures of Faisal, a young frog, and his friends – grasshopper Saleem, butterfly Laila, snail Professor Aamir and fish Mrs Jamila – who all live in or next to a pond. The set of characters represent family figures: Professor Aamir is fatherly, Mrs Jamila is motherly. Faisal, Saleem and Laila are the younger members within the group. The characters also have different skin colours. Lots of bugs and insects feature in the stories; these play the part of being extras in the series, so when the friends play games they are the cheering spectators and if they are building something the bugs act as helpers. At the end of each episode the friends always try to remedy their mistake or highlight the positive.

Character notes

Creating some key character notes is fundamental to the consistent construction of a main character, both for an individual animator and for a jobbing animator using the information 'bible' of a commercial series. It is often the case, particularly in children's entertainment, that the character has a dominant arguably stereotypical trait, in order to have complete immediacy for the audience. The characters from 'Faisal' are character 'types' and have particular narrative functions so must have clarity and specificity both in their design and the way they behave in the story itself.

REFERENCES
2) Faisal and Friends © Aladdin Media 2004

Faisal the frog's character notes

– Main character – the hero.
– Lovable frog, but gets into mischief.
  Once he realises that he has done wrong he
  always tries to remedy the situation. He is
  sometimes like a lovable rogue.
– Wears football kit and loves sports.
– Cheeky leader in the circle of friends. Favourite
  pastime is playing with his best friends Saleem
  and Laila.
– A 'regular', confident voice, sincere sounding.
– Athletic in his appearance, he is the link
  between the pond life and dry land.
– Facial expression – happy. Large eyes with a
  cheeky glint.

Faisal's Den

– Faisal lives in a den by the edge of the pond.
  Lots of vegetation – lilies and other pond
  foliage. Hanging foliage.
– His wooden door has a handwritten sign on it
  saying 'Faisal's Den'.
– Inside view – bed, picture of Faisal playing
  football. Side table with a few knick-knacks,
  desk with some books, football boots by the
  side of it, chair etc. Typical young boy's
  bedroom (furniture possibly made out of things
  found around the pond).

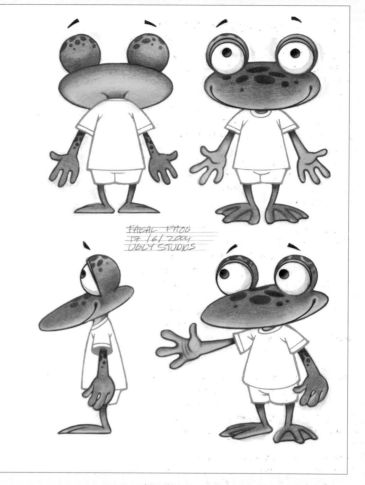

Mrs Jamila (Mama Jamila) the fish's character notes

– Beautiful mature fish.
– Caring about characters.
– Stern, but fair. Concerned about environment.
– A voice of authority.
– Facial expression – kindly.
– Mrs Jamila lives in the pond.
– Motherly figure in the stories.
– Very caring towards the characters.
– She is normally the one to tell them when
  they have done wrong.
– She has beautiful geometric patterns instead
  of scales on her body.
– She tells the friends to take care of their
  environment as this is their home and they
  should look after it.

Saleem the grasshopper's character notes

– Friend of Faisal, he's rather unsure of himself and relies on Faisal and Laila for support. He often gets into sticky situations. He provides the humour in the stories.

– He has lots of legs so he is a bit clumsy. Wears trainers.

– Clumsy-voiced with a slight stutter when nervous, speaks a bit fast.

– Saleem is very fast as he can hop long distances very quickly.

– He is cute and lovable – the sort of character that mothers would love. He has a puppy dog look about him. He provides the 'aaahh' factor in the series.

– He wears a typical and distinctive Arabian waistcoat.

– Facial expression – looks a bit nervous sometimes. His antennae droop down when he is sad or worried.

– When he is happy his antennae point straight up.

Saleem's Home

– Saleem lives in a boot.

– He gets into his home by hopping in from the the boot lip.

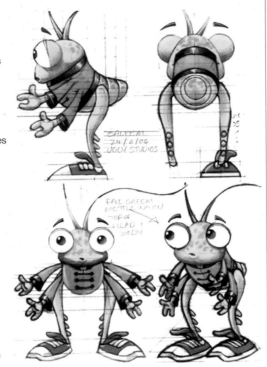

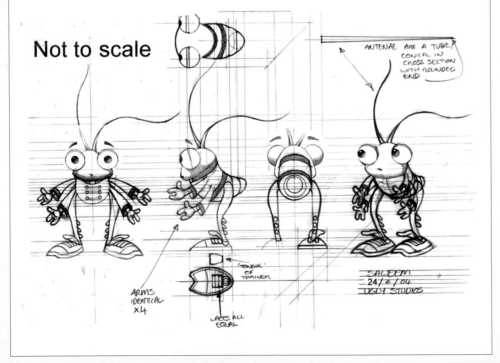

Not to scale

Laila the butterfly's character notes

– Female. She is from North Africa. She has
  darker skin tones like the Nubian race in Egypt.
  Strong African features.
– The inspiration figure for young girls, she is like
  the African version of Barbie, but more
  confident.
– She has striking patterns on her wings and
  wears a beautiful scarf.
– Strong, but feminine and gentle. Very beautiful.
– Laila enjoys playing with Faisal and Saleem.
  Laila influences the kind of games they play
  and Faisal and Saleem will often turn to her for
  ideas, especially how to remedy the mistakes
  they have made.
– Soft-voiced, feminine, but not girly, confident.
  Laila is a good flyer and can therefore see into
  the distance from a good height.
– Facial expression – long lashes and dark skin.
  She has strong defined features.

Laila's Environment

– Laila lives among the flowers in the flower bed
  growing by the side of the pond. Her house is
  found by zooming in between the flower
  stalks. She has a beautiful room that is spick
  and span. She has a large mirror decorated
  with petals. She has shelves with books,
  beautiful plants and colourful pebbles. At the
  end of her bed hangs a long silk scarf.

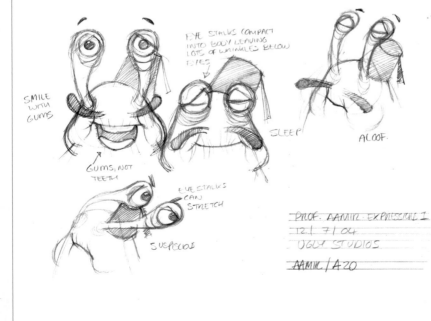

Professor Aamir the snail's character notes

– Learned, very old and laidback.
– Acts as a father figure in the stories.
– The friends laugh at him because he is always
  sleeping and makes funny sounds (snoring).
  They turn to him for advice because he knows
  everything in the world. He reads a lot too.
– He wears a Fez and a monocle. He is wise.
– Professor Aamir is forgetful about things that have
  just happened, but is crystal clear about events in
  the past. He is like the nutty professor. He likes to
  tell the friends stories about the years gone by
  when he can keep his eyes open long enough or
  when he is not reading.
– Slow-voiced and deliberate, a cross between
  Owl and Eeyore in Winnie the Pooh.
– Facial expression – sleepy-eyed and dozy looking.

Professor Aamir's home

– Professor Aamir lives in a tree hundreds of years
  old. His walls are lined with shelves filled with
  books. He has a comfortable rug and big
  comfortable floor cushions. He has a fireplace
  for the cold nights.

Layout and Thinking Cinematically

Layout is essentially the technical version of storyboarding in which camera movement, effects work, and specific design elements to enhance action and performance are addressed. The layout artist creates the settings and architectural environments of the scenes, and must consider time, place, scale, mood, atmosphere, the dynamics of the proposed action, lighting and the overall 'style'.

During the 'Golden Era' of animation – from the late 1920s to the mid-1940s – the Disney Studios effectively established an 'industrial' model of studio production, which survives with some technological modifications into the contemporary era. One of the most important stages of production stressed by Disney was 'layout' – the scene-by-scene appearance of the

↑ **Still of Max Miller and background of**
↗ **wartime London from Heroes of Comedy: Max Miller – Brian Larkins**
Miller depicted in one of his famed suits presented against a background of a period wireless, using iconic branded microphones, in a literal depiction of the radio broadcast. The animation focuses on Miller's notable performance style informed by open hand gestures and stop/start movement in which he always seemed to be furtive, telling a secret or a naughty story, before he sought rapid exit from an assumed pursuer.

Wartime London is rendered simply through the iconic silhouette of St Paul's, air-raid beams, and a bombed environment. The use of 'iconic' associative imagery is a useful visual short cut to locate an audience with the immediacy the Disney veterans suggest.

- One quick look is all the audience gets – keep it simple, direct, like a poster; it must sell an idea.
- Fancy rendering at a later date cannot save a poor original conception.
- Always keep screen directions clear. This will be your biggest headache – don't overlook it.
- Keep informed on: art in history – architecture, costumes and landscapes.
- Keep informed on: styles, media, textures, surfaces, composition, and drawing.
- Keep informed on: technical information – effects given by different lenses, ground glass, filters, gels etc.
- Mood can be established by timing and movement.

film, taking into account the staging and dramatisation of the narrative in relation to backgrounds and context; the blocking of characters (i.e. their movement and action in a scene); and the most effective camera shot/angle to support the animation in the sequence.

Simple layout strategies

Take the illustrated examples from the Heroes of Comedy series, concerning wartime Music Hall comedian, Max Miller. These adopt a simple strategy to get across information with immediacy and skill. Cathal Gaffney has a strong understanding of the relationship between fine art perspectives, cinematic 'genres' and the need to use animation to enhance an 'observational' style. This is cleverly combined in his film, using a variety of highly self-conscious filmic devices.

Using the key codes and conventions of cinema

Gaffney cleverly combines his understanding of 'live action' documentary and the traditional

ways in which it captures 'actuality' footage, with the graphic freedoms afforded by animation. He uses traditional shots from the documentary style and exaggerates for comic effect through animation.

Gaffney: 'The history of Give Up Yer Aul Sins stems back 40 years. A teacher, Margaret Cunningham, brought in an old battered tape recorder to record her seventy pupils in the classrooms of Rutland Street National School, and she told them they were all going to be on the wireless. So the little kids – probably beaten into the catechism – were so excited and rattled off the story of John the Baptist. These tapes were ultimately just played back to the pupils as a kind of learning aid for them.

'So later on, Margaret got sick, and the tapes were going to be thrown away, and someone told Father Brian Darcy, and he brought them into the RTE (Irish Public Service TV and radio stations) and had a slot on a radio show and played them. →

Preparation: Layout and Thinking Cinematically

→ It was an instant success and went on several radio shows, and eventually, EMI Records put them on CD, which sold 80,000 units and money went to Cunningham's care, and to the School. It went five times platinum in Ireland, and that is pretty big by any standards. It had been around for years. I knew of it. I had never listened to it, and I was driving down to Galway and I heard the story of John the Baptist and I fell about laughing. I bought the CD and contacted EMI, and responded to the Framework Scheme, funded by the RTE and the Arts Council, which gave out £30,000 to make a five-minute short film. We managed to get the funding and I designed the film, and worked with Alan Shannon who did the animation. We worked out the storyboards and scenes, and worked on it between commercial briefs. We did the film in downtime really. The soundtrack, no matter how many times you heard it, remained fresh.'

Gaffney (cont.): 'The soundtrack itself, was actually dreadful – dogs barking, desks falling and the like – so partly as a response to that, and the era it came from, we decided to make it as an animated documentary. We had the cutaway shots and at the end of the film, we have the film itself coming out of the camera, because the soundtrack ends so abruptly. It was a technique we had to adopt because the story just stops. We animated all the scratches on it and had the microphone coming in and out of the frame. If we had approached that as a computer animation it would have looked dreadful, or if we did some arty-farty style to it, it would not have worked. We just had to do classical animation – 12 drawings per second – to make it work. The response has been overwhelming. Adults and children love it. Adults feel nostalgic about it because you couldn't have such a view today.'

REFERENCES
3) Johnson, O & Thomas, F. The Illusion of Life, New York: Abbeville Press, 1981, p215

↑ **Still of seaside postcard-style art**
↓ **direction from Heroes of Comedy: Max Miller and seafront background – Brian Larkins**
To animate one of Miller's notorious sexually innuendoed gags, the choice was made to adopt the style of saucy seaside postcard artist, Donald McGill. The tone of Miller's gags was

matched by a period visual style also concordant with similar material. Visual sources in popular culture may be just as significant as those drawn from more notable art cultures.

This seafront design draws from designs and photographs of the period, and uses an air-brushing technique for a particular texture.

**Stills from Give Up Yer Aul Sins –
Cathal Gaffney**

← **1.** This traditional establishing shot shows the context in which the story is to take place. Taken from a high and wide perspective, it highlights the way in which the film-maker – in true Hitchcock style – is almost surveying a scene in order to select a story possibility. Here the camper van, driven by the documentary film-makers, begins its approach to the school.

← **2.** This medium shot focuses on the camper van, but also draws attention to the character of the streets and the people strolling along going about their business.

↑ **3.** This medium shot sustains the sense of place, but directs the viewer to where the camper van is heading – the school in the distance.

→ **4.** The camper van moves into close up. Throughout this introductory sequence, the key questions for the viewer have been why are we following this camper van? Who is inside it? Where are we going? The shots have provided the narrative 'hook' at the start of the story, and this is crucial to all successful narrative fiction. Note the background detail of the props supporting the buildings, and the general sense of an old-fashioned and run-down part of the city.

← **5.** The close up of the camera sustains the self-reflexive aspect of the piece – this is an animated film about the making of a documentary, so it deliberately calls attention to the film-making process itself.

← **6.** This 'proscenium'-style medium shot effectively frames the key protagonist – Mary, the little girl on the left – in the context of her classroom and colleagues. There is a general sense of excitement about the presence of the camera and the opportunity to be filmed.

← **7.** This close up of Mary in the act of telling the story of John the Baptist defines her character. As in all close ups, specific character detail and information are revealed. Most importantly, a sense of empathy and engagement with the viewer also takes place in this case.

← **8.** This close up again stresses the nature of the character, but also the 'cartoonal' aspect of the film in its design and character performance/movement. The shot also uses the convention of the faded extremities of the frame as a reference to the act of dream, memory, or fantasy. This is not the 'real world' where the little girl tells the story, but the world of the imagination, signalled also by the change of time, space, period etc.

9. This low angle shot showing both the little girl talking and the camera recording her is a classic shot from the vocabulary of documentary film-making, signalling the presence, but supposed unobtrusiveness of a 'fly on the wall' crew, who are, of course, in this case, the makers of the animated film.

10. A traditional medium shot focusing on the conversation between two characters.

11. A close up always accentuates 'emotion' and the fundamental relationship the characters have with the audience.

12. The vitality and affecting expressiveness of the little girl as she gets carried away with telling the story is captured in this exuberant leap.

13. Here the animation itself becomes important, both in the literal re-enactment of the girl's storytelling – Jesus curing the lepers – and in the facilitation of a visual gag not possible in live action.

14–15. This extreme close up accentuates the physical action in the frame and exaggerates the emotion even more than when held in close up. Here the blind lady can see again.

Key Principles and Processes

The Fundamentals of Animation

↑ **16–17.** The image here supports the perception of the 'lame' as imagined by the little girl, and the apparent 'ease' of the miracle as God enables them to walk again.

↑ **18.** Here the medium shot accentuates the comic movement of the character as he celebrates the miracles performed by Jesus.

↗ **19.** An important functional use of the medium-close shot to give specific and significant information to the viewer, but here also operating as a gag – a modern party invite for Salome, 'the wicked lady'.

→ **20–23.** Salome's dance played out not as an erotic fantasy, but as an exaggerated show dance, foregrounding the possibilities of accentuation and exaggeration of the body in animation.

↘ **24.** A good example of composition of crowds: John is diminished in status by being placed towards the background, but remains the focus of the scene as he is in the middle at the key point of perspective. The soldiers, though overpowering him as a group, still defer to John – the central protagonist in the story and the key figure of empathy within the image – because of this composition.

Sound

While sound design, music and animation can be thought of as separate practices with independent techniques and discourses, it is within the establishment of relationships between these art forms that we begin to recognise contemporary animated film.

Tom Simmons is an accomplished sound designer and combines his professional work with lecturing at the Norwich School of Art and Design, UK, encouraging students to see the intrinsic relationship between 'sound' and the animated film, drawing upon historical examples and promoting experimentation.

Simmons: 'Combining sound and animation is a complex activity for which there is no single correct or magical formula. Just as Disney and PIXAR have established models for the creation of characters, narrative and plot within animated film, so too have a community of smaller independent companies and auteur practitioners. From early examples of the use of music within the films of Oskar Fischinger and Hans Richter, to the wittily zany soundtracks in Warner Bros. cartoons created by Carl Stalling and Treg Brown, or Scott Bradley in the Tom and Jerry shorts, to the complex layering of sound and image in Peter Jackson's versions of The Lord of the Rings, many strategies have been developed for working with sound in relationship to the moving image.

'The following examples present a view of some of the strategies animators and sound designers have used to articulate relationships between sound and image. Examples are presented according to their role within the production process. Some have generic applications and can be heard similarly deployed in many animated films, others are film or artist specific.'

Music video and animation inspired by music

Simmons (cont.): 'Michel Gondry's animation to the Chemical Brothers' Star Guitar is an example of musical structure informing visual decision-making. A simple train journey becomes the platform for an image sequence in which a passenger's window view is shaped by the repetitious patterns of the music. Similar examples include Shynola's video to Go With the Flow by Queens of the Stone Age and Jonas Odell's video to Take Me Out by Franz Ferdinand.

'Tim Hope delivers a visual-lyrical interpretation in the video to Don't Panic by Coldplay. The video opens with an animation representing the water cycle to the words "We live in a beautiful world". Hope moves through a visually stunning image sequence detailing industrialisation and pollution before returning to a domestic setting for the closing lyrics "… all that I know, there's nothing here to run from, because yeah, everybody here's got somebody to lean on".

'Welsh animator Clive Whalley presents a fascination with musical structure in several animated films. Examples include the six films from the S4C-commissioned Divertimenti series, each of which was collaboratively produced with a different musician or performer. In the pre-production of Divertimenti No.2, Love Song, Walley made analyses of the breathing of the performer, the meter bars on the recording desk and of a hand dance to the melodic phrases of a harmonica track, which were then visually interpreted in layers of animated paint on glass.'

Character animation that is informed by, reacts to, or visualises sound, normally speech

'Aardman's Creature Comforts series takes speech characteristics such as accent and dialect as the basis for designing and animating stereotyped animal models. A number of people are interviewed on a particular topic, recordings of which are analysed and used to develop and animate clay models. Speech effects, such as gulping, burping and coughing are often animated if they are contained within the original vocal recordings.

'Disney's Aladdin features the voice of Robin Williams as the genie trapped in the lamp. In order to create an animated genie that would visually match Williams' character, Williams was asked to improvise speech recordings from which a genie character was drawn. A number of character transformations were brought about by changes in the sonic qualities of Williams' voice.'

Sound recording, usually speech, which lead a narrative or a narrator

'Gemma Carrington's Coming Home is a film concerned with memories, conveyed through several generations of a family. A radio, which is rarely seen, plays information about the era and provides a narrative metaphor for →

↑ **Pop promo stills from Go With the Flow by Queens of the Stone Age – Shynola**

↖ One of the intrinsic problems faced by directors of music videos is to create something that is original and distinctive, both in relation to the band and the song being promoted, and in regard to the now extensive back catalogue of music videos. Inevitably, animation is often deployed to create something different. Here in Queens of the Stone Age's Go With the Flow, Shynola – Richard 'Kenny' Kenworthy, Gideon Baws, Jason Groves and Chris Harding – refresh the 'band-in-fast-car-on-the-road' genre with some distinctive design and computer animation. It has its sex – some show girls; its drugs – the 'acid' style design; and its rock 'n' roll – some villains chasing the band, but the look is altogether fresh. First Shynola painted the band black and stood them on the back of an old Chevy pickup. They were shot on Hi-Definition Video against a green screen and in post-production the band were keyed out, the camera moves were tracked and a virtual environment was created for them to drive through.

→ moving between generations. Generational transformations are led by the sound of static interference in the radio, acting as a "portal" for tuning into different eras.'

Simmons (cont.): 'Dad's Dead, directed by Chris Shepherd, employs a principal character whose voice delivers the story in all but a few occasions, but who is similarly never seen. In moments when the narrative is visually presented, the narrator's voice becomes the property of other characters, which are uncomfortably lip-synched to the voice of the narrator.'

Examples of sound strategies and techniques that are based in post-production are explored later in the book.

Sound advice

When developing a project, try to establish the idea and map out the sound and animation strategies, and the relationships between sound and image in the pre-production stage. If there is a script, it is a good idea to test it by undertaking a sample recording before settling on a final version; certain constructions that look good on the page just don't work in practice. Likewise, voicing the script will help to ensure that the 'right' voices for the characters will develop in the film. Think about the properties sounds will have in the film and how these will relate to the environments used. It is a good idea to work out which sounds should be recorded 'dry' in a sound studio and processed

digitally, and which should be recorded on location. When working with music, decide how this will affect the editing decisions and how this will work with such ideas as anticipation, tension and relaxation in the film's structure. After compiling the sound material and working it into the dope sheet, clarify the strategies for working with or against the images: what occurs; how, where and when? By complementing or counterpointing the music and image, narrative and meaning are implied.

Use of dope sheets

Arril Johnson is an animator, model-maker, writer and actor, who worked for Potterton Studios in Canada and now delivers animation courses at the University of the West of England, Bristol. For traditional animation the 'dope sheet' has been the most invaluable aspect of the production process. Here Johnson talks about its role and explains its function.

Johnson: 'In the industry, camera instruction sheets are often called "dope sheets" from the early 1900s slang use of "dope" to mean "information". Dope sheets relating to any given scene or shot are kept in a production folder along with the layout and drawings or final artwork required for that shot. In some cases, however, as with personal films or shorter commercial projects, it is possible for a set of dope sheets to incorporate all the shots planned for the entire film. Administrative convenience and clarity determine the choice. Although developed for organisational use on animation productions involving drawn animation, these sheets can also be useful when planning and shooting animated action using other techniques. There are variations in dope sheet design between studios, but all of these forms (and they are forms) represent a vertical timeline running from the top of the page to the bottom.'

Dope sheet specifics

Johnson (cont.): 'Typically, each sheet holds four seconds of screen time. The sheets that are used on projects to be shown at the film speed of 24 frames (exposures) per second have spaces representing 96 frames running down their length. On the other hand, where television is shown at a multiple of 25 frames per second, as in the UK, 100 frames represents four seconds of televised time. Because so much animation is made for television, you are more likely to encounter this type of dope sheet.

'The dope sheets shown here (see pages 60–63) were designed for duplication on standard A4 photocopier paper and are smaller than industry standard sheets, representing only two seconds of time instead of the usual four. The top of the dope sheet provides spaces for information that typically would only appear on the first camera instruction sheet. The obvious exception is the sheet number, which appears on the top right in each case and is consecutive.

'Reading from the left, the other information provided is the title of the production and episode (if any), the number of the sequence (made up of interrelated scenes), the scene (or shot) number, the name of the animator (and sometimes the assistant as well), the duration of the shot in whole seconds with residual frames, the total frame count, and the length of the shot in feet. This last item relates to film and the way animators were often paid. In one foot of 35mm film there are 16 frames. If you were making animation drawings to be filmed at two exposures per drawing you would have to produce eight drawings to create a foot of filmed animation. If you were being paid a set rate per foot you would have a fairly clear idea of how productive you would need to be to make a living.'

Preliminary script recording

PIXAR Director, Pete Doctor and Editor, Lee Unkrich note that in the process of the preliminary recording of the script, with additional improvisation by the actors, they can make particular choices about 'performance', which will finally take its place on the 'dope sheet' variants.

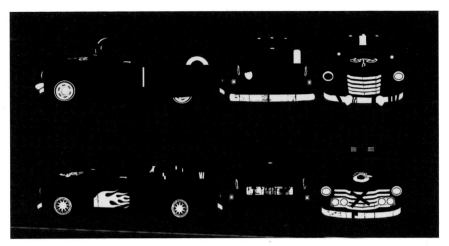

Doctor: 'So we have all this great material and we have to make all the difficult selections – which line is the funniest, which one do we want to use. In more cases than not we end up cutting performances together, so that what seems on the screen to be "one line" is actually the editors assembling the perfect take.'

Unkrich: 'It is a real luxury for our medium that you do not have in live action because you don't have to "opt" for the performance you have. You can make choices, syllable by syllable sometimes, but if we have done it so seamlessly that the audience doesn't notice, you end up with a really great performance.'[4]

Lip-synching

Lip-synching can be problematic for some animators, but basic approaches can sometimes work well. Animator Bill Plympton explains:

Preparation: Sound

Plympton: 'The minimal approach to "lip-synch" is all about money and time – four drawings with four different mouth positions. Everything else is exactly the same – I just colour pencilled each one. With those four drawings I think I got two minutes of animation out of it. And the secret is to work with the soundtrack to make sure all the mouth positions work for you. What I do is say the words in front of the mirror – basically I do a slow motion version of the words like "The secret of li-fe-e" – and find the appropriate mouth positions first. One of the things that I didn't realise, and the famous Warner Bros. animator, Preston Blair told me – I met with him before he died – was that people don't actually close their mouths after they say something. Mouths remain open. So I leave the mouths open for about half a second longer, and it makes it more natural, makes it more real.'

REFERENCES
4) Quoted in the PIXAR Animation Masterclass, London Film Festival, National Film Theatre, November 2001

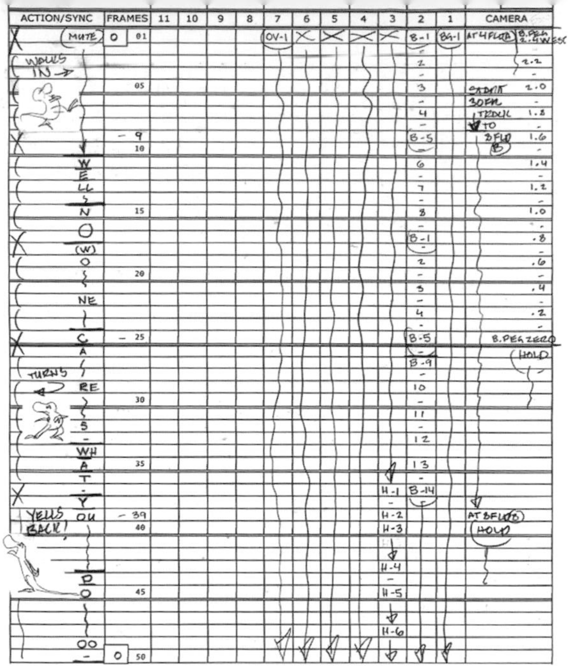

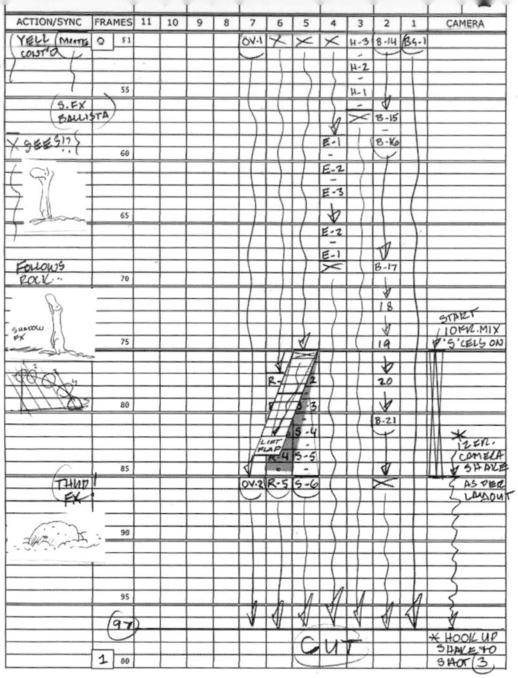

Tutorial – Dope sheet basics

Diagram 1

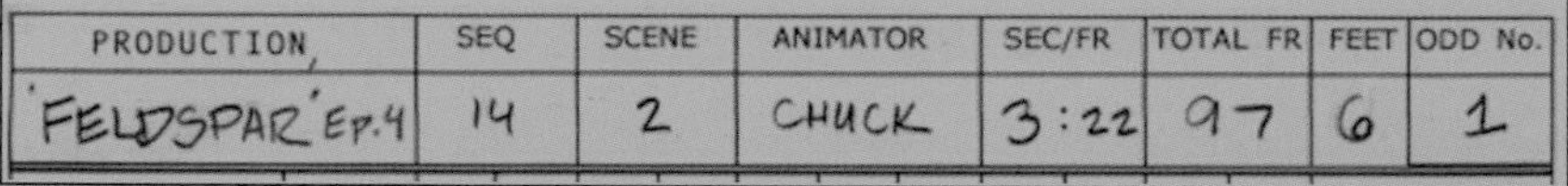

PRODUCTION	SEQ	SCENE	ANIMATOR	SEC/FR	TOTAL FR	FEET	ODD No.
'FELDSPAR' Ep.4	14	2	CHUCK	3:22	97	6	1

In traditional drawn, cel animation and stop-motion animation, the 'dope sheet' – essentially the information required to execute the animation in relation to the soundtrack – is crucial to the planning and timing of the work. Here Arril Johnson explains a basic dope sheet, and though with the advent of more and more computer-generated work this is now less used, its principles are still helpful to all aspiring animators in terms of embracing core animation skills.

Diagram 1

In this case, in order to help with the numbering of the frame count, there are two types of sheets; odd numbered and even numbered. The sheet marked 'ODD No.' shows a frame column starting at '1' (see far right column of Diagram 1) and ending at '50'. The 'EVEN No.' sheet shows frames marked running from '51' to '00'. Put a '1' in the box to the left of '00' and you have an indication of '100' frames. Sheet 1 is odd, sheet 2 is even, sheet 3 would be odd, 4 even, and so on. If you put a '1' next to the '01' at the top of odd sheet 3 it would read frame '101' and at the bottom a '1' next to '50' means frame number '150'. On even numbered sheet 4, a '1' goes next to '51' and a '2' goes next to '00'. In other words, at the end of sheet 4 you will have reached your 200th frame; eight seconds of animation at 25 frames per second. This is easier than it reads and it does give you control.

So, this is your first exposure, frame one, at the top of dope sheet one.

Diagram 2

This is your sample scene's last frame, 97 shortly followed by the last frame on sheet 2, frame 100; four seconds of screen time on these A4-sized dope sheets.

Diagram 2

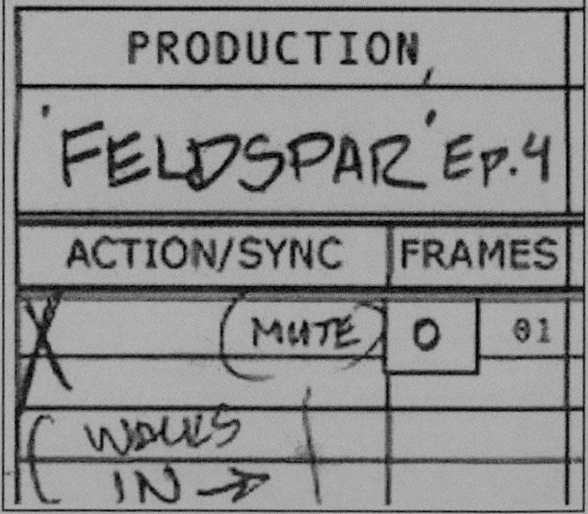

PRODUCTION		
'FELDSPAR' Ep.4		
ACTION/SYNC	FRAMES	
X (MUTE)	0	01
WALKS IN →		

Tutorial – Dope sheet basics

Diagram 4

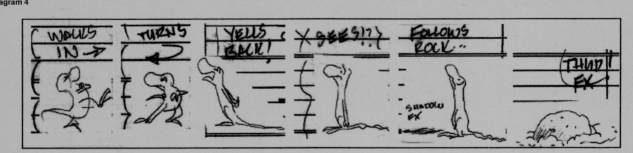

Diagram 3

Almost anyone animating can make use of the information (on the facing page). You need to know how long your scenes (and whole film) will last if you're going to manage the pacing of the film, fill a predetermined broadcasting time slot, or just manage your own time in order to finish a personal film.

The column on the left of the dope sheet, next to the frame count, is often marked 'Action/Sync'. This refers to a description of the action as it unfolds and any specific information about the soundtrack. Something that is equally useful to both graphic and model animators often appears in the action column of dope sheets: thumbnail sketches.

Diagram 4

Thumbnails are simple, expressive drawings of certain key moments in the performance of the action and on many dope sheets, are often less than an inch high. They can help clarify the body language needed in the final animation. Another rough diagram also appears in the action column on the second sheet of the sample doping.

Diagram 5

This describes the trajectory and acceleration of the stone that eventually lands on the character. In addition, it shows the angle of light that determines where the stone's shadow should be as it moves.

The 'X' and '(' symbols in the action column are my personal method of indicating where the main drawings, the keys, and the linking drawings, the in-betweens, occur on the timeline.

Diagram 6

The 'X' represents a key and the '(' an in-between. In this case, each is photographed or captured for two frames. Called animating on twos, this cuts your work in half. When timing the intended animation in order to know where the keys, in-betweens and pauses should occur, I find it useful to make up vocal sound effects that mimic the physical rhythm of the action. That way it is possible to stop flailing around the room as I repeatedly act out the animation and, instead, sit down with the stop watch and analyse the 'music' of the action.

Next to the action notes in the 'Action/Sync' column is a detailed analysis or breakdown of the soundtrack, which synchronises with the animation.

Diagram 6

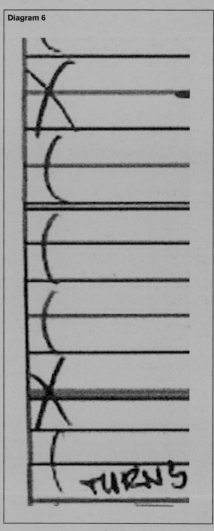

Diagram 3

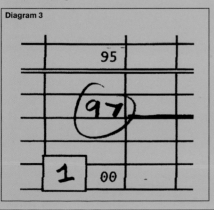

Diagram 5

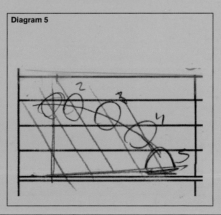

Tutorial – Dope sheet basics

Diagram 7

It could be anything, sometimes music, but in this example it is the pre-recorded voice of the character. In addition to creating a believable performance of the action, the animation must convince the audience that this voice is coming out of the character as the action occurs. It must remain synchronised to the character's lips and be integrated into the total performance. The character's body language, however, usually anticipates the spoken words by several or sometimes more than several frames. First of all, most people think before they speak and the gestures of the face and whole body reflect these thoughts and feelings. Secondly, if the character assumes a new position just as an important word is being spoken the audience might be distracted enough by the visuals to miss the vocal emphasis on that word. The picture and sound need to integrate, not compete, and the character's body language needs to create the illusion of thought.

To the right of the 'Action/Sync' and 'Frames' columns are the numbered columns indicating different levels of artwork. These are only applicable to drawn animation, whether it is scanned into a computer and composited or traced on to clear cels and photographed.

Diagram 8

Number 1 is the lowest level and, in this case, is reserved for the background, BG-1. Here level 7 is used for OV-1, an overlay of some scenic element that exists above (in front of) all other artwork.

Diagram 9

As the shot progresses, additional artwork appears on various levels with prefixes indicating the nature of the numbered drawings or cels; 'E' for eyes, 'H' for head, 'B' for body, and sometimes a large 'X' indicating a designated level, which currently has a blank cel doped because no artwork is required on that level yet.

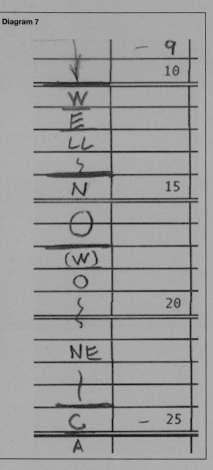

Diagram 7

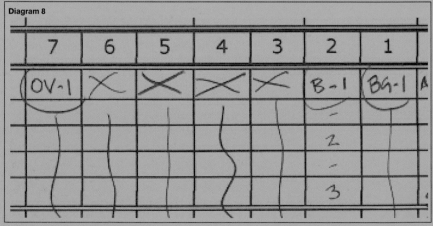

Diagram 9

Diagram 8

Diagram 10

The 'camera' column shows any moves planned for the artwork or camera, as well as any transitional or special effects. In this case, the shot starts at 4 field 'A' with the camera showing a specific portion of the artwork four inches wide. The bottom pegs are indicated as starting at 2.4 inches west (left) of their normal zero position and immediately panning east (right) at a rate of .2 inches every two frames. On the ninth frame of this shot the camera has to start recomposing the picture so that it will end up cropping the artwork at 8 field 'B' at a specific moment in the action 30 frames (one second and five frames) later. Further down the camera column is an instruction in the camera column to 'Start 10 frame mix "S" cels on'.

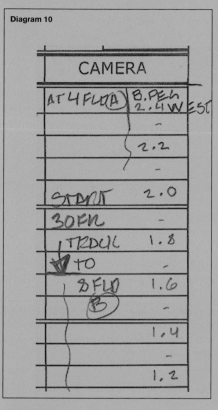

Diagram 10

CAMERA

computer, however, it might be easier to dope the outgoing and incoming artwork on separate levels. In the virtual world there are no physical limits to the number of levels available.

When this mix does end, there is an indication of a camera-shake lasting 12 frames to give the effect of a vibration induced by the rock hitting the ground (and Feldspar, the dinosaur). Because the rock hits the ground from above, the first movement of the artwork is downward (south), a specified distance below the current position. This is usually followed by a similar, but slightly smaller move up (north) above the start position, followed by alternating and decreasing repositionings down and up until the artwork is back in its original position. Although it is necessary to shoot such an effect with one frame per repositioning in order to make the vibration feel real, I tend to shoot two frames of the first move so that the impact is emphasised before the vibration begins. There are some wonderfully eccentric variations on camera-shakes and it is worth experimenting and carefully considering the

context of the shake. At the end of this shot the word 'CUT' appears, but there also is a request for a 'Hook-Up' to the next shot. This means maintain continuity; in this case, between the animated vibrations that end this shot and the ones that start the next.

Diagram 13

In certain cases it is possible to prepare drawn animation and then improvise the final timing on the virtual dope sheet in a computer program. It is also possible to improvise the timing of model animation and computer-generated images. What filling out the Action/Sync column of a printed dope sheet does, however, is develop your sense of timing and provides a structure that might change in part, but is extremely useful when a deadline is approaching and you've just enough physical strength to do the job, but very little energy for analytical or creative thought. It's your plan; the framework within which small changes can take place.

Diagram 11

A mix or a dissolve is usually used as a transitional effect between scenes and is basically the overlapping of a fading out of one set-up and the fading in of the next. It also is possible to use a mix within a shot or scene as a special effect, for example, when making a ghost materialise or smoke dissipate. In this case, the 'S' cels are the approaching shadow of the rock and the mix allows the rock's shadow to become darker as the rock comes nearer to the ground. The use of a flap, like that shown on dope sheet 2, can help deal with the doping of cel changes that occur during the mix.

Diagram 12

The mix-out is doped on top of the flap and the mix-in underneath it. This can be a useful conceptual device when shooting film on a rostrum camera where the film is physically wound back before the mix-in starts. On a

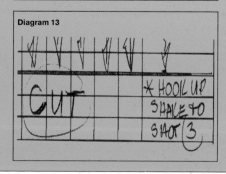

Diagram 1

Diagram 13

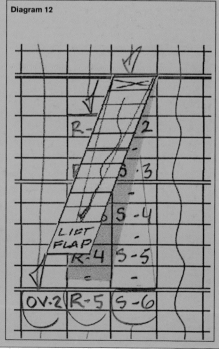

Diagram 12

Technique

The choice of technique for an animator is fundamentally related to key skills, artistic intentions and practical considerations. For some, this is straightforward – traditional drawn/cel animation; stop-motion animation using clay, puppets or objects; or computer-generated animation, using a variety of software applications. For others, there is the desire to work in different ways, or to mix media.

Film-maker and lecturer at Norwich School of Art and Design, Suzie Hanna, mixes media in her own films, deploying traditional and digital techniques. Her approach enables her to constantly refresh the imagery in her films, reflecting different positions in the narrative, and often shifting from interior states – memory, fantasy, dream – to exterior states – observed, concrete 'reality'.

Rising popularity of mixed media

Hanna: 'Mixed-media animation is more prevalent within independent and small studio practice as most commercial animation studios are structured for mass-production relying on one main process, be that 2D, CGI, or stop-frame animation. Brad Bird's popular film The Iron Giant is an early example of a mainstream mixed-media animated film. Collaboration between studios in the production of mixed-media live-action and animation films is

becoming more common. In the 1999 BBC series Walking with Dinosaurs, traditional puppets appeared on screen with virtual ones in a live-action landscape.'

Convergence of digital and traditional techniques

'Recent animated feature films, such as Hayao Miyazaki's beautifully drawn Spirited Away, employ a range of digital techniques to enhance the visuals including mapping hand-drawn backgrounds on to 3D CGI models and 2D texture and material shaders for aspects such as the creation of a realistic, ever-changing sea surface. Sylvain Chomet's Belleville Rendez-vous, although primarily 2D, uses CGI 3D backgrounds, and Aardman's claymation feature Chicken Run has digitally imposed weather effects. This expansion of mixed-media production has been engineered by computer technology, the digital interface allowing all sources to be imperceptibly combined.'

Independent animation allows media experimentation

'Independent animators are free to experiment with any media they are attracted to, and have done so since the early days of animation. Ladislas Starewicz, Hans Richter, Oskar Fischinger and Norman McLaren, received critical acclaim for their mixed-media experiments in the first half of the last century and are sometimes referred to as 'artist film-makers'. Contemporary animators who employ a →

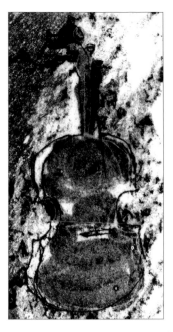

↓ **Stills from Paganini's Dream –
Suzie Hanna**
These stills show a cut-out replacement sequence illustrating a simple animated movement.

↑ **Stills from Paganini's Dream –**
↓ **Suzie Hanna**
Here are three different representational techniques to show a violin, which reflect a range of mixed-media approaches in a single film.

→ diverse range of media, although perceived as experimental practitioners, use configuration as well as abstraction in their work, orthodox as well as experimental components.'

Examples

Hanna (cont.): 'Some examples that demonstrate the diversity of methods and approaches include the following films: Jane Aaron's Remains to be Seen contains animated drawings that are captured as stop-motion elements in live environments. This pre-digital work evidences complex planning and rigorous attention to detail. The outcome is not only visually engaging, but draws the viewer's attention to the actual production process. Daniel Greaves' Manipulation also self-references animation methods through the creation of a drawn character who when discarded, emerges from the bin as a 3D crumpled paper stop-motion puppet. Feeling My Way by Jonathan Hodgson uses a mixture of digital and traditional methods, print-outs from live-action video overdrawn with paint and pencil, re-scanned and edited to create a moving collage. Chris Shepherd's Dad's Dead combines live action with a broad variety of drawn animation styles to create powerful messages through transformation, literally warping and defacing the frame content. Compositing programs such as After Effects and Flame make this layering more accessible, and whereas Jane Aaron physically placed all her elements in front of the lens and captured the information in one go, contemporary mixed-media animators tend to incorporate a host of post-production methods in their film-making.

'As with all animation, planning and design must be rigorous, and when mixing media it is important to imagine how the elements will interact or combine. It is a good idea to test the processes and develop your creative techniques through experimentation. If you are using stop motion as the method and your mixed media is in the physical content of the set, check the stability and registration of anything you may intend to move, and if indoors, pay strict attention to the lighting.'

Rotoscoping

'Rotoscoping by printing digital live-action video frames is common, but can be very expensive and time-consuming. Only print selected frames, eight or 12 per second, and export them from the timeline as small TIFFs. Combinations of analogue and digital techniques, for instance using directly animated

Catagories of mixed-media animation artists

1. The animator who moves from one medium to another in search of stretching boundaries and preconceptions about animated film-making techniques and processes. They may well only use one or two ways of working in each film, but their oeuvre has a mixed-media identity. *Examples: Oskar Fischinger, Norman McLaren, Caroline Leaf and Daniel Greaves.*

2. The artist whose engagement with a range of materiality and techniques is a significant factor in their inspiration, whose concern seems to be that the audience should enjoy the processes shown in the making of the film as much as any other part. This may take a primarily three-dimensional or two-dimensional form. *Examples: Jane Aaron, Robert Breer and Joanna Woodward.*

3. Collaborating animators who combine their own preferred techniques, or directors who commission passages from other animators to enrich the breadth of material and style in their productions. *Examples:*

Marjut Rimminen and Christine Roche, Joanna Priestley, Tim Webb, Paul Vester.

4. Artist film-makers who animate with widely varying techniques and materials as a way of bringing ideas and narratives to life in a physically symbolic manner. *Examples: David Anderson, Kayla Parker, Jan Svankmajer, Yuri Norstein, Simon Pummell and The Quay Brothers.*

5. Digital mixers who wish to go beyond the traditional uses of commercial software and use computers, during part or all of the process, to combine images (and sounds) from a variety of sources in experimental ways. *Examples: Jonathan Hodgson, Andreas Hykade, Run Wrake and Chris Shepherd.*

6. Performing artists who use the animated film they have made as a prop or part of another kind of exhibition that creates a 'live' mixing of media. *Examples: Kathy Rose and Tim Hope.*

sequences within a CGI landscape, can humanise a homogenous scenario. After learning the principles of animated movement, chroma-keying and compositing techniques are probably the most important skills for the modern mixed-media animator.'

Dad's Dead

The multi award-winning Dad's Dead, made by Chris Shepherd is an excellent example of a mixed-media animation, and one that also points out the relationship between live action and animation.

Shepherd had returned to his roots in Liverpool and discovered that the Eileen Craven Primary School, which he had attended as a boy, had been vandalised and burnt out. The destruction of the school prompted Shepherd to consider his memories of school and the formative context that it had been, and his mixed feelings about its influence. He was keen to find an approach to the subject matter where the

animation could facilitate a film taking place in someone's head, and that the assumed 'innocence' of animation could be contradicted by dark, fantastic and subversive things taking place in an ordinary, run-down, derelict, everyday terrain.

Having completed a provisional shooting script, Shepherd cast 'real scouser', Ian Hart for his voice-over, and shot live-action material in six separate shoots over seven months, attempting to 'build the film up like a painting', creating an animatic alongside the live-action material that would suggest how the animation would interact and counterpoint the dramatic action featuring Johnno, the dysfunctional youth at the heart of the story. Shepherd wanted to make a film that people might find disturbing and perhaps not like, but ironically, the film has been embraced as a challenging portrayal of the way that 'nostalgia' is easily triggered, but may not be comforting if remembered actually as it was.

Stills from Dad's Dead – Chris Shepherd and Maria Manton
Shepherd is highly successful in offering a commentary on the uses and meanings of animated imagery while using animation to re-invent controversial documentary-style domestic drama.

→ Johnno steals the Mr Whippy cap and boxes of 99s before he burns out the ice cream van he burgles.

↑ The innocuous child-friendly images on the side of the ice cream van are animated to echo Johnno's brutality. The sharp-toothed figure beats up the rabbits. Simultaneously, the innocence of animated animal characters is subverted and revised.

→ This theme continues throughout the film as an elephant, which is animated dancing on a child's birthday card and inevitably suggests Disney's Dumbo, is later hanged as Johnno torches a flat. All innocence has been completely lost and the image works as a metaphor for a personal, social and cultural world in decline.

Shepherd encourages the view that the only effective way to make a film is to be 'true to yourself' and to explore your own world carefully for the inspiration it can bring, stressing 'what can be boring to you can be interesting to someone else if presented as an engaging story'. This chimes with the view of John Lasseter (the director of Toy Story and Toy Story 2), that research and observation are absolutely vital because 'nothing is more interesting or rich than what is actually there, once you look at it with a truthful, but creative eye'. Shepherd's story, the memory of the relationship between the narrator and Johnno, recalled in a range of challenging vignettes – destroying an ice cream van; spray-painting dead pigeons and torturing animals; Johnno lying about his father's death; Johnno's abuse of a blind man he supposedly cares for; and the torching of a run-down flat – also explores the received associations of mediated imagery,

← **Stills from Dad's Dead – Chris Shepherd**
← **and Maria Manton**

↙ The narrator, when fleeing from Johnno's house, finds a Ladybird book – one actually found on the ground at the location – and when animated, this initially embodies happy memories with 'Auntie May', and the apparent stability of a family structure. The images for the Ladybird books were drawn by Martin Aitchison and John Berry, and clearly represent a safe, middle class, trouble-free England, which was clearly not the experience of Johnno and his kind. The film represents his disempowerment by animating obscene graffiti on the Ladybird images.

↙ The traditional 'cartoonal' imagery of animals is subverted by the use of animation to show Johnno throwing a cat from a tenth floor flat. A highly realistic depiction of a cat lying dead becomes very challenging in this light.

↙ The translucent, almost supernatural figure
↓ of Johnno as he throws stones at ducks on a pond; one animated to show a fleeing 'cartoonal' duck and to once more point out the difference between fantasy and reality; innocence and experience; life and death.

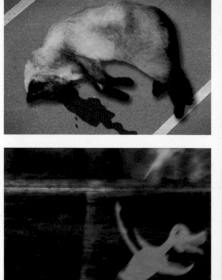

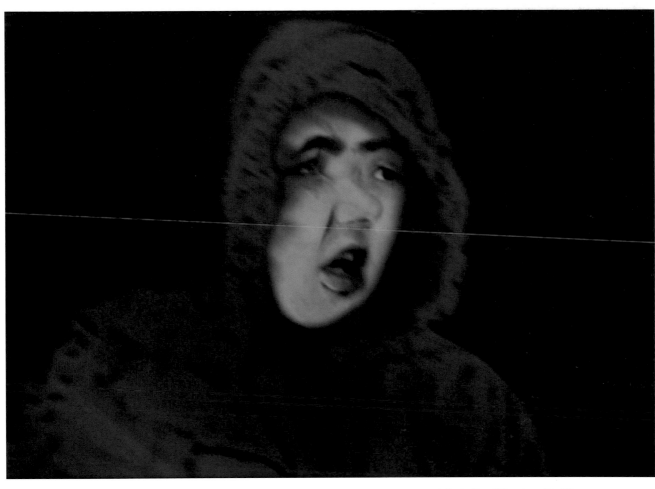

↑ **Stills from Dad's Dead – Chris Shepherd**
↓ **and Maria Manton**
Shepherd distorts Johnno's face at certain
moments to show the psychological and
emotional complexity of the character as he
plays out his conscious frustration, anger and
brutality. It was Shepherd's desire to create
a 'live-action Francis Bacon' painting with
such imagery.

↓ **Production still from LearnDirect Bus –
DFGW/COI/Maria Manton/Chris
Shepherd**
Ironically, this graffiti style prompted a
commission from LearnDirect to make a
public information film based on the 'doodling'
readers do on newspapers when considering
an advertisement.

The Animator as Interpreter

Inventing scenarios, writing scripts and creating funny material are all particular interpretative and creative skills needed by the animator – what solutions are dramatically viable, offer comic situations and are particularly suited to animation?

Script and Scenario

All animation practitioners approach the execution of what they wish to create in a variety of ways. Some receive a script and interpret it; others write their own. In either case, it is crucial for the writer to engage with the distinctive 'language' of animation, the core principles of script-writing and often, the issues that inform the creation of an original and particular

'world' that only animation can facilitate. All these issues are considered here:

The distinctive language of animation can be summarised as follows – any one element or more might be intrinsic to an individual approach:

– Metamorphosis (the ability to facilitate the change from one form into another without edit).
– Condensation (the maximum degree of suggestion in the minimum amount of imagery).

– Anthropomorphism (the imposition of human traits on animals, objects and environments).
– Fabrication (the physical and material creation of imaginary figures and spaces).
– Penetration (the visualisation of unimaginable psychological/physical/technical 'interiors').
– Symbolic association (the use of abstract visual signs and their related meanings).

```
                 64 Zoo Lane
          © COPYRIGHT ZOO LANE PRODUCTION 1996

             The Story of Zed the Zebra.

CAST

1 Zoo      Lucy
           Georgina the Giraffe
           Giggles and Tickles
           Nelson the Elephant
           Molly the Hippo
           Snipsnip Bird

2 Story    (narrated by the Snipsnip Bird)
           Zed the Zebra
           Ronald the Rhino
           Nelson the Elephant
           Herbert the Warthog
           Georgina the Giraffe
           Nathalie the Antelope
           Snipsnip Bird

----------------------------------------- page 1


64 Zoo Lane

The Story of Zed the Zebra.


1. EXT. ZOO -NIGHT
Lucy slides down Georgina's neck into the Zoo.
When she's landed she ignores the animals and instead
starts to do exercises.

             1. LUCY (touching her toes)
One Two ! One Two!

             2. MOLLY
Lucy, what are you doing?

             3. LUCY
Can't you see? I'm doing exercises.
(Bends sideways)
One Two! One Two!
```

```
Lucy runs round Nelson.

             4. LUCY (while running)
I have to get ready for the race tomorrow.

             5. GEORGINA
What race?

             6. LUCY (impatiently)
The potato sack race at school of course.

             7. GIGGLES AND TICKLES (excitedly)
Faster Lucy! Faster!

Lucy keeps on running.
Suddenly Nelson's trunk picks her up.

             8. NELSON
Hey hey hey! Wait a moment!

             9. LUCY(protests)
Put me down. I have to practice for the race!

             10. NELSON
Aren't you taking this all a bit too
seriously, Lucy?

             11. LUCY
But I want to win!

             12. MOLLY
We all want to win. But you can't always win.
Sometimes you win and sometimes you lose. . .

             13. SNIPSNIP BIRD (off screen)

----------------------------------------- page 2


. . . but the most important thing
is to have fun!

The SnipSnip Bird lands in the Zoo next to Lucy.

             14. LUCY
You're the Snipsnip Bird, aren't you?

             15. Snipsnip Bird
```

```
That's right. And I know all about races!
Let me tell you  a story . . .

Nelson shapes his trunk like a swing and Lucy sits down .

             16. Snipsnip Bird
. . . about Zed the Zebra.

2. EXT. AFRICAN SAVANNAH WATER HOLE - DAY
CUT to empty savannah. Grass curtain opens.
Suddenly a black and white blur whizzes past from left to
right. Then it whizzes past from right to left.  Then it
stops. It's a zebra.

             17. SNIPSNIP BIRD (V/O)
Zed the Zebra was  fast. . .very fast!
He was the FASTEST RUNNER
in all of Africa.

Zed  looks at his own reflection in the water hole and
smiles.

             18. ZED
Just look at those Go Faster Stripes!
I'm so cool!

Suddenly an elephant's trunk slams down in the water hole
spoiling Zed's reflection and slurping  up all the water.
It's Nelson the Elephant. Zed looks annoyed.

             19. ZED (has an idea)
Hey Nelson, you're a SLOW runner, aren't you?

             20. NELSON
Slow . . .me? I wouldn't say I was slow.
(Thinks)
In fact I can run quite fast. . .

             21. ZED
. . .for an elephant! Haha!
But you can't run as fast as me !

             22. NELSON (annoyed with Zed)
Says who?

----------------------------------------- page 3
```

Having considered the 'language' of animation and how it might be applied to a potential work, developing a script is essential, especially in 'narrative'-driven works. Award-winning animation scriptwriter, Alan Gilbey of Peafur Productions suggests the following when approaching the task:

Gilbey: 'The tough truth is that if you wish to make movies an audience will watch to the end you must win, hold and deserve their attention. Your holy creative duties are:

– To intrigue your audience.
– To take them on a journey that exceeds their expectations.
– To leave them somewhere that made their trip worthwhile.'

There are many books about screenwriting and most will tell you the same things: the orthodox theories of film structure. These are not the only ways to make movies, but they are very effective. Any rule of writing can be broken with great success (Belleville Rendez-vous, Tarantino and the Cohen brothers all appear to go their own way), but if you break rules without understanding them first you stand a very good chance of screwing up.

Creative Considerations

It is important to think about how your visual and textual pre-production work relates to a wider scheme of issues with regard to a potential film:

– The need to create a specific 'world' defined and limited by its own terms and conditions.

– The consideration of the relationship between narrative and aesthetic requirements, and the economy of the chosen technique.

– The relationship between character and story events, and the specific elements that will be animated.

– The imperative of the soundtrack in the determination of the imagery and the timing of the animated elements.

– The realisation of the performance of character action implied in the script and mediated through voice artists and animators.

An Vrombaut and John Grace created a highly specific world for the popular children's series, 64 Zoo Lane, which had clear instructions about its characters,

plot, structure, language and humour, as well as the following dos and don'ts:

– Animals can move freely within one continent, but cannot travel to other continents.

– Stick to native animals (no dromedaries in Australia or penguins in the North Pole).

– If a character appears in a story set in one continent, it cannot appear in a story set in a different continent.

– No humans, human footprints, litter left behind by humans or any other signs of human civilisation.

– Props should always be made of materials the animals can find in their natural environment. Keep props simple (no machines).

– Don't set a story within a story.

– Avoid flashbacks.

This gave a consistency to the piece that children could engage with and soon grasp the parameters of.

Award-winning animation scriptwriter, Alan Gilbey of Peafur Productions has co-developed shows with Aardman Animation, Cosgrove Hall Films, the Disney Channel, Universal Pictures and Fox. He also created and wrote Aaagh! It's the Mr Hell Show and Bounty Hamster.

Gilbey has presented highly entertaining workshops on script development. Here are some of the key points he stresses to animators eager to write better material:

Show don't tell

In every book this is rule number one, yet it's one of the hardest to master.

Always strive for the most visual ways to tell your story. Let your pictures do the talking and save the talking for things that pictures can't do. When you add words make sure they make a real difference to what we're seeing. If you removed the words from your pictures (or the pictures from your words) and the film still made the same sense then something has gone wrong.

Characters are important

An audience loves characters who intrigue or enchant them. They might be Bart Simpson. They might be an anglepoise lamp. They might be a cute mouse or a reprehensible monster, but if the viewer feels a degree of empathy for them, they will stay the course because they like the things that happen when that character is around.

If you are creating a new character, find out a lot about them before you start writing.

Beware the stock cast of characters you have in your head. They've been put there by a lifetime's exposure to other people's stories and it's easy to repeat too accurately something we've all seen before. Often the best new characters are a blend of something a little familiar (the stoic, silent suffering of Buster Keaton) and something from left field (a dog). Put those together and you get Gromit.

Parodi's Amazing Life, written by Massimiliano Grassini, has a simple visual concept of setting a young girl's rapidly passing life in a single room. Childhood passes into young adulthood into motherhood – one characterised by an absent father and three sons; one a suicide victim, one a drug addict, one a TV obsessed 'zombie' – and maturity, where in despair, she 'rewinds' her life on a TV remote control and punches her childhood sweetheart who is ultimately the cause of her later unhappiness.

What is your script about?

I don't mean what is the story? That's just the surface. What is it really about?

The theme? What's the secret objective of the tale you are telling?

Is Buffy The Vampire Slayer about vampires? No, it's about the pains of growing up, using monsters as metaphors. If you have an idea for a story, but no idea of what it is really about, you have a truck but no cargo. Think about something you really want to say, then make your story serve that higher purpose.

Before you start a script answer these questions…

–What does your film seem to be about?
–What is it REALLY about?
–What do you want to make your viewers feel?

Your film may not reach any firm conclusions, but it does need a sense of closure or it won't satisfy. It'll just stop. A good ending is the natural, but entirely unpredictable result of all that has gone before. It is your ultimate weapon for leaving the audience in the state you want to leave them – be it laughing, crying or arguing about what you meant.

Three-act structure

There are many ways to hold an audience, but the oldest and most well-known is the three-act structure:

Situation Welcome to my world. I'm going to make you wonder what happens next.

Complication Ooh! I bet you didn't see that coming. My characters are sent on a journey and no one knows where it will lead them.

Resolution Blimey, I didn't expect them to end up here!

I believe many scripts go wrong because they only have two acts; the initial idea and its development. Reaching for the third act – the surprising, the less obvious, the twist in the tale – is what will make your film unique. So…
– Draw a flow chart of your film – with three boxes.
– Then scribble out your story so it divides into them.
– If the divisions feel slight or forced, do some more thinking. Is there more that could happen? Is the story really over or is there somewhere else you could go that would bring fresh perspectives to your theme?

B-plots

In a visual medium a single idea can be put over pretty quickly, so you'll need more than a single idea to stop your audience thinking about popcorn.

B-plots can do this. They are miniature three-act tales that weave around your major story and may concern a supporting character. They usually conclude before the main tale does and often reflect another aspect of your secret objective. Or not. Sometimes they are just the comic relief. But profound or preposterous, they make a film richer.

Riffs and rhythms

Riffs and rhythms can also make films richer. Think of a film as a piece of music. Verse and chorus pace a song and the best songs usually have more than one hook.

– If we meet an incidental character bring them back later, then later still. If they eventually change the course of the main story in some way all the better.

– Give minor characters teeny three-act stories of their own, even if they're just the cat on the mat in the corner of the room (part of the success of Creature Comforts).

– If a train passes a window, keep the train passing the window at regular intervals. Then let the train passing somehow move your plot forward (at first it was there to show that your characters lived in poor housing, but later someone misses an important part of a conversation because of the noise it makes).

Go back to your flow chart and scribble out some parallel sets of boxes.

Preparing to script

Got everything sorted? Know what your film's about? Good. Next do the following:

– Write a two- or three-page synopsis of your story with a paragraph for each scene.

– Write a one-page synopsis with a paragraph for each act.

– Write a single paragraph for the back of the video box. Make us want to rent your movie.

– Write a one line teaser for the poster.

Then go back and rewrite your long synopsis. Does it achieve the aims you set yourself when you did the 'What is your script about?' exercise (see page 73)? If it doesn't, rewrite it so it does, THEN start on your script.

Cut, cut, cut and cut again!

As you may have gathered by now, writing really is the act of rewriting. Scripts tend to get better the more you go over them.

Having read a lot of scripts and watched a lot of student films I can confidently state that:

– Many are far too long.
– Few knew when to stop.
– Most would benefit from harsh, critical cutting.

So be brutal – too brutal – with your cutting. If you want a pacy film start your scenes late and end them early. Hit the road running and let your audience catch up. If I told you to cut three minutes from a fifteen minute script, then a week later said you could put the cut scenes back in again, I'm willing to bet good money you'd decline! Comparing the two drafts, you will see that in screenwriting less really is more.

Animated Gags and Comic Events

A high number of animated films aspire to be funny. The American cartoonal tradition effectively established the 'gag' as the lingua franca of the animation vocabulary, and much can be learned from simply watching the sight gags in Disney's Silly Symphonies or the work of Chuck Jones, Tex Avery and Bob Clampett at Warner Bros. Theories written on comedy argue that there are only a limited number of gags – between four and seven depending on who you believe – and all else is merely variation or dressing on these core comic structures. The following suggested 'gag' structures are particularly suited to visual humour:

– Misdirection and juxtaposition
– Illogical logic
– Dramatic irony
– Puns and parody
– Exaggeration and understatement
– Repetition

Misdirection and juxtaposition

Most comedy is about undermining expectations. Establish one idea or principle, which has a predictable outcome and then deliberately misdirect the audience to an unexpected conclusion. This is usually done by linking or juxtaposing two unlikely ideas where the incongruity or mismatching of the two ideas creates the joke. John Kricfalusi's Son of Stimpy controversially mixes the two ideas of Stimpy's lost 'fart-child' – itself a bizarre incongruity – with the story of Christ.

Illogical logic

Most animation uses its distinctive language of expression to create worlds with their own codes and conventions, however surreal or apparently 'illogical' these principles are, but this is especially important in comic scenarios, where a particular distortion of everyday logic can create jokes. As with misdirection and juxtaposition, this might also resolve itself with a revelation – perhaps a pertinent observation of something that supposedly might or should remain unsaid. Simply telling the truth about a situation is sometimes the most 'illogical logic' of all. Bill Plympton's I Married a Strange Person sets up the narrative premise that Grant, the hero, has a satellite-induced boil, which enables him to literally enact his every thought or desire – suddenly his girlfriend's breasts enlarge to take over the house, during sex, or are twisted into a variety of balloon animals!

Dramatic irony

This is an important device in any narrative, but is especially useful in comedy. Simply, it is concerned with giving the audience more information about a situation than the characters themselves have. This can often be the prelude to 'bad' things happening to characters, which might result in their humiliation, and that we are permitted to laugh at, rather than have sympathy for. Simple definition – it is 'humour' when it is happening to 'them'; it is 'horror' when it is happening to 'you'. Pure 'irony', of course, is merely saying or implying the opposite of what is meant, knowingly. Effectively, the joke is coming out of the viewer or listener's recognition of the 'sub-text' of what is being said. This is essentially the premise of Matt Groening's work in The Simpsons, where both Homer and Bart are unknowingly playing out their own limitations, ineptitudes and shortfalls with complete self-belief, unaware that they create social disruption and cultural mayhem. The series itself, though, is wholly self-conscious about the way it parodies American sit-com and exposes social hypocrisy and double standards in society at large. Consequently, its comedy works on a number of levels.

Puns and parody

Visual puns play on the possible double meaning in certain kinds of images. Verbal puns play on the double meaning in words. Some images 'substitute' for others and create an amusing juxtaposition or discontinuity; some words 're-direct' the suggested meaning of one interpretation of the word on to another possible level of meaning, sometimes, for example, creating 'innuendo'. Graphic and verbal puns often underpin cliché and stereotype – which, while vilified in much creative expression is extremely useful in comedy as a shortcut to an immediate and accessible comic possibility. Parody follows on directly from this, in that an existing and well-known person or popular work of art is exaggerated, exploited or critiqued in an act of what might be called 'excessive' reproduction –

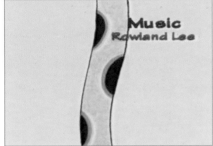

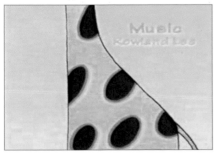

← **Screengrabs from the opening sequence of 64 Zoo Lane – John Grace and An Vrombaut**
Humour for children is often based on simple distortions of the physical realities they are beginning to understand and embrace. This extended neck of a giraffe simultaneously refers to the 'truth' of the long neck, but at the same time plays with the idea.

↓ **Still from Creature Comforts – Nick Park**
Much of the humour of Creature Comforts comes from the juxtaposition of what is being said with the type of creature chosen to say it, together with the background slapstick gags that accompany the 'interview' with the animal.

British Film Institute

in animation, this is largely in the act of caricature, and is often for political or subversive purposes. Right from the earliest animation, the graphic pun was an important comic device. Felix the Cat uses his tail as a range of objects; castle turrets become ice cream cones etc. The parody, too, was often the best way in which the Warner Bros.'s cartoonists could send up the aesthetic and ideological sensibilities of Disney cartoons, mocking Disney's aspirations to art and culture, or sending up its 'tweeness' and sentimentality.

Exaggeration and understatement

Presenting something in an overstated and extreme fashion can successfully draw the humour from a situation. Similarly, its opposite – the understated or deadpan can also draw the comedy into relief. Excess can often lead to physical or emotional 'cruelty' in comedy, and often needs a 'victim' figure who can be insulted and abused. The main aspect of exaggeration, though, is its flouting of convention, routine and conformity. By 'breaking the rules' of social and cultural

representation in a context that signals this is for 'humorous' and not 'harmful' ends, the joke can be successful – but there is arguably sometimes a fine line between the two. Most animated cartoons thrive on a tension between excess and subtlety, but the concept is perhaps best epitomised by Marv Newland's Bambi Meets Godzilla in which Disney's Bambi is unceremoniously crushed by the massive foot of Godzilla; end of cartoon. Excessive yet understated, but full of symbolic and metaphoric meaning.

Repetition

Repeating something often enough, and in the most surprising contexts, can have the effect of becoming funny. Most catchphrases work in this way, even if they don't seem to intrinsically be 'a joke' in their own right. Similarly, a repeating visual idea or situation can inspire a comic context. Sometimes, for example, in the case of Chuck Jones's Roadrunner cartoons, these repetitions become the minimalist conventions for the maximum of narrative and comic invention.

The Animator as Performer

Whether working through the pencil, a puppet or pixels, the need to express thought, emotion and action is fundamental to effective animated sequences, and while many voice artists are given credit for the performances in animated films – particularly so that 'stars' can sell animated features – it is the animator who creates the performance of the character through visual means.

British Film Institute

← **Still of Gollum from The Lord Of the Rings – Peter Jackson**
The universally acknowledged 'Gollum' from The Lord of the Rings trilogy is a combination of a motion captured performance by Andy Serkis, and an extraordinarily nuanced use of computer-generated animation. Audiences forget that they are watching a CGI character – in a way, for example, that they don't with Jar Jar Binks in Star Wars – because of the capacity for Gollum to think, feel and express his tragic contradictions.

↗ **Still from The Iron Giant – Brad Bird**
Director Brad Bird has suggested that the art of character animation is like 'catching lightning in a bottle one volt at a time', because the animator must work on brief seconds of complex personal exchange over a long period of time; time which passes in live action, literally at the moment of its execution. This attention to detail is reflected in the relationship between the boy and the iron giant in Bird's adaptation of Ted Hughes' poetic narrative.

Many of the performance issues in relation to animation are intrinsically related to the casting of the voices. Getting this right can enhance the character considerably. John Lasseter and Pete Doctor of PIXAR animation commented on this in their PIXAR Animation Masterclass at the London Film Festival, 2001:

Lasseter: 'The casting of the actors is something we are considering as we are developing the storyboard. We cast for not how big a star they are, but how good an actor they are – how well their natural voice fits in with the character's persona that we are trying to put across. We also hope to get actors who are quite good at ad-libbing. Working on a feature that takes four years to make is like telling the same joke every week for that time; it gets awfully old. We try to look for spontaneity as much as we can.'

Doctor: 'What is great about people who can improvise well is that they don't just shoot off and go somewhere else with the material, they stay true to the subject matter that you are trying to put across. They put it into words that are much more natural and believable, without completely going off script. The spontaneity is so valuable.'

Lasseter: 'In casting an actor, we oftentimes take a line of dialogue from a movie or a TV show that they have been in, take away the picture, and put in a drawing or image of the character that we are interested in them playing, and it is remarkable because sometimes when you take away the physical image of these really great actors there is something really lacking – it is flatter than you would expect – but other times it really comes alive with just that voice, and we go with those actors. The next stage is animation. We have the actors' voices. We have the layout. As directors we will first talk to the animators from the standpoint of acting. What is the sub-text? We do talk to them also about the practicalities of moving a character from one place to another, but we don't tell them how to do it. Sometimes the animator has a problem about how a character is going to do a certain thing. So the animators will use a video and they will act things out. We have a room that is all mirrors and they will act things out. Even though we are creating fantasy worlds we want to make it believable.'

Top ten tips to make your characters act

Ed Hooks, a major acting practitioner for the American animation community, offers ten tips to animators when thinking about 'acting' for their characters:

– Thinking tends to lead to conclusions; emotion tends to lead to action.

– Your audience only empathises with emotion, not with thinking.

– It is good for your character to have an obstacle of some kind.

– A gesture does not necessarily have to illustrate the spoken word. Sometimes a gesture can speak of a different inner truth (study Gollum in The Lord of the Rings).

– Animate the character's thoughts. All of them. The more specific the thoughts are, the better it will be. (Look at The Iron Giant scene in which the giant eats the car in the junkyard. You will count something like 13 different thoughts in a 12-second time frame.)

– A character plays an action until something happens to make him play a different action. In other words, there should never be a moment when your character is doing nothing.

– Definition of acting: Playing an action in pursuit of an objective while overcoming an obstacle.

– Scenes begin in the middle, not at the beginning. You want to enter a scene as late as possible.

– Dumb people and dumb characters do not think they are dumb. They think they are smart.

– Don't start animating until you have your story set. Storyboard everything first. If a sequence lacks conflict or negotiation, try to fix it before starting the animation.

The Animator as Editor

Animators as a rule and not unsurprisingly think about animation, but it is important to think, as has already been stressed in this book, about the wider craft of film-making too. Considering 'editing', for example, might be important at the script, storyboarding, layout and shooting script stages, as well as in the final execution of the work.

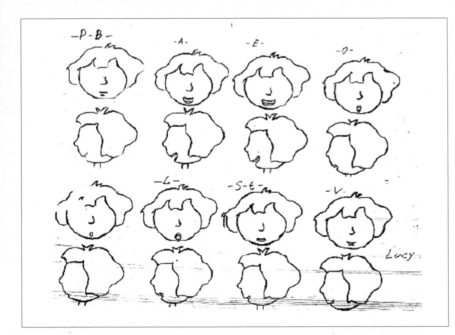

← Sketches for lip-synching –
Animation Workshop

Animation Workshop, created by John Grace, Andy Chong and Brian Larkins, demonstrates a number of the core skills in traditional 2D animation, and shows, for example, aspects of 'lip-synching' that in themselves might be related to the ways in which a scene is edited.

Jamie McCoan, an experienced editor of both live-action drama and animated films, offers some points on the place of editing in the visualisation process and the later stages of production.

McCoan: 'If possible get involved in the storyboarding. The obvious difference between editing live action and animation is the lack of coverage (the filming of the same piece of action from several camera positions) in the latter. The bulk of what would, in live action, be considered the editor's work (selection of shots, sizes and angles) is carried out at the storyboarding stage and the contribution of an editor with a strong grasp of film language can be invaluable.

'You should encourage the director to discuss any particularly difficult shots or sequences with you well ahead of shooting if possible. There is always a chance that an editing solution can be found that will save hours of animation time. 'If you are cutting while the film is being shot you should feel free to suggest any changes or additional shots that will improve the film. You shouldn't be overly inhibited by the knowledge that any additional footage will represent a lot of work – from time to time you may be able to redress the balance by suggesting a shot that is more easily achievable than what was originally planned.

'Animators, with good reason, are loath to shoot footage that will not be used, but if you can encourage them to shoot some overlapping action (ideally a whole line or action – and possibly even a beat before and after), this will afford you some degree of choice and later, during fine-cutting will enable you to make subtle changes of emphasis that will give the film's editing precision and crispness.

'There are of course opportunities open to the editor in animation that are generally not available in a live-action context. Frames can be removed to speed up action or maximise impact (Tex Avery apparently used to do this at the animation stage, removing in-between drawings from animators' work before shooting to get the extreme actions and reactions he wanted).

'It is sometimes possible to take apparently outrageous liberties with synch – especially if you are dealing with talking birds or crocodiles, or the like. Take a look at the crows in Dumbo – at times their beak movements have only the most tenuous connection to their dialogue. This is because they arc unable to produce the accurate mouth shapes that humans and 'soft-mouthed' animals do. This can give the editor a great deal of license if dialogue needs to be changed or a shot 'cheated'. Even with painstakingly animated lip-synch you can get away with a lot; so long as the mouth movement starts at the beginning of a phrase and ends at the end there's a good chance that you can cheat the synch – it's always worth a try!

'Ultimately body language may be more critical in maintaining the illusion of synch than the slavish matching of mouth shapes. I was cutting a musical sequence some years ago and it became apparent that whilst the characters' mouths were in perfect synch, their gestures, foot taps and hand movements were somewhat off the beat. We found that if we slipped the synch so that the body movements hit the beats, then nobody queried the lip-synch. 'A small note about lip-synch: most animation

manuals give examples of consonant and vowel mouth shapes showing the 'plosives' (P, B) as closed mouth-shapes. The truth is the actual sound of a P or B is emitted on the first, small, opening of the mouth – that's when the pressure, built-up whilst the lips arc pressed together, is released. Try it yourself! I suspect that this is at the root of the myth, rife in animation circles, that synch looks better if the sound is two frames late – what's really happening is that the sound is being repositioned to where it should have been in the first place!

'Every cut should have a positive motivation stemming from the needs of the story. It is not unknown in animation for seemingly arbitrary cuts to appear because shot A ran into difficulties or it was physically impossible to show a particular piece of action. Obviously these situations do occur and have to be addressed – the trick is to make the solution appear to be dramatically motivated; whatever you cut to should enhance the audience's understanding of the scene otherwise it will feel let down and your momentum will have been lost.

'To illustrate consider this example: a character is running along and jumps into his waiting vehicle; we're talking puppet animation here so jumping is difficult or perhaps even impossible to execute. The director suggests a cut from the long shot of the character running to a detail of his running feet, which begin to jump up out of frame so we can then cut to a close shot of the character landing in his seat. Would this work?

Could it be made to look convincing? I had no doubt that the shots would all cut together to make a reasonably convincing continuity, but in dramatic terms what would the shot of the feet add? It would neither impart new information nor give greater insight – in short there would be no dramatic justification for cutting to the character's feet. In the event, what we arrived at was a perfect example of an editing solution to an animation problem – we decided to cut directly from the long shot of the character running to the close shot of him landing in his vehicle. It worked beautifully, propelling the action forward and maintaining the energy and pace of the sequence.

'Having said all this, as far as possible the editing of an animated film should be approached in the same way as that of a live-action film. The grammar of visual storytelling applies. We are still dealing with actions, reactions, motivations and emotions, and the editor's job is to meld these elements into a dramatically satisfying whole through the selection, juxtaposition and timing of the material provided. Bold, and sometimes, painful decisions have to be made and some of these can involve painstakingly produced footage being cut from the film. People may not see it this way at the time (and there's a good chance you may be overruled), but the best service anyone can give the animators and everyone else working on the film is to make it the best film possible.'

The Animator as Director

The animation director operates in much the same way as the live-action director in that the work is normally the vision of that person, and the personnel attached to a project needs to be directed to facilitate the director's requirements. In animation, though, the director is very often 'hands on', too, actually animating.

Martin Pullen is a highly experienced animator and director of children's animation from Paddington Bear to his own creation Tom and Vicky. In having clear knowledge of the demands of the animator and how this relates to the needs of the director, here he offers some insights to both roles, and talks about the creative agenda for Tom and Vicky.

Comparing CGI and stop-motion

Pullen: 'People who do stop-motion hate sitting at a desk or at a computer all day long. The process of CG is similar with key positions and in-betweens and so forth, but it is so boring! I need a real puppet under hot lights all day; actually touching, actually moving it and creating a physical end result. I animated and directed at Filmfair, sometimes working with four animators on a programme. I did storyboards and framed up shots, and talked animators through the blocking. →

↖ **Stills from Tom and Vicky – Martin Pullen**
The director has to have a clear sense of the 'emotion' he or she wants the characters to project – in this case 'surprise' and 'shock' – as it is played out through the expressive limitations of the puppet.

→ **Magician sequence from Tom and Vicky – Martin Pullen** It is sometimes the case that characters engage in a self-conscious 'performance' themselves. Tom and Vicky's grandfather is a magician. The puppet must adopt the known codes and conventions of performance observed in a traditional magician.

→You have to delegate to a crew and work as a team because of the volume of work needed. In live action you direct actors, but in animation you have to direct a person to move a puppet a certain way in accordance with the storyboard, and in relation to how you anticipate cutting a story together. If a shot is 200 frames long and has some specific dialogue, you need to trust the animator to execute that; other more complex moves might need particular direction.'

A team spirit

Pullen (cont.): 'Being able to work as part of a team is vital. Everyone must enjoy the job and bring their creativity to it. In stop-frame, drawing is less important, but being "an actor" much more significant. You are performing through the puppet and it is crucial that you study other people to recall the gestures and looks; to know how someone walks; and to "see" the timing in someone's movement. People say I stare at them, but I love to observe the details of eyes, nose and mouth in an expression, and then bring that personality to the puppet.'

Tom and Vicky

'I was trying to develop an idea and one day I saw a child's drawing and thought you could do something in the style of a three-dimensional child's drawing, making props out of calico and using big stitches, crayons etc. I thought I could do that myself. I thought that I would set it in a garden with two young children – Tom and Vicky – cared for by their grandad. I did designs for the main characters – a pet dog and a pet cat; then I thought, what do you get in a garden? So I came up with a pond and from that, two frogs emerged. I really wanted to focus on "style", so the look would be significantly different, and I knew I could make a pilot. As I was watching TV or travelling on a bus I would be making props and eventually within a year, I got the puppets made and developed a pilot, which I took to Central TV. Everyone really liked it, but it was eventually financed by Granada and ITV commissioned it.

'Central to it were the frogs, Fred and Bert. I loved the children's animation The Herbs, where all the characters had a signature song, so I thought we would put a song in every episode. The stories were quite fantastical, but they would often start with a sort of logical starting place, for example, Tom and Vicky looking for a pot of gold at the end of the rainbow, or hunting for dinosaur bones, or encountering the squid who lived in the pond – fish are such a pain to animate, I thought it would be more fun! Alright, it is my Harryhausen moment as well, but he's a squid who lives in an old tug boat and knows everything, and the frogs are behaving like Laurel and Hardy, so the combination of "know-it-all" and foolishness really works. There were 26 shows and they were very popular. I think children liked the tactility and invention of it.'

→ Every aspect of the mise en scène is handcrafted. Here the barbecue food is made distinctive by its material tactility.

↘ The dinosaur bones that figure in one of Tom and Vicky's adventure stories demonstrate the breadth of subject matter covered in minute detail.

← As well as the articulations of emotional expression through the gestures of the puppet, the Director must be able to engage with 'action' sequences that necessitate particular preparation – here the 'dive' of the frog and the effect on the pond.

Applications and Outcomes
Introduction

Learning how to animate and make animated films is best done through a combination of reading the available literature, taking the advice and support of others with more experience and knowledge, and doing as much 'hands-on' practice as possible.

However, it is important to reiterate that all creative practice needs a great deal of thought and preparation, as well as technique. There is no practice without theory and no theory without practice. Bringing together historical knowledge, conceptual and technical insight, and the desire to create something distinctive is crucial, but not necessarily enough. Being able to articulate the 'art' of creative practice, as well as demonstrating it through the work is a vital component in proving its worth and effect.

This section offers an historical and critical context for the four core disciplines of animation – drawn/cel; 3D puppet/clay stop-motion; computer generated; and 'alternative' or 'experimental' animation – and draws upon the work of students and professionals across the animation disciplines, with discussions about the working process. Consequently, it offers a range of insights and 'best practice', which will be highly valuable to anyone embarking on making an animated film.

Drawn and Cel Animation

British Film Institute

British Film Institute

A Brief History

The history of animation is normally written as the history of the animated cartoon, and the history of the animated cartoon is normally written as the creation of an animation 'industry' by the Walt Disney Studio. While this rightly privileges the place of the Disney organisation in the development of animation as an art and a distinctive production process, it also neglects the animation of the pioneers in the United States, and overstates the 'ownership' of animation as a singularly American phenomenon. Indeed, it may still be the case that all animation both within the United States and elsewhere in the world, remains a response to 'Disney' – aesthetically, ideologically and technically. This is both a tribute – many individuals and studios across the world have aspired to the Disney style – and a model of resistance, challenging and

implicitly critiquing the process, design and meaning of the Disney output, at the same time preserving indigenous traditions and other approaches to the art form.

The animated cartoon essentially emerged out of the experiments towards the production of the cinematic moving image. As early as 1798 Etienne Robertson created the Phantasmagoria, a sophisticated 'magic lantern' to project images, and this was followed by Plateau's Phenakistiscope in 1833; Horner's Zoetrope in 1834; von Uchatius' Kinetoscope in 1854; Heyl's Phasmatrope in 1870 and Reynaud's Praxinoscope in 1877 as devices that in some way projected drawn moving images. With the development of the cinematic apparatus came the first intimations of 'animation'. At first, accidents or trick effects in the work of figures like Georges Méliès and the emergence of 'lightning cartooning' – the accelerated movement of drawings by manipulating camera speeds –

particularly in the British context where Tom Merry, Max Martin, Harry Furniss and Lancelot Speed defined an indigenous model of expression related to British pictorial traditions in caricature and portraiture. It was also Britons, Albert E. Smith and J. Stuart Blackton working in the USA, however, who saw the potential of a specific kind of animation film-making in The Enchanted Drawing (1900) and Humourous Phases of Funny Faces (1906), though these were essentially little more than developments in lightning cartooning.

While stop-motion 3D animation progressed in a number of nations, it was only with the creation of Émile Cohl's Fantasmagorie (1908) – a line-drawn animation based on the surrealist principles of the 'incoherent' movement of artists in France – that the 2D animated film was seen to be a distinctive art form.

Cohl was later to work in the USA animating George McManus' comic strip, The Newlyweds

Applications and Outcomes The Fundamentals of Animation

← **Still from Humourous Phases of Funny Faces – J. Stuart Blackton, 1906**

Blackton's film was essentially a development of the 'lightning sketch' – the speeded up creation of a hand drawing – but its effects suggested that 'animation' would soon become a distinctive art form.

↙ **Still from Gertie The Dinosaur – Winsor McCay, 1914**

Gertie, who featured in Winsor McCay's vaudeville routine, was arguably the first example of the kind of 'personality' animation much admired and developed by Disney. The dinosaur clearly had an identity and point of view of its own, and was very appealing and amusing to audiences.

→ **Still from Animal Farm – Halas & Batchelor Collection Ltd., 1954**

Animal Farm, based on George Orwell's famous parable of the Russian Revolution, was the first full-length British animated feature, and was an important milestone in animation history as an animated film that was a serious film, appealing to adults, and which treated animals not as anthropomorphised comic figures.

(1913), one of a number of popular comic strips that characterised early American cartoon animation, including Krazy Kat, The Katzenjammer Kids and Mutt and Jeff. Winsor McCay, an illustrator and graphic artist made Little Nemo in Slumberland (1911), based on his own New York Times comic strip and made one of the first self-consciously reflexive cartoons in the aptly titled Winsor McCay Makes His Cartoons Move (1911). McCay's influence on the history of animation cannot be understated as he created one of the first instances of the horror genre in The Story of the Mosquito (1912); 'personality' animation in the figure of Gertie the Dinosaur (1914), who featured in an interactive routine with McCay in his vaudeville show; and 'documentary' in an imitative newsreel style depiction of The Sinking of the Lusitania (1918). McCay had previously suggested that he only wanted to use animation to show things that couldn't be seen in everyday life – dragons, dinosaurs and dreams – but he realised that animation could also re-create things that had not been documented in another way, thus the realistic detail in his Lusitania film. McCay championed the art of animation, but feared too, that it would become an industry driven by other motives.

As early as 1913, John R. Bray and Raoul Barré were developing systematic, 'industrial' processes, for the production of animated cartoons using variations of what was to become the 'cel' animation process, where individual drawings, later cels, were created with various stages of a character's forward movement, and these were aligned with backgrounds that remained the same, using a peg-bar system. By replacing each stage of the movement and photographing it frame by frame, the illusion of continuous movement occurred, but more importantly, a production system was emerging that echoed the economies and hierarchical organisation of Taylorist production processes that characterised the industrial progress of modern America, most notably, in the production of Model T Fords at the Henry Ford car plants. Though the Fleischer Brothers, Paul Terry and Pat Sullivan with Otto Messmer, all emerged as viable producers of cartoons, it was Walt Disney who effectively took the Ford model and created an animation 'industry'.

With Steamboat Willie (1928), Disney, in the face of increased competition from the technically adept Fleischer Studio, created the first fully-synchronised sound cartoon, simultaneously introducing animation's first cartoon superstar, Mickey Mouse. Within ten years, Disney had made Snow White and the Seven Dwarfs (1937), the first full-length, sound-synchronised, Technicolor animated film; along the way making the seminal Silly Symphonies, including Flowers and Trees (1932), the first cartoon made in three strip Technicolor; Three Little Pigs (1933); The Band Concert (1935); The Country Cousin (1936); and The Old Mill (1937), all of which made aesthetic, technical and narrative strides in the field. Disney effectively defined animation and created a legacy that all other producers learn from, →

British Film Institute

British Film Institute

→ respond to and seek to imitate or challenge.
As Disney made Pinocchio (1940) and Fantasia
(1941), the Warner Bros. studio continued its
emergence, and following the Disney strike of
1941 (which arguably ended 'the Golden Era' of
animation), provided a context in which Chuck
Jones, Frank Tashlin, Tex Avery, Bob Clampett and
Friz Freleng became the new heirs to the
animated short. Altogether more urban and adult,
the Warner Bros. cartoons were highly inventive,
redefining the situational 'gags' in Disney films

through a higher degree of surreal, self-reflexive,
and taboo-breaking humour. While the Fleischers
had Betty Boop, and a strong embrace of Black
culture and underground social mores, and
Hanna-Barbera had the enduring Tom and Jerry,
Warner Bros. had the zany Daffy Duck, the laconic
'wise ass' Bugs Bunny, and gullible dupes, Porky
Pig and Elmer Fudd, who became popular and
morale-raising figures during the war-torn 1940s
and its aftermath.

Jones and Avery, in particular, altered the
aesthetics of the cartoon, changing its pace and
subject matter, relying less on the 'full animation'
of Disney, and more on different design
strategies and self-conscious thematic
concerns, for example, sex and sexuality;
injustice; status and social position. In many
senses, the innovation in cartoons as varied as
The Dover Boys (1942), Red Hot Riding Hood
(1943) and Coal Black and de Sebben Dwarfs
(1943), anticipates the more formal
experimentation of the UPA (United
Productions of America) studio, a breakaway
group of Disney animators, including Steve
Bosustow, Dave Hilberman and Zachary
Schwartz, wishing to work more in the style of
modernist art (actually pioneered at the Halas &
Batchelor and Larkins Studios in England), less
in the comic vein, and on more auteurist terms
and conditions. Works like Gerald McBoing
Boing (1951) and The Tell-Tale Heart (1953)
used minimalist backgrounds and limited
animation, and were clearly embracing a
European modernist sensibility that itself was
developing in the 'reduced animation' of the
Zagreb Studios, and its leading artist, Dusan
Vukotic. As the Disney studio arguably entered a
period of decline, Chuck Jones created three
masterpieces – Duck Amuck (1953), One
Froggy Evening (1956) and What's Opera,
Doc? (1957) – all exhibiting Jones's ability to
deconstruct the cartoon, work with literate and
complex themes, and create cartoon 'art' in its
own right.

In retrospect, it is clear that these were the last great works of the theatrical era, as the major studios closed their short cartoon units and the television era began. It is pertinent to note, too, that Halas & Batchelor's adaptation of George Orwell's Animal Farm (1954) had also progressed the cartoon feature, addressing serious subject matter and representing animals in a more realistic and less 'Disneyfied' way. Many critics see the Saturday morning cartoon era as the true demise of the American cartoonal tradition, but arguably, especially in the pioneering efforts of the Hanna-Barbera studio, it was the very versatility of animation as an expressive vocabulary that enabled its continuity at a time when its cost may have prevented its survival altogether.

At the same time, the Japanese animation industry expanded its production specifically for the television market, and series like Astro Boy debuted on US television. Echoing the popularity of Manga in Japanese culture, animé of all kinds have emerged in the post-war period, and by the early 1980s Japanese studios were producing some 400 series for the global TV market, and by the early 1990s over 100 features were produced a year. Katsuhiro Ôtomo's Akira (1988) was the 'breakthrough' animé, which introduced Western audiences to the complex, multi-narrative, apocalyptic agendas of much Japanese animation, and the works of Hayao Miyazaki, Mamoru Oshii and Masamune Shirow that followed competed with Disney,

Dreamworks and PIXAR in the global feature marketplace. Filmation and Hanna-Barbera continued to produce cartoons for American television, and Disney consolidated its place on the new medium with Disneyland and later variations like Walt Disney's Wonderful World of Color. Individual works continued to emerge from the National Film Board of Canada (NFBC), established in the early 1940s by John Grierson, and led by the innovative Norman McLaren, but in the American context, radicalisation appeared in the frame of Ralph Bakshi, who explored adult themes and the spirit of the late 1960s counter-culture in his sexually explicit and racially charged films Fritz the Cat (1972), Heavy Traffic (1973) and Coonskin (1975). In effect, this was the first time that animation in America was used by adults to engage adults with contemporary adult issues and cultural politics.

Jimmy Murakami's adaptation of Raymond Briggs' When the Wind Blows (1986), like Animal Farm (1954) and Yellow Submarine (1968),

represented attempts in Britain to innovate in the traditional 2D cartoon, but it was Hayao Miyazaki in Laputa, the Flying Island (1986), My Neighbour Totoro (1988) and Porco Rosso (1992) who sustained and enhanced the quality of the animated feature, and the partnership of Ron Clements and John Musker with The Little Mermaid (1989), Aladdin (1992) and Hercules (1997), who revived Disney's fortunes. While the cartoon short enjoyed continuing innovation in the work of Paul Driessen, Cordell Barker and Richard Condie at the NFBC, it was clear that the impact of digital technologies would revise the animated feature, and indeed, production for television. The TV cartoon has enjoyed a renaissance in the works of John Kricfalusi (The Ren and Stimpy Show), Gendy Tartakovsky and Craig McCracken (The Powerpuff Girls; Samurai Jack). Matt Groening's The Simpsons has become a national institution, but feature animation essentially changed with the success of PIXAR's Toy Story (1995), the first fully computer-generated animated feature.

Walk Cycles

One of the core practices in drawn animation is the walk cycle – essentially the 'benchmark' model of movement that is pertinent to other depictions of physical activity in animation.

Creating walk cycles and activity in motion is fundamental to the craft of animation. Motion studies created by Eadweard Muybridge are still a valuable source in achieving such movement, which in the early years of animation was drawn and captured by painting on cels.

Tutorial – Walk Cycles

In a book of this length, it is not possible to include tutorials on a range of technical approaches, but over the next pages, a consideration of the 'walk cycle' will be undertaken by Arril Johnson, as it is one of the traditional and key aspects of animation, which should be mastered by all aspiring animators.

Diagram 1 – This detail from a dope sheet shows a thumbnail sketch of Feldspar the dinosaur not just walking, but walking with attitude. Think about the length of the step the character takes. Is it a long, bold step? Is it a short, tired shuffle? Think about the speed of the step. Is it slow and fearful? Slow and lazy? Quick and nervous? Quick and aggressive? Or is it just average and relaxed? When walking, as in Diagram 2, does the character lead with its head, its chest, its pelvis or its feet? Does it walk in a flat-footed way or does it have an adolescent bounce? What is its purpose and mood?

Diagram 2 – Generally, when a series of drawings is produced showing the right foot swinging forward while the left foot slides back and then the left swinging forward while the right slides back, the foot doing the sliding while it bears the weight of the character will slide in regularly spaced stages. This is because this collection of drawings, called a 'walk cycle', is usually designed for use over a panning background that pans in a consistent and fluid way. This is done in order to create the illusion of a camera following the character as the character walks along in front of the background.

The same set of drawings and background can be used in another way; the character can walk forward into, through, and out of the scene while the background remains static.

Diagram 1

Diagram 2

The point is, once the foot supporting the character's weight is placed on 'ground' its position relative to the background is fixed until it can be lifted up for the forward swing.

If the character is walking across a slippery floor, however, this fixed relative position rule might not apply. If the character also has a very awkward walk with an irregular rhythm then the regular spacing of the sliding foot also would not apply because the character's speed would keep changing. So, these rules are only general and are there to help you organise a difficult job.

Diagram 3 – This shows the character's full step and mid step positions. Here, the mid step position is drawn with its supporting foot registered with the rear foot of the full step position. This is how it would be used if the character were walking through the scene. If the character was supposed to walk in place while the background panned, then the toe of this mid step pose would be lined up with the middle mark, five, of the chart under the character. Because the character has a bit of energy, the foot that is about to be lifted is only resting on its toes instead of suggesting a heavy, flat-footed walk.

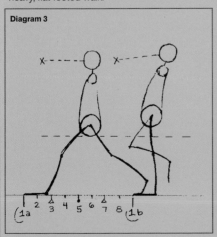

Diagram 3

In the drawing showing the mid step position, the straight leg supporting the character has lifted the hips higher. This gives the leg swinging forward more room to clear the ground before it and for the character to settle down again. What does the top part of the body do? Does it also bounce like a piston? Does it tilt back, as in this example? Should it tilt forward, or maybe curl into itself in order to absorb the shock of the bounce and keep the head steady? If the head does bounce a bit, what does the character's eye line do? In this example the face tilts slightly downward when the head rises so that the character seems to be looking at a particular point in space instead of staring blankly ahead like a robot.

Diagram 3 also shows the spacing of the sliding foot, with its middle position and other in-betweens. The full step position is a key drawing showing the extreme extent of the stepping action. The mid step position is the first in-between drawing you'll do and is called a breakdown drawing. In this case, it shows the passing point where the swinging leg and the sliding leg overlap each other if the character is viewed in profile. A breakdown often determines the flavour of the finished action more than any other drawing because, while the key positions indicate where the character is going to be at main points during an action, the breakdowns show how the character moves to get from one key pose to the next. The drawings that exist in-between are in-betweens.

Diagram 4 – This shows what generally happens to the angle of the foot that is being lifted, swung forward, and placed to take the character's weight on to the next step. This example is, of course, an exaggeration of the norm. Usually a human being lifts the foot just enough to keep from dragging it on the ground as it swings forward. This is fine on a flat surface, but walking in a forest, over rocks, or in deep snow, for example, would require more

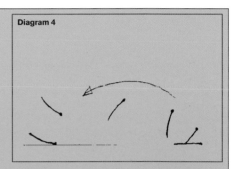

Diagram 4

effort and concentration. With this in mind, how would the character walk over such terrain if they were tired, confused, and a strong wind was blowing? As with most things in animation, find the answer by observing when you can, remembering what you observe, imagining what you haven't been able to observe, and acting.

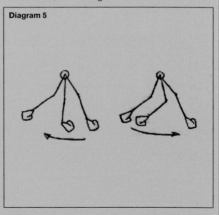

Diagram 5

Diagram 5 – This shows how the locking of the elbow joint affects the swing of the arm. On the forward swing the arm tends to straighten and, if it is relaxed, the hand might drag slightly at the wrist. On the back swing the hand will straighten more and the dragging effect will be seen very slightly at the elbow joint as the lower arm follows through on the action initiated by the upper arm.

Diagram 6 – Maybe the character needs to turn around while walking because it's trying to finish a conversation while still leaving a room. Maybe it needs to leap, run, and eventually skid to a stop. Does it skid to a stop because it is frightened or has it forgotten something? When the skid finishes, has the character recovered its balance or is it in danger of falling over, as in Diagram 6? If it falls over, which way does it fall and does it have time to cushion its landing? In these instances you might be linking a variety of cycles with additional drawings or executing the entire animation without the use of any cycles because the action is organic and specific to a complex environment. In this case you need to think carefully about key poses and, for example, which foot the character might be leading with so that it is in the right position to begin a new action.

Diagram 7 – When pulling a heavy object you try to maximise the use of the power in both legs. Walking normally won't do the job. You lean away from the object so that the weight of your body assists you and, as much as possible, keep both feet on the ground. This means that each leg swing is done quickly so that each foot spends as much time on the ground as possible in order to double your pulling power. Diagram 7 is a working drawing for just such an action. There were 37 drawings in this painfully slow walk cycle, but each foot only spent five drawings in the air.

Diagram 8 – It is also possible to give very different rhythms to the front and back feet of a quadrupedal animal for comic effect and still make the movement logical. This diagram shows short, heavy limbs at the front and long, bird-like limbs at the back. Each limb cycles in 12 drawings and each limb slides backwards at the same speed when on the ground. The difference is that the front limbs have a shorter stride and take longer to lift up and swing forward to the start position. The bird-like

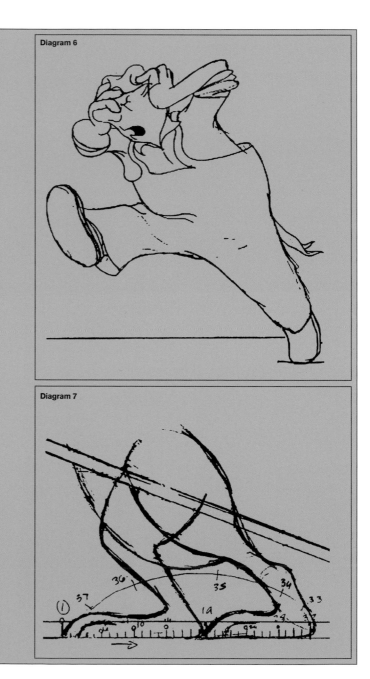

Diagram 6

Diagram 7

Applications and Outcomes The Fundamentals of Animation

limbs at the back have a longer stride, with more time spent supporting the animal, but swing forward more quickly.

Diagram 9 – This is a simplified plan for a character running forward in three-quarter view. Initially, a master or key drawing was prepared, which showed the character with a double set of limbs so that the alternate positions of the left and right feet, for example, could be seen in one graphic. This was constructed within a wedge that matched the required perspective of the character's path. In this case the drawing was copied over three generations and each time reduced to about 65 per cent of its previous size. Of course, a reduction in size has no effect on the angle of the wedge and so it was then possible to easily position the three copies where they needed to be within the wedge of the original drawing. Now that a rigid framework existed to control the perspective and proportions of the character's key positions, the required in-between drawings could be improvised in order to give a more organic and varied feeling to the final animation.

Diagram 10 – Of course, there are other ways to get to where you're going.

Diagram 8

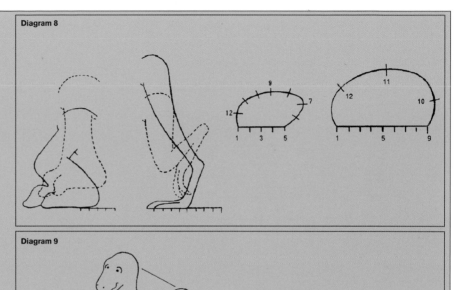

Diagram 9

Diagram 10

Muybridging

Animation Workshop, the brainchild of the late John Grace, and Andrew Chong and Brian Larkins, is a comprehensive workshop package for animators wishing to attain the core skills of 2D drawing for animation. The workshop includes a complete case study of the phenomenally successful children's series, 64 Zoo Lane, and is also characterised by a number of exercises of key movements, gestures and actions that are used in classical animation. Here is a movement sequence based on Muybridge's horse gallop – essentially a core sequence of eight repeating movements, showing the shifting dynamics of bodily weight, compression and extension through the stride pattern.

↓ **Cels for a gallop sequence from the Animation Workshop, The Animation Academy, Loughborough University, UK**

→ **Cels for a gallop sequence – Eadweard Muybridge**
Animation imitates live-action movement by distilling the essence of the action and stressing the differing relationships between the movement itself and the consequent distribution of weight as the horse gallops forward. It then becomes a repeating movement cycle.

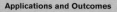

SA 4040   Sc 2x 202   cBRR-35

Cel Painting

Cel painting – the application of paint to the reverse of a celluloid sheet in the colouring in of a design or character, which then represents one frame of the film – has largely been made redundant by the economy of using digital ink and paint. Where cel painting was the core technique for making animated film in the 'Golden Era' in American studio work – for many years after, and throughout the world as part of the 'industrial' technique – it is now merely one of a set of technological and aesthetic choices to be made as part of a project.

Slinky Picture's road safety campaigns featuring endangered hedgehogs near roads have been very popular with children's audiences. Director, Chris Shepherd wanted to use traditional hand drawn, cel-painted techniques to get the particularly lush density to the colour expressed in Joe Simpson's original designs for the ad.

Visual Vocabulary

Shepherd wanted to capitalise on the visual vocabulary children possess from Disney films and book illustration to get the safety message across quickly and accessibly. His own memory of road safety campaigns from childhood was influential too, in the sense that he had little empathy for 'Tufty', the squirrel, the main figure of identification in those ads, and indeed, felt sorry for the weasel, the domestic villain of the piece. Shepherd's tougher Liverpool background cast Tufty as a 'mummy's boy', and for many of his friends, prompted the desire that the car would swerve and hit him!

Far more persuasive, suggests Shepherd, were Richard Taylor's Charley Says films, because the children feared that a pet might be harmed and it was therefore important to take responsibility so that it wouldn't be, which in turn meant that the child would be safe too. This underpins the Stayin' Alive ad and those that follow it. The children singing were also chosen as 'natural' rather than 'stage-school' voices, to create greater association and to encourage the memorable 'sing-along' aspects.

↖ **Untrimmed cel from Hedgehog Road Safety Campaign – Department of Transport/COI/Darcy/Maria Manton/Chris Shepherd**
The campaign appeals to children and adults on the basis of the children's attraction to an animated animal and the adult knowledge of the presence of hedgehogs on the roads, and the dangers that befall them.

Drawing and Aesthetic Tradition

There are different traditions of 'drawing' in animation that respond to the indigenous traditions of the arts in any one nation. Here is an example of the ways traditional drawn animation works in a Japanese context.

Koji Yamamura's work is effectively 'anti-animé' – a response to what is an increasingly mainstream, homogenised, industrial product, boasting some outstanding figures like Tezuka, Miyazaki, Oshii, Ôtomo and Shirow, but nevertheless characterised by many forgettable genre movies. Yamamura returns to an indigenous, traditional Rakugo (comic strip) story Atama-yama for his multi-award winning short film, Mt. Head, which tells of a mean-spirited man who swallows a cherry pip and grows a cherry tree out of his head.

Metamorphosis

Yamamura's return to a traditional narrative is accompanied by a return to traditional hand-drawn animation. This privileges his particular skill in using metamorphosis, as one thing transforms into another, enabling a sometimes literal space to become an emotional space or even the realm of fantasy or dream, without any of the elements being discernably different. Is the cherry tree a metaphor for the man's psychological state? Is it a charming and surreal storytelling device? Is it a vehicle to play out oppositional tensions between nature and culture, reality and fantasy, bureaucracy and art, life and death?

Yamamura's experience

Clearly, the film works on a number of levels. The film was completed over two years and is composed of over 10,000 drawings.

Yamamura: 'First I worked for a while at the company of animation background art, then I quit and started to make my own animation films. I have learned all animation by myself. When I was 13 I read a column on how to make an animation film using Super 8. That was a start, and I have kept making my own animation for fun. While I studied Fine Art at Tokyo Zokei University, I saw the retrospective of Ishu Patel at the first Animation festival in Hiroshima in 1985. That made me decide to create animation films as my life work. I had worked for ten years to make short animations for children, but from the start I had always wished to make shorts that adults can enjoy. The theme throughout Mt. Head was a recognition of a mystery of life and an absurdity that you can never handle rationally.'

↙ **Sketches and stills from Mt. Head – Koji Yamamura**
Mt. Head is a story about a mean-spirited man who swallows a cherry pip, and grows a cherry tree out of his head. The tree then hosts parties of beer-drinking business people letting free their inhibitions, as part of a traditional ritual of 'blossom viewing'.

↙ To make the 'absurdity' of growing a tree from a man's head, Yamamura supports his proposition by depicting everything realistically, as if it were actually taking place and affecting real people. This is reinforced by the realistic stylisation of light and shadow across 2D flat, drawn planes.

→ Yamamura works from a traditional base of
↓ observational drawing, contextualising the cherry tree within the environment. Within the Japanese tradition of the arts this enables him to create an 'aesthetic distancing', which recasts the cherry tree in a more symbolic light when he uses it in his film as a central visual motif. Cherry blossom has particular significance in Japanese culture – where the falling blossom symbolises something beautiful and perfect that is about to conclude or die. This sense of beauty in transience provokes 'mono no aware' – an awe or sublime feeling in the passing. In Japan many heroic figures or characters going through rites of passage are linked to the impermanence, but unparalleled beauty of the blossom.

→ Here is some of the character development work for the central figure in the film. This character shifted from being a gaunt, near skeletal figure to a more appealing, rounder faced one.

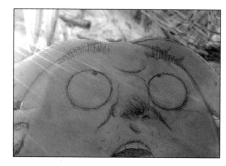

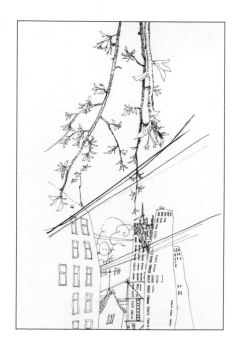

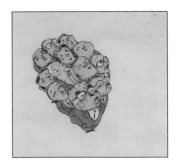

→ **Sketches and stills from Mt. Head –
Koji Yamamura**

'I have kept a theme of identity since my
twenties and I've finally formed this into
animation using every skill that I have learned
up to this point.'

This sequence illustrates Yamamura's
preoccupation with metamorphosis as a literal
change in the animation and 'change' in the
attitude of characters and situations.

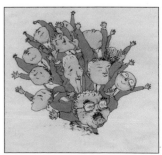

3D Stop-motion Animation

→ **Still from King Kong – Merian C. Cooper & Ernest B. Schoedsack, 1933**
Willis O'Brien's groundbreaking stop-motion animation in King Kong proved profoundly influential on generations of film-makers from Ray Harryhausen to Phil Tippett, to Barry Purves to Peter Jackson.

← **Still from Tale of the Fox – Ladislaw Starewicz, 1930**
Starewicz's work corresponds to the darker, amoral universe of the European fairy tale, and uses animals as highly conscious, dramatic characters, often with complex motives, again a far cry from the use of animals in the American cartoon tradition.

A Brief History

3D stop-motion animation has two distinct histories. The first is the largely European tradition of short stop-motion films made by individual artists, and stop-motion series principally made for children's television. The second, and predominantly Hollywood tradition, is the 'invisible' history of stop-motion animation as a branch of special effects for feature length films. This is complicated further by the fact that 3D stop-motion animation has got two principal approaches using either puppets or clay models, but also includes films made with objects and artefacts.

Though J. Stuart Blackton and Albert E. Smith, Britons working in the USA, have been credited with making the first puppet film called The Humpty Dumpty Circus (1908), there remains

the possibility that British film-maker Arthur Melbourne-Cooper may have made the first 3D advertisement as early as 1899 called Matches: An Appeal, animating matches, an approach shared in Émile Cohl's 1908 film, The Animated Matches. Cooper's 'toys come to life' stories became a staple of early British animated film and included Dreams of Toyland (1908) and The Toymaker's Dream (1913). Similar preoccupations informed Giovanni Pastrone's The War and the Dreams of Momi (1913) and later, Alexander Ptushko in The New Gulliver (1935), but it was another Russian, Ladislaw Starewicz who first developed an extraordinary technique, following his interest in entomology, animating three-dimensional insect characters. The Cameraman's Revenge (1911) is a melodramatic love triangle, and highly self-conscious in its reflexive tale of cinema about cinema. His later films Town Rat, Country Rat (1926) and Tale of the Fox (1930/released 1938) are masterpieces of the stop-motion form, and remained singularly unsung until recent years.

Related area of study
Not Disney

Animation made outside the American cartoonal tradition, and the long shadow of Disney, has often been marginalised in animation histories. This does more than neglects important, aesthetically different work; it dismisses significant indigenous works that reflect national cultures and alternative perspectives on human experience. It is also true to say that the American tradition, particularly in its formative years, is largely a comic tradition. Other countries have aspired to different kinds of storytelling and have different thematic and artistic preoccupations. The recovery of this work is paramount to a full understanding of the place of animation not merely in international film culture and history, but as an articulation of the distinctiveness and diversity of the art form in general.

Applications and Outcomes   The Fundamentals of Animation

In the USA, though, it was pioneer Willis O'Brien who inspired generations of what would be called 'Effects Artists'. Amused by his brother, who playfully changed some of the postures of clay figures created for the exhibits in the San Francisco World Fair of 1915, O'Brien experimented with his first stop-motion film of a boxing match, soon to be followed by a prehistoric 'comedy', The Dinosaur and the Missing Link (1915). In 1925 he made The Lost World, based on a Sir Arthur Conan Doyle story, assisted by gifted model-maker Marcel Delgado, who constructed 18" models influenced by Charles Knight's acclaimed dinosaur paintings in the American Museum of Natural History. RKO then employed O'Brien on the groundbreaking King Kong (1933), which changed the status of special effects work, fully deploying O'Brien's 'rear projection' system, which combined background live action with foreground miniature animation, first seen in O'Brien's aborted project, The Creation (1930).

O'Brien later became mentor to the most famous of all stop-motion animation artists, Ray Harryhausen, who, inspired by King Kong, sought to copy the technique in his own short films. After working with the renowned George Pal on Puppetoons, he made his own short educational films, the first of which was called the Mother Goose Stories, and ultimately he joined O'Brien in making Mighty Joe Young in 1949. This began a long and distinguished career in which he created many fantastical and mythical creatures in films like The Beast from 20,000 Fathoms (1953), The 7th Voyage of Sinbad (1958), Jason and the Argonauts (1963) and Clash of the Titans (1981). Harryhausen is constantly cited as a major influence by contemporary animators and artists from Phil Tippett to James Cameron, and enjoys knowing references in Henry Selick's Nightmare Before Christmas (1993), in the underwater skeleton battle, and in PIXAR's Monsters Inc. (2002), in which a top class restaurant is called Harryhausen's. Selick's battle echoes one of →

Related area of study
The special effects tradition

The special effects tradition is often understood in a way that effaces important work. Even though an audience is required to embrace the spectacle of an effect, it is crucial that it seems authentic enough for it to seem 'invisible' as an effect in the live-action context it is presented within. This has also had the consequence of marginalising a great deal of animation work, and its major artists. While Ray Harryhausen is now properly lauded, it is nevertheless still the case that his work is seen as 'old fashioned' and of another time. For stop-motion animators, it is crucial that his work is viewed as 'state of the art'; his technique in regard to the movement of full bodies, often with multiple limbs, and complex actions, is still unsurpassed.

Related area of study
Concept-driven animation

Jan Svankmajer's work is an important example of the ways in which the principles of modernist thought and political insight may be accommodated in experimental film. Svankmajer's 'agit-prop' – his strident critique of authoritarian regimes and political repression – and 'agit-scare' – his use of surreal images drawn from the unconscious to prompt moments of fear and revelation in his audience – are conceptual applications to the medium and should be understood as a methodology in the creation of distinctive imagery and alternative narratives. By adopting a 'conceptual' premise to an animation, a highly original outcome can sometimes be achieved.

British Film Institute

→ Harryhausen's most famous sequences – Jason's fight with six skeletons in Jason and the Argonauts, which was so technically demanding it took over four months to make, at 13 frames per day.

Harryhausen's legacy is great, but George Pal, his one time employer, also exemplified fine work. His 'replacement' technique was of a slightly different order. Where Harryhausen manipulated his models by small increments and recorded them frame by frame, Pal created replacement pieces of his models – faces, arms, legs etc. – which progressed the cycle of movement he was creating, and which he changed and inserted, once more recording the incremental progression frame by frame. Though a more cumbersome technique, it survives into the modern era, particularly in clay animation, and has been used in films by Aardman Animation. After making early films in Germany, Pal moved to Holland, fleeing the rise of Nazism, and established the biggest puppet studio in Europe, principally making striking advertisements for sponsors like Philips and Unilever. His Puppetoons, made in Hollywood, included Jasper and the Beanstalk (1945), Henry and the Inky Poo (1946) and Tubby the Tuba (1947), and were highly successful, securing Pal a reputation that enabled him to produce and direct feature length sci-fi and fantasy films like The War of the Worlds (1953), Tom Thumb (1958), The Time Machine (1960) and The Wonderful World of the Brothers Grimm (1963).

Pal's legacy in Europe has been sustained, consolidated and advanced by two major figures of Czechoslovakian origin. Influenced by the indigenous marionette and theatrical traditions, Jiri Trnka and Jan Svankmajer have produced a range of extraordinary films pushing the boundaries not merely of the stop-motion technique, but of other approaches, too. Trnka's politicised if romantic-vision inspired masterpieces like Old Czech Legends (1953), A Midsummer Night's Dream (1955) and The Hand (1965), while Svankmajer's more subversive and challenging view, genuinely taboo-breaking in its daring, meant he created films like Dimensions of Dialogue (1982), Alice (1987) and Little Otik (2001). This altogether darker work was to inspire The Quay Brothers working in England; Kihachiro Kawamoto working in Japan; and Tim Burton and Henry Selick working in the USA.

The contemporary era has seen the emergence of the Will Vinton studios in America and Aardman Animation in the UK as masters of clay animation. The two styles vary, but both studios value the 'clay' aesthetic as something visually distinctive and engaging. Nick Park, Aardman's most famous son, has created Wallace, the eccentric inventor and his altogether smarter dog, Gromit, a now globally famous partnership, that has featured in Park's shorts, A Grand Day Out (1989), The Wrong Trousers (1993) and A Close Shave (1995). Park's work, though speaking to a wider tradition of English wit and whimsy, nevertheless has clear affiliations with the stop-motion animation made for children's

television in the UK by Gordon Murray and Bura and Hardwick – Camberwick Green (1966) and Trumpton (1967); Oliver Postgate and Peter Firman – The Clangers (1969) and Bagpuss (1974); and Ivor Wood at Filmfair – The Wombles (1973) and Postman Pat (1981). The high quality of three-dimensional animation for children in the UK has been sustained by Cosgrove Hall, S4C, and BBC Animation, and has only been echoed in the American context by the early 1960s' work of Jules Bass – Rudolph the Red-Nosed Reindeer (1964) and Mad Monster Party (1968) – and Art Clokey's simple clay figure, Gumby (1955 onwards). Inevitably, Will Vinton's Martin the Cobbler (1976), The Adventures of Mark Twain (1985) and the 1990s' advertisements for the Californian Raisin Advisory Board, featuring raisins singing popular songs, have in their various ways created a benchmark in clay animation in the USA, which has always had to compete with the Disney tradition, but also in recent years with the now dominant CGI aesthetic.

The fundamental belief in the sheer 'difference' and visual appeal of stop-motion animation has also prompted the emergence of important individual artists, from Serge Danot – The Magic Roundabout (1965) to Joan Gratz – Mona Lisa Descending A Staircase (1992) to Barry Purves – Gilbert & Sullivan (1999), each bringing a specific vision to the materials, sense of theatrical space and fluid timing of their narratives.

← Still from animated sequence in Jason and the Argonauts – Don Chaffey

The skeleton fight, which features Jason and two of his fellow Argonauts fighting six skeletons, still remains one of the most celebrated and complex animation sequences in feature film. Harryhausen's work as a 'one man' effects unit has only been equalled and surpassed by the rapid advances in digital technology and huge investments in post-production effects personnel.

→ Stills from Chicken Run – Peter Lord & Nick Park

Chicken Run, Aardman's parody of The Great Escape and other Second World War movies, combines English eccentricity and whimsy with Hollywood-style spectacle and adventure, sustaining the tradition of 3D stop motion into the contemporary era.

British Film Institute

Related area of study
The craft aesthetic

Stop-motion and clay animators have always championed the 'materiality' and 'textural' aspects of their work as the distinctive appeal of 3D stop motion, but one of the most significant aspects remains the necessarily 'artisanal' approach to the work, which is not reliant on 'off the shelf' software, but the ability to make and build things, as well as to respond to the miniature demands of theatrical practice and live-action film-making techniques on a small scale.

British Film Institute

Sound and Stop-motion Animation

Master animator, Barry Purves, sees a strong relationship between sound and the sense of performance in stop-motion animation, preferring nuanced vocal performances, specific and suggestive sound effects, and above all, an inspiring musical score to create a distinctive soundtrack for animation.

Purves: 'Like most elements that make up animated films, sound is usually a celebration of artifice. In my own films I am personally reluctant to use straightforward dialogue, as this inevitably leads to a static, talking-heads approach to shooting (that's a bit of a naive generalisation, but not untrue). I favour a more movement-based form of storytelling, seeing the whole body of the character as much as possible – using the body language to tell the drama and emotion. I guess I find a body more interesting than a generally over-animated mouth flapping away.'

Using artificial constructs

'I prefer to use words, not as dialogue, but in enjoyably artificial constructs like singing (in my Rigoletto and Gilbert & Sullivan films), or stylised nods towards Kabuki (Screen Play) or Greek Drama (Achilles). It has to be said that a lot of my favourite short animated films, like The Monk and the Fish, and Three Misses, are wordless.'

The cliché of voices for animation

'When I have worked with voice artists I definitely try to avoid the usual characterisation of animated characters – wildly over the top and silly cartoony voices. This may seem to contradict my words about celebrating the artifice, but nothing would make me switch off quicker than squeaky vocal gymnastics. These untruthful performances, on way too many shows to mention, are not the same as honest and detailed character work, such as The Simpsons, however flamboyant they may be. The voices in Babe strike me as some of the most beautiful voice acting I have heard for ages. They manage to suggest the animal as well as the human qualities, without ever having to resort to cheap tricks.'

Methods of voice recording

'With working with voices, I prefer to have the whole cast in one room and allow them to bounce off each other, and happily let them tread on each others' sentences and fluff the odd line; it's these unexpected details that seem to make a character live. Obviously it is sometimes impractical to have the cast all together, but I'd always encourage some spontaneity from the actor. I'd also be very specific about the physicality of the situation...I hate those moments when the clearly static voice performance in a studio bears no relation to the physical efforts of the character in the film.'

Applications and Outcomes   The Fundamentals of Animation

Purves uses the tight construction and
specificity of the musical score to help him
structure the dynamics of the dramatic
performance in his animation.

Purves concentrates on the physical gestures
of characters as the determining emotional
vocabulary of his work; each figure literally
embodying the suggested feelings in the
musical narrative.

→ **Still from Gilbert and Sullivan: The Very
Models – Barry Purves**
The wit and whimsy of a range of Gilbert and
Sullivan operettas is combined in a musical
narrative, which tells the story of Gilbert and
Sullivan themselves. Purves illustrates this
combinative score with the rich textures of
design drawn from the staging of the D'Oyly
Carte performances.

Core study
Movement as meaning

Express as much narrative information as
possible through looks, gesture and physical
movement that has a particular purpose or
objective.

Lip-synching

'Lip-synch is something that seems to get
students and young animators bogged down. I
think I would probably concentrate on the eye
acting than over-synched mouth shapes. It is the
eyes we watch in a conversation and too often
than not, we do not have the necessary anatomy
on an animated character (such as teeth, or a
tongue) to do accurate lip-synch. We don't have
enough frames in a second either. The secret
probably is to suggest the mouth shapes,
suggesting the syllables rather than meticulously
closing and shutting the mouth with every letter.
The rhythm and vocal effort are probably more
important than accuracy.'

The value of impressionistic sound

'Likewise, with sound effects. It's all too easy to
add an effect for every rustle of clothing or every
footstep. This leads to a very cluttered
soundtrack, especially as music is nearly always
an essential element. And, again, I'd suggest that
often the effects are too literal. Since we are
playing with things of the imagination, we have
the freedom to surprise, to emphasise, and to
challenge the expected. It is inevitable that sound
effects usually get left to the end of production,
and added when filming is finished, but I'd
encourage the use of sound as a storytelling
element in its own right, and not just as
atmosphere. I'm afraid I find that for most
colleges, working with sound is usually an
afterthought. As a practical point, sound can
often be used to suggest things that the budget
won't allow to be seen, and is often the more
effective and surprising for that.'

Music

'And as for music, several chapters should be
devoted to this essential element of storytelling.
It's often music that starts me thinking about a
film, and I love the discipline of using a precise,
fixed piece of music. Having the musical score at
the start of a film certainly works for me, and
probably stops the composer's frustration of
having to make his or her music fit with
mathematics. Music seems to focus me and
allows me to make every moment count, as well
as giving the films a natural rhythm and flow. I've
seldom used music just as background, and have
always been lucky to have specially composed or
recorded music. To me, it is just as important a
part of the storytelling as the visuals, and this has
occasionally, only occasionally, led to conflict in
the mixing where most engineers are used to TV
dramas and insist in putting the music timidly
"behind" the picture. To me, it is right there up
front. Animation, in my eyes, is a great marriage
and celebration of movement, music and design,
all equally telling the story and illuminating the
characters. I think that is why I respond to ballet
and dance so instinctively and constantly refer to
animation as a relation of dance.'

Stop-motion Animation and Satire

With its ancestry in caricature, political cartooning, and the comic strip, its tendency to exaggeration and comic invention in the cartoon, and its ability to subvert and distort, animation has always been a ready vehicle for satirical approaches. Animation has the capacity to safely engage with excess, and in 3D stop motion, to even engage with the material world.

Eric Fogel is creator and co-executive producer of Celebrity Deathmatch. Fogel, seeking to contemporise 3D stop-motion animation, sought to use the phenomenon of modern 'celebrity' as his subject and the comic 'plasticity' of clay as his material, to create one of the most successful animated series for adults.

The Mutilator

Eric Fogel's early life was characterised by an addiction to drawing his own comic strips and prototype animation in flip-books. Illustration and design became an overwhelming interest, which ultimately prompted his taking a course at the Tisch School of Arts at New York University between 1987 and 1991. He developed his initial film-making technique on live-action short films before adapting one of his own comic strips – The Mutilator – into his debut animated

film. Though he was strongly advised by his tutors against making the film, Fogel wanted to experiment with cel animation, and felt that he wanted to work with a personal story – The Mutilator was essentially a satire about the time Fogel lived on Manhattan's Lower East Side, but played out in a post-apocalyptic quasi science-fictional form. The film enjoyed immediate success and won New York University's Award for Excellence in Animation, and gained theatrical distribution through Spike and Mike's Sick and Twisted Festival of Animation.

MTV and iconoclastic animation

Fogel continued to make animated shorts for such Festivals including Mutilator II: Underworld and Expiration Date, which served as an impressive portfolio, gaining the interest of Abby Terkuhle, President of MTV Animation, who invited Fogel to tender any new and potentially innovative concepts that would be suitable for the station's commitment to distinctive and iconoclastic animation, which would be readily identified with the network. Fogel's debut series for MTV, The Head (1994), featured a relationship between a man with a giant cranium and an alien that lived inside it. This spawned a graphic novel and enjoyed success for two seasons. Celebrity Deathmatch became Fogel's second series and was MTV's first clay animated work. The series successfully combines the excessive and playful brutalities enabled within the animated form, drawing a great deal from the Tom and Jerry films made by William Hanna and Joseph Barbera at MGM, and the satiric vision

that seeks to undermine not merely celebrities themselves, but the whole concept of 'celebrity' as social preoccupation.

A contemporary critique

Further, the programme enjoyed a parallel exposure to WWF wrestling, long predating the recent cross-gender bouts in the live-action spectacle with male and female contests self-evidently legitimised by the artifice of the medium. There was the desire too, to move beyond what Henry Jenkins has described as 'masculine melodrama' in the sport, while embracing the way that 'conventional melodrama, externalises emotion, mapping it on to the combatants' bodies and transforming their physical competition into a search for moral order. Restraint or subtlety has little place in such a world. Everything that matters must be displayed, publicly, unambiguously, and unmercilessly.'[1] This readily chimes with animation's capacity to safely engage with excess; indeed, extending its potential further

Related area of study
Enunciation

'Enunciation' in animation sounds a more
complex concept than it actually is. Simply,
when animation comes on the cinema,
television or computer screen, the audience
'knows it' to be animation. The form has got a
particularly distinctive 'look', 'feel', and 'style'
that it literally 'announces' itself, and in doing
so shows a scale of artifice or illusion that
implies the presence of a creator – the
animator or auteur.

both in the interrogation of the form and the
explicitness of what is suggested by each
celebrity. Fogel essentially plays out known
variables of the publicly determined and
constructed mediations of popular celebrity, and
in this echoes what Peter Brooks has called the
necessary characteristic of 'self-nomination' in
the melodramatic imagination; in other words the
specific and particular 'narrative' that informs the
physical, emotional, psychological and material
characteristics of any one identity.[2] This is
especially significant because the coherence
and pertinence of the work lies in the coupling of
this 'self-nomination', and what Donald Crafton
has called the implicit 'self-figuration' of
animated forms in which the animator is directly
or indirectly present in the film as a signature
presence by virtue of the enunciative
distinctiveness of the form used.[3] Fogel's
presence as an animator and a satirist moves
the animation beyond the mere cartoonal
pleasures of extended slapstick and into a
critique of the status and illusory agenda of
contemporary celebrity, and perhaps as
importantly, the American populist tradition
which supports it.

Strategic choice of media

Celebrity Deathmatch gained high viewing
ratings and led to Fogel being named in
Entertainment Weekly's top 100 most creative
people in the industry. It is certainly clear that
Fogel's commitment to stop-motion animation
was not merely an aesthetic decision, but also a
political one as he saw the advent of computer-
generated animation and the huge investment in
it by all the major studios as potentially
endangering the survival of the process. Having
committed to stop-motion, it was clear, however,
that for the fast turnaround required for a
television series, it would be necessary to
eliminate the use of clay as the wear and tear
was extensive, and the consequent
degeneration of the characters meant the time-
consuming necessity of re-sculpting. Having
addressed this issue, the team making the show,

some 20 full-time animators, worked on 15
sound stages, producing 10 seconds of
animation per day, and a half-hour show in five
weeks, sometimes using elaborate wire systems
for 'flying' characters that echo the full scale use
of similar processes to create spectacular
imagery, drawn from Hong Kong cinema, in live-
action works like The Matrix and Crouching
Tiger, Hidden Dragon.

The process

The animation is created against chromatic
backgrounds, and various 'plates' of crowd
characters from an archive of audience
responses are digitally mixed with the key action
in the computer. While computers are an integral
part of the process, it is important to stress that
Fogel most values the importance of pre-
production and the work of the scriptwriting
teams, and the singular and distinctive
'authorship' in manipulating one frame at a time.

Influences

Fogel: 'Growing up, I had a love affair with
animation in general, but I soon realised that
there was work that I liked which was not the
"kiddie-toon" stuff you would find on a Saturday
morning. We had something in the States called
Science Fiction Theatre on Saturday afternoons,
and on those sort of programmes you would find
the work of Ray Harryhausen – Sinbad movies
and such – and there was one particular movie,
The Mysterious Island, where you had a gigantic
crab crawling up out of the sand and attacking
the tiny people. I was always frustrated and →

→ **Stills from Philips Broadcast of 1938 –**
← **George Pal**
One of Fogel's seminal influences, George Pal,
created animated advertisements, which like
Celebrity Deathmatch, playfully parodied
elements of Hollywood culture, from movie
stars to dance crazes and subcultures.

→ amazed at the same time, because without
the aid of a VCR you could not pause the
animation and study it, and you had no means
to find out the "tricks" – how was it done – so I
was mystified and delighted, and knew that I
wanted to find out about the process of
animation, and become an animator.'

Various comedic approaches
Fogel (cont.) 'I got behind a camera and
experimented. I have an art background in the
sense that I always sketched, doodled and
sculpted – it wasn't traditional, in the sense
that I wasn't trained. Everything that I have
learned was achieved through experience. I
was always a fan of professional wrestling
because those characters seemed to me to be
so much like cartoon characters, so much
larger than life, and then there was another
show out of the UK called Spitting Image, and
during the 1980s they were running these
specials in the States, and I remember seeing
the Ronald Reagan and Michael Jackson

caricatures, and finding them so well observed
and funny. Just the image of these already
exaggerated people as puppets blew me away,
so I thought if I combined these two elements –
the wrestling and the celebrity satire – it would
make a great stop-motion series. Animation has
always embraced different kinds of approach to
comedy, and satire, while attractive to the
animator can also create problems if
mishandled.

'On the one hand, if you do it incorrectly, you
can come across as mean spirited or angry,
and we did not want that to happen; all we
wanted to do was to have fun, and laugh at
these characters at their expense, and that was
a much easier sell in animation. Also these
celebrities are proud to be seen that way;
being represented in animation is like a vain
tribute to their work. Before I got to MTV I had
been developing the idea for about a year and
just as I was to prepare to finance the
first short films, I was fortunate that MTV

decided that they would go ahead, and we
made the first fight – Charles Manson versus
Marilyn Manson. We knew that we would only
have two weeks to make this five-minute
animation and it was only myself and one other
animator doing the work, and we knew that clay
was not going to work. I had worked with clay a
lot in the past and I knew that within the
timeframe available that it would slow us down
tremendously. Again, with this first fight, we
knew it was essentially a pilot, a test, so we had
a model shop create foam latex versions of the
clay puppets and it proved much more efficient
to work with these models. We still used clay
heads to sculpt the good expressions and get
the exaggerated reactions that we wanted, and
when we wanted to do extreme reactions, we
made a series of replaceable heads and
actually sculpted the expression into a series of
six heads, sometimes combining these heads
with a digital morph. Later on, we went on to
use resin heads to preserve the look of clay
and reduce the weight of the head so it would

animation. We completed a Halloween special, for example. We have a character growing – it starts as a skull on the floor and slowly morphs into a full sized human, and you see all the layers of anatomy – the flesh, the muscle, the skin – everything is growing from the skull and expanding into the limbs, the arms and the legs. We use a combination of on-set clay-sculpting for the musculature; then morphing to make the transition between several replaceable bodies; and then we had a 2D artist treat the musculature with a variety of techniques, and this is combined in one shot. It was amazing! Metamorphosis is still the central preoccupation of the art, I think.'

Celebrity Deathmatch has been extraordinarily successful with both the public and the figures it playfully satires.

Fogel: 'We had an extraordinary response from Steven Spielberg when we pitted him against Alfred Hitchcock – of course, he had to lose to "the Master" – but he wrote to us demanding a re-match, so that was a great moment.'

not keep tipping over, but we kept the area around the eyes soft so that we could still sculpt there and widen the expressions. We also manipulate the eyebrows and change the mouth; these are the only things that are moveable on the heads.'

While embracing the techniques of George Pal and Ray Harryhausen, Fogel also readily engaged with new production software:

Fogel: 'We are using the same technology as we were when we started off – we use Adobe Premiere to capture the animation and Adobe After Effects to apply the digital effects. These are off-the-shelf software packages, but what has happened is that our digital team has got better through doing, and this has improved the look. They are constantly using different kinds of software to improve the visual impact of the work, and I am always looking for shots that we can enhance digitally, to make them more memorable, and ways to enhance the

REFERENCES
1) Jenkins, H. 'Never Trust a Snake...': WWF Wrestling as Masculine Melodrama in Baker, A and Boyd, T. (eds) Out of Bounds: Sports, Media and the Politics of Identity, Bloomington and Indianapolis: Indiana University Press, 1997, p48
2) Brooks, P. The Melodramatic Imagination: Balzac, Henry James, Melodrama and the Mode of Excess, New Haven: Yale University Press, 1976, p4
3) Crafton, D. Before Mickey: The Animated Film 1898–1928, Chicago: University of Chicago Press, 1993, p11

A First Experience

Students aspiring to be animators undertake courses, not merely learning from their tutors, but from one another. The following work is made by students, and may be viewed as an example of peer-learning, identifying important issues in the creative process and the technique.

Hide and Seek is an undergraduate student animation made by Kerry Drumm and Aaron Wood. Kerry Drumm and Aaron Wood are formerly students of Surrey Institute of Art and Design, Farnham, UK, and aspire to be professional animators and film-makers.

Intention

Wood: 'This was based on a short story. Our intention was to make a dark atmospheric piece that relied on mystery and suspense throughout. Aesthetically we wanted to create a slightly fairy tale feel, but at the same time add a horror aspect without slipping into "pantomime".'

Drumm: 'We wanted to try and make the audience work with the film. We watched lots of Hitchcock, who was able to pull you into his films; you always knew something wasn't quite right. We wanted to achieve the same feeling with our film. The narrative structure I think above all was the most important element during the pre-production of the film and it was something we worked on over and over until we felt it was right.'

↗ **Mood-board for Hide and Seek –
Aaron Wood and Kerry Drumm**
Collected on the mood-board are the various textures and sights that compound the imaginative world of the narrative. This is an effective method in collating diverse images and materials that define the look or atmosphere of the piece.

→ **Preparatory work for Hide and Seek –**
↑ **Aaron Wood and Kerry Drumm**
Preparatory set design sketches, stylised to convey the atmosphere wanted.

You had to be able to follow the narrative of the film to understand the ending; if it became lost it would just fall apart.'

Story

The story is simple. Some children are playing hide and seek in a deserted house, and in the midst of the game, something occurs that has dark repercussions for the house in the future. The stop-motion animation brings a 'realistic' aspect to what is in essence an increasingly surreal and supernatural narrative. Citing influences including Tim Burton, Henry Selick, Barry Purves and Paul Berry, Drumm and Wood were interested in the technical, as well as the thematic and aesthetic challenges of creating an atmospheric piece. These influences are clear in some of the preparatory design work.

Personal influences

The sensitive combination of fairy-tale innocence and gothic threat in some senses emerges from the simple design strategy and the textures of the materials, evidenced early in Drumm's research work and sketchbook. Her own background is fundamental to her approach:

Drumm: 'Animation was never something I've always wanted to do. I knew I wanted to do something in relation to art, perhaps illustration. I had always loved books, and being dyslexic (although I didn't know that at the time) I always found the illustrations within books more appealing. I would create my own story within the illustration to save me reading, which took too long. Pop-up books fascinated me: you opened them up and suddenly this world opened up to you. The scene would often allow you to open windows and doors, slide characters across the page of the book.'

Drumm's observation here, about finding her own narrative within the illustrative images, is important in the sense that animation, first and foremost, offers the possibility of visual storytelling through highly specific choices of pictorial 'association'. The viewer 'reads' the film literally through 'design in motion'. This informs the creation and construction of characters, script development and storyboarding, and in this case, the role of the set.

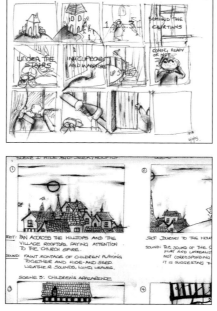

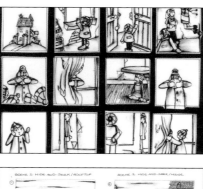

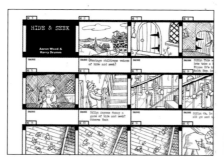

← **Storyboard and attic design for Hide and**
↙ **Seek – Aaron Wood and Kerry Drumm**
The evolution of the storyboard is essentially the development of both the story, told in pictures, and also the recognition of the 'movement' within the frame and consequently, the decisions about what is to be animated and what is to be shot. Wood notes: 'The majority of the film was executed using stop-motion animation (the games of hide and seek, and the mother searching). The scenes that did not involve puppets were shot in live action. This was to establish the location/house (opening shot), show the passing of time (autumn to winter to spring) and to reveal Billy's whereabouts (ending).'

↓ The attic design had to accommodate a significant portion of the action.

3D Stop-motion Animation: A First Experience

→ **Set model and sketches of house from Hide and Seek – Aaron Wood and Kerry Drumm**
From creating the initial sketches to the construction of the final working models was a complicated process of trial and error.

Set design

The design of the set was important narratively, as well as in regard to practical concerns. The attic becomes a significant story context and needed to accommodate being shot in a certain way. The house overall had to be built in a fashion that walls etc. could be removed or pushed back to accommodate a moving camera, or specific kinds of angled shot.

Wood: 'We had to manoeuvre the Bolex camera around and get it to zoom down stairs and hallways for the ending few shots. This idea became a problem as firstly the camera was too huge to just dolly from room to room and secondly, we were not using a zoom lens so had to deal with zoom shots manually. We got around this by building a complex set in which every wall or even half a wall could be removed and the set still support itself.'

Drumm: 'We both enjoy being in a studio, challenging camera shots, experimenting with light, changing scenes and working with puppets. The complexity of the set and the way we had to build it to allow us to move the camera through the walls meant we had some awkward shots. We were often lying on the floor squeezing between the tripods of the camera and pepper lights, or balancing on top of stepladders to get to the puppets to animate – it was good fun!'

The important point to take from Drumm and Wood's efforts is that their work took a great deal of planning and construction, yet there still had to be a high degree of improvisation. This is what the creative process is about, and it sometimes requires some 'low-tech' invention to create seemingly 'hi-tech' outcomes.

Characterisation

Simple ideas can also be the best. Drumm and Wood use a group of children, but in such a short film it is difficult to differentiate them, except in the case of one child, who the viewer is led to mistrust and even dislike. Differentiation, therefore, comes easily through the different designs of the character's costumes.

There were further challenges – particularly in facilitating the 'acting'. Crucially, in this particular case this is achieved through simple 'blocking' and shot choice. 'Blocking' is the placement and desired move to be executed by the character.

Snow

Another specific challenge was the snowfall on the house.

Wood: 'At first we thought of green-screening flour, washing powder or a similar material, but all of these were too fine to be picked up on screen. The other problem was it was snowing while the camera panned, so the snow had to at least look like it was floating/hovering instead of falling in a straight line down. This was done using Adobe After Effects and blue-screening over the film in editing.'

Assessment and advice

Drumm and Wood are clear about what is distinctive about 'animation' as a creative expression and the things they learned from their work on the film.

Wood: 'Everything is much more in your control. The style and design; the atmosphere created; and the "little world" created in the film. I think animation has so few boundaries, which allows for so much artistic freedom, so much more expression and different possibilities in representation and interpretation.'

Drumm: 'Again, I think it comes down to storytelling and maybe it's connected to the way I visualise a story from just a picture, photograph or a painting. Everything that I look at I visualise in 3D and begin to build a story from that image. Animation is such a powerful tool; you can create an imaginary world and bring it to life to tell a story.'

Applications and Outcomes

The Fundamentals of Animation

Production shots from the making of Hide and Seek– Aaron Wood and Kerry Drumm

→ 'Our tutor suggested it would be interesting to feel as if you were floating through the house, so that set us an early challenge. We began to plan how we could achieve this. These shots were filmed live action and as the Bolex camera could only run for 10 seconds, it was frustrating. We used a shopping trolley to 'dolly' for the opening scene (we did return the trolley to the supermarket we borrowed it from!).'

↘ The placement of the characters and their exchange uses the stairs to good effect, offering the possibility of demonstrating their relationships and prompting specific story events.

↘ Characterisation of the individual children was mainly achieved through differences in costume.

↘ Although the settled snow was actual, the snowfall was added digitally, since panning the camera across the screen meant the snowfall couldn't fall straight to the ground and still look realistic.

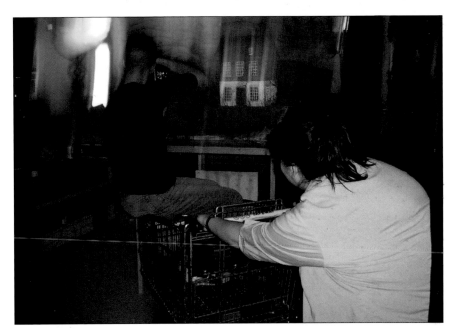

Core skill
Being practical

3D stop-motion animation can require:
- Possibly making and maintaining material objects.
- Familiarity with technical equipment in the facilitation of sets.
- Attention to scale and perspective in preparation and shooting.
- The ability to improvise solutions to practical problems.
- Patience and attention to detail.
- A sense of 'theatrical' performance and 'live action' cinematography.

Animation for Children

3D stop-motion animation has become extremely popular with children, who perceive its physical and material world as intrinsically different from the 2D cartoon. This sense of a real and appealing 'place' with consistent and amusing characters is central to keeping a child's attention, and gaining a strong emotional investment in the stories. Here are two examples, The Koala Brothers and Engie Benjy, addressing the particular issues raised by this kind of work.

Stop-motion animation has a particularly rich tradition in children's animation, where it is often the case that a high number of episodes need to be made. This means the core concepts need to be of high quality; the characters need sustained appeal and the contexts in which they inhabit

need to facilitate as many storytelling possibilities as possible.

Point of view
Dave Johnson is the creator of The Koala Brothers, one of the most successful of recent stop-motion animations on Cbeebies, Nick Jr. and the Disney Channel. He offers some key advice about making animation for children:

Johnson: 'Try and see what you are doing from the children's point of view. Will they enjoy this? Any decision you make you must be guided by what they understand and what they might find funny. You have to remember what it was like to be a child.

'Ironically, it is often the case that people who have children are not necessarily the people to make children's television because they are too close to it, or might create work that speaks to their own understanding of their own children. You have to have a desire to do it, and you need to use

language that is not too sophisticated or concepts that are too difficult. For example, we had a script submitted for The Koala Brothers, which was about a shopkeeper who wanted to promote his shop and deal with advertising, and for a four-year old this is not in their world, it simply isn't relevant, so it is a matter of thinking what might be relevant to a four-year old – it might be that there is something that they want and can't have that is in that shop, and that is what you would focus on.'

Concept
'If you are making a children's series you've got to have a simple concept that people can grasp straight away. Basically, if you said, "What is the Koalas about?", I would say, it is about two koalas who fly around in a plane and help people in the Outback, that's it. So it is about "helping". BBC Worldwide really embraced this as this was what they termed "core values". That perspective was helpful because it forced me to understand exactly what the show was about and in terms of purpose, suddenly I realised that if you are making

Applications and Outcomes   The Fundamentals of Animation

a show that is saying "it is good to help others", that is not a bad thing to be doing because it crosses religious and political boundaries. It is not a contentious thing to say and is important enough to sustain the work across a long series.'

Execution

'The big thing we try to do with The Koala Brothers is to strip the possibilities down – it is set in a desert. I've worked on many shows where you spend 90 per cent of the time doing set dressing and lighting, and the animators get to work for 10 per cent of the time on what is in essence the most important thing of all. So we set this in the Outback, which is sky, ground and a rock, so you are spending your time on the personalities of characters, and the story. The Outback setting focuses everything on those characters, and in the real Outback the whole thing of people being isolated and having to work together, make their own entertainment, and help each other, feeds into this. It just happens that the Outback community is one where they stick together and live under difficult conditions.'

Story issues

'The "help" in each episode, as such, is often very small and unsensational. One was about a wombat who saw that everyone else seemed to have visitors, but no one came to see him, so he invented an invisible friend. While some thought this was a bit silly, the Koala Brothers were very supportive, and asked the wombat and his friend for dinner, and there they encouraged him to invite people over, and they also arranged for all the townsfolk to visit. It is not a big issue, but children see such small things as big in their own lives. Another story was about a cricket match where teams are picked and a penguin is left out. The Koalas bring the penguin in, and everyone realises that it is not nice to feel left out.

'There are running themes, too, about affection, for example, and there is a lot of hugging and physical warmth and supportiveness, which is possible with animal characters, though sometimes more problematic with human characters, especially for American markets. The Koala Brothers' world is in the middle of nowhere, but offers the children the possibility that if they went far enough they would encounter this place and community, like in Pingu, for example, or most famously, in Lucas' "galaxy, far, far, away". It chimes with the real world, too, in that it is like the Flying Doctor Service and Outback communities pulling together. The message throughout is a positive one.'

Engie Benjy

Cosgrove Hall has a rich tradition in children's entertainment and is careful to align entertainment with educational principles. Two of their most recent series speak very specifically to a concept inherently related both to children, to the possible concerns of parents, and their potential role as accompanying viewers.

Engie Benjy – who 'makes things better' – is a character who mends different types of vehicles, with the help of his friends Jollop and Dan. Voiced by youthful UK TV show hosts Ant and Dec – Anthony McPartlin and Declan Donnelly – the programme is explicitly based on the kinds of stories made up by children as they play with their favourite toys. This enables a highly fantastical, yet plausible model of storytelling, which reflects how children think, behave and react to certain situations, and looks at the idea of 'problem-solving' from a child's perspective. Like The Koala Brothers, the centrality of the idea of helping each other is a core aspect of the narrative development.

↗ **Publicity stills from Engie Benjy –**
Cosgrove Hall Films Ltd. 2003
The colourful design is key in appealing to children, as is the overall concept of 'invention' – many inventors and DIY experts have figured in British Children's TV from Fireman Sam to Bob the Builder to Wallace. This provides a ready context for amusing machines and contraptions.

→ British TV personalities Ant and Dec with Engie and Jollop are shown on the right. The voice casting of the characters is very important in creating empathic performances for children. McPartlin and Donnelly have considerable experience in children's television and youth programming, and provide engaging vocal interpretations for the anticipated audience.

Core skill

– When conceiving an animation for children, focus on a simple and accessible concept children can immediately understand and empathise with.

– Try to create a colourful, but simple design strategy that clearly depicts the characters and the environments they participate in.

– Use simple language and try to tell the story as much as possible through 'emotion', 'action' and established codes and conventions of 'performance'.

– As well as creating amusing and dramatic situations try to include a constructive and humane theme to encourage and support child development.

Clay Animation

**Clay animation offers the possibility of
working with an 'everyday' material and
fashioning work, which at one and the
same time demonstrates the 'hands-on'
nature of the process and the manipulated
outcomes of the process itself. The
presence of the 'human hand' gives the
work itself a sense that in being 'made',
it is highly accessible and could have
been achieved by the viewer accordingly.
Clay animation is the most obviously
'artisanal' animation.**

Michael Frierson is both an animation
practitioner and historian working at the
University of North Carolina at Greensboro,
USA. He has created a number of clay animated
works for children's television and wrote the
pioneering history, Clay Animation: American
Highlights 1908 to the Present (New York:
Twayne, 1994). Frierson provides an insightful
engagement with history, theory and practice in
discussing an ident he made for Nickelodeon.

Early experiences
Frierson: 'My very first exposure to clay
animation was meeting Barry Bruce, a character
designer at Will Vinton Studios at the University
of North Carolina at Greensboro in April, 1979. It
was at the Carolina Film and Video Festival and
the same weekend that Three Mile Island
nuclear plant almost melted down. He did a
workshop and was incredibly open and

supportive of the students who were making
animated films at the time, and he really inspired
me to make a clay film. We took him to a
basement where someone was shooting a
puppet film and said. "What do you think?" And
he wasn't even looking at the set, he was just
looking at all the junk on the basement floor and
he said, "You got a lot of cool junk here you can
use to make a set, or a camera rig." That showed
me it was all about tinkering, finding some low-
tech way to make it work.

'I studied film-making at the University of
Michigan and ran the Super 8 film festival there
for a few years, which was a fabulous learning
opportunity for me. We saw the first Tim Hittle
films in Super 8 there and invited him out to the
festival and picked his brains. There was no
formal animation programme at UM, so I just
read books and talked to people at festivals and
wherever I could corner someone.

'My animation work grew out of my interest in
manipulating time in 16mm film. I have always
been fascinated by time lapse images. When
Koyaanisqatsi came out in 1982, I thought I had
died and gone to heaven. I saw a lot of clay
animation in Super 8 and the 16mm festival in Ann
Arbor, MI. It had amazing experimental films that
manipulated time in myriad ways. Time and the
visual representation of time has been a primary
theme in motion pictures since the beginning,
and when you see that tradition expressed in
hundreds of independent, experimental films,
you want to jump in and try it.' →

1. Kangaroo hops into frame ...

2. pulls kitten out of pocket - looks confused ..

NEW?

3. Pulls everything including the kitchen sink ...

4. pulls giant baby out of pocket with great difficulty ...

RATTLE RATTLE

5. Looks up at baby adoringly ...

6. BABY drops rattle on mother's head ...

↑ **Storyboard images from Nick Jr. ident –**
↗ **Michael Frierson**

Applications and Outcomes   The Fundamentals of Animation

Playing with and manipulating clay can be a helpful experience in understanding three dimensionality, proportion, weight, texture, and the creation of a 'knowable' creature or figure in a plastic form. Even if there is the intention to pursue another kind of animation, working with such a material can still be helpful in the preparation or understanding of other forms.

→ **Frierson (cont.):** 'My wife, Martha Garrett, has always been a big influence on me because she is a talented ceramic artist. When she was a kid, she would build clay models and keep them for years in her refrigerator. We played with cut-out animation for a while, then in 1980 built cardboard sets and clay chickens for a film called Chickens in the Louvre, based on a wacky song by some friends of mine. Since there was so little clay around then, it did great on the festival circuit and was picked up by this little cable company that was just starting in New York called Bravo.

'There's little of working with actors in animation, which I like. You only have to work with voice talent and a storyboard. Also, I like the low-tech nature of clay animation. If you work with a Bolex, single frame is a natural thing to do. You just automatically start pushing that trigger forward instead of backward – that single click is a very satisfying sound.'

The challenges
'I have a love/hate feeling about animation. I hate animation pre-production. I have a short attention span, so actually figuring out what every shot is going to be in advance and counting a voice track in 16mm mag on a squawk box was no fun for me. It's only marginally easier in a computer. Consequently, I constructed a very basic storyboard for the ident I discuss later. But once you're over that hurdle, the production part feels very good. It may be slow, but you have a clear idea where

you are going and it becomes like fine needlework: each frame, like each stitch, is moving you closer to the end. You get four or five seconds in the can in one day, and it feels great.'

Loony Tunes
'My touchstone has always been classic Looney Tunes. The best Looney Tunes are the greatest short films ever made. I never saw Disney's Wonderful World of Color because it was on NBC and the tuner knob had broken off our TV and it was stuck on CBS. So when I was a kid, Looney Tunes WAS the entire body of animation. There wasn't any other animation on TV except an occasional Popeye, and Davey and Goliath on Sunday morning, because it had a religious message and was sponsored by the Lutheran Church.'

Clay animation milestones
'In 1974, Bob Gardiner and Will Vinton won the Academy Award for their clay animated film Closed Mondays. That film had a big impact on me, because we had not seen much 3D puppet animation in the US. It also forced the Academy of Motion Picture Arts and Sciences to change the name of the category from "Best Cartoon" to "Best Animated Film", and that is indicative of how independent animation from the period was shaking up the scene.

'In the late 1970s, Will Vinton was producing half hour clay animated films like Martin the Cobbler (1976), Rip Van Winkle (1978) and The Little

Prince (1979). Even though some of the stories were a bit corny, the technique was very strong: it's classic clay animation, very rich and very detailed. It has the same sort of appeal that intricate doll houses do, this kind of miniature world that is delicate and detailed. Seeing that material, I began to wonder where clay animation came from. I started researching the history of clay animation. I met Art Clokey, creator of the popular Gumby series, and wrote an article about Gumby in Funnyworld in 1982. Then I found some early American clay films from 1908 and the first woman clay animator in the US, Helena Smith Dayton, who was making clay films in 1917. So I ended up writing a book called Clay Animation: American Highlights 1908 to the Present (New York: Twayne Publishers, 1994). I feel like telling that story has been my contribution to clay animation more than my films.'

The appeal of clay
'Clay has an inherent visual appeal because it moves in 3D space and it's very plastic. Art Clokey told me once that clay has this appeal to the collective unconscious because we are all basically made from it. I thought that was far fetched at one time, but now I see that he is right. It's a visceral medium that speaks to us at the prelogical level.

'My wife has always been my partner on any animation I have ever done. She's the sculptor, she makes great characters and she has an intuitive grasp of facial expression and body movement. I hold the poses I want, and she →

→ studies me and makes them. So clay is right for us. It's challenging, but also a very forgiving medium: you can be sloppy with it and it still looks great. I tell my students to start loose: don't try to be slick with it at first. Just move it around and watch the fingerprints in it.'

The Nickelodeon ident

'The ident is a short piece of branding for television channels, designed to capture the attention before ending with the channel's logo. I like working within those constraints, presenting a very slight narrative in a very short amount of time.

'Like any puppet animation, clay is difficult to fly in the air. Whenever you have to fight gravity, clay can be very problematic, particularly if you're not using expensive armatures. There's a moment in this piece where the baby kangaroo is supposed to squeeze out of the mom kangaroo's pouch, and we had not thought hard enough about how to achieve that technically.

'So we started building the baby growing out and it immediately got too heavy to support, and now you're stuck. You either have to trash the shot and go back and reframe and do a cut in, or just keep going and power through the problem. In those hard frames, where you're just hanging in there and trying to keep it from falling apart, it gets very intense and sometimes very ugly between Martha and I! We just kept building on the back end of the baby and moving the clay forward and trying to keep the mom balanced.

'We tried some traditional "squash and stretch" movements – where the mother kangaroo jumps into frame – that worked much better than I thought they would.

'And a Tex Avery moment when she pulls out about 40 things from her pouch. We added multiple arms to her and just kept them moving every frame, in the same way Avery uses multiple limbs in a rapid motion segment in a classic cartoon. With the sound there – a series of whipping sound effects – it's a funny flash in the midst of some normal movement.'

Lighting

'The one thing I would change is to try to light the set more dramatically. This piece is lit high key for comedy, but I've learned that you can actually use foam core above the set and just cut holes where you want to place the light and you can achieve a much more realistic look on the set. Foam core with properly placed holes withholds the light where you don't want it, lets the corners fall off more and highlights the areas you want the audience to look at.

'I teach animation at the University of North Carolina at Greensboro, and my wife teaches animation to 8th grade students. We find that clay is really a wonderful medium for beginners. It's one of the easiest things on the planet to animate. It's detailed, it's 3D, it's plastic, it's colourful, it's visceral, it's forgiving. Anyone can animate clay. You may not be Nick Park or Will Vinton, but you don't have to be: clay can be a low-tech, funky, dirty medium and it still works great.'

In summary

Frierson's achievement here is considerable. Clay animation has a strong 'material' presence. By using the kangaroo characters and the idea that anything of any size, shape or condition can be produced from the mother's pouch, the 'impossible' nature of what can be created in the animated form is fully expressed. There is comic value in all sorts of incongruous things emerging from the pouch, 'including the kitchen sink', but also in 'topping' that gag with the use of a giant baby, whose rattle ultimately falls on his doting mother, revealing the Nick Jr. logo. The timing is highly effective in that the fall of the rattle is postponed until the audience sees the kangaroo's mother looking up proudly at her son, establishing a mood of pride and status that is then collapsed by the physical slapstick of the giant rattle hitting her in the midst of her dotage. With the 'punchline' of the gag comes the tagline of the ident, making it memorable in the child's mind.

↑ **Stills from Nick Jr. ident –
Michael Frierson**
Frierson's knowledge of cartoon gags helped
him determine the comic scenario of the ident.
Drawing from historical precedents and
previous work is an important aspect of creative
work in speaking to the expectations of the
audience, while also including surprise and
original elements.

Digital Animation

A Brief History

The history of digitally produced animation begins outside the sphere of the entertainment industry, emerging out of the work of military and industrial research teams seeking to use computer graphics for the purposes of simulation and technical instruction. The ENIAC (Electronic Numerical Integrator and Computer), created by the US Army at the University of Pennsylvania in 1946, can claim to be the world's first electronic programmable computer and, though a vast contraption, it had little processing power. With the first silicon transistors made in 1954 and integrated circuits in 1958, computers became more powerful and their uses more various, but they were still largely untouched by creative endeavours.

British Film Institute

John Whitney was a pioneer in this respect, establishing Motion Graphics Inc., and making analogue computer-generated light effects, inspiring his son, John Whitney Jnr. He, in turn, was aware of the more commercially orientated innovation prompted by Ivan Sutherland, with the invention of the 'Sketchpad' in 1962. This device enabled 'drawing with light' into the computer and underpinned the establishment of Evans & Sutherland as the first company to promote computer graphics as a creative technology. Whitney Jnr. worked for the company for a short period before joining Information International Inc. (Triple I), specialising in 3D CG simulations. By 1964 when the first digital film recorder became available, John Stehura had made Cibernetik 5.3 using only punch cards and tape, imagining his abstract, computer motion picture in his mind and only seeing its outcome on screen for the first time when using the recorder at General Dynamics in San Diego, USA.

Having worked on an analogue video graphic system for his projects in the early 1970s, Ed Emshwiller made the pioneering Sunstone (1979) – a three-minute 3D computer graphic work using traditional frame-by-frame transitions and the use of colour in motion to create movement in static images – which preceded the development of any software or hardware to more easily facilitate such work. Another pioneer, Larry Cuba, made First Fig in 1974, and later worked with John Whitney Snr. on Arabesque (1975), each effectively working not merely as an experimental film, but as an act of research in the relationship between geometry, mathematics and graphics as they could be expressed through the computer.

One of the most crucial developments in the field, however, was George Lucas' creation of the initial teams that were later to become the nucleus of Industrial Light and Magic (hereafter ILM) and PIXAR – a company later created by Steve Jobs, the founder of Apple Computers, following the purchase of Lucasfilm's Computer Research and Development Division in 1985.

Robert Abel, a pioneer in motion control camera techniques, had joined Lucas' team and, as well as development work on Star Wars (1977), effected research with Evans & Sutherland on applications of computer animation in the entertainment industries. It was not until 1982, however, that the first fully persuasive applications of computer-generated imagery emerged, first with Disney's Tron (1982) and second, in the Genesis sequence of Star Trek – The Wrath of Khan (1982).

It was clear though that the research and development undertaken by ILM aspired to move beyond using computer graphics as purely an effect, wishing to prioritise the technology as a new model for the core process of film-making. Ironically, this would create a post-photographic mode of cinema. John Whitney Jnr., having left Triple I, established Digital Productions and was responsible for the next key development in CGI (computer-generated imagery) by creating

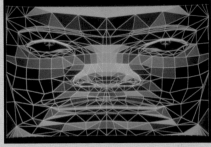

← **Stills from Tron – Steve Lisberger**
↙
↓ Tron was a landmark film in its creation of computer graphics and simulated animation techniques, and its presentation in Super Panavision 70mm. Illustrator Syd Mead, later to work on Bladerunner, worked on the visuals with comic artist Jean Moebius Giraud and commercial artist, Peter Lloyd. The light cycle sequences and innovative environments remain its lasting achievements.

over 25 minutes of material for The Last Starfighter (1984), and with it a watershed of doubt about the economic and aesthetic viability of the technique. In 1985, three key works ensured that CGI would have a key role to play in future productions however: John Lasseter's ILM research project The Adventures of Andre and Wally Bcc, with early signs of Lasseter's trademark combination of traditional cartoon character animation with the computer aesthetics; Daniel Langlois' Tony de Peltrie, the first convincing CG character performance of an aging pianist, using the software that would underpin the creation of Softimage, along with Alias | Wavefront, one of the major computer animation software companies in the world; and Robert Abel's Canned Food Information Council-sponsored commercial Brilliance, featuring a sexy robot, employing some primitive, but nevertheless effective motion capture.

Although initially the progress of CGI as a

process was compromised by its cost, its technical rather than creative base and its slowness of execution, and the lack of a standardised software package, James Cameron's Terminator 2: Judgement Day (1991) demonstrated that CGI could be used for effective storytelling and aesthetic ends, and could work on a different scale than anything previously envisaged. With the increasing standardisation of the requisite software, production facilities proliferated and CGI was an intrinsic tool of expression throughout the commercial and entertainment sector, not merely in films, but in video games and multimedia applications.

Jurassic Park (1993) consolidated CGI as a crucial cinematic tool in the creation of its highly realistic dinosaurs, just as King Kong (1933) vindicated the importance of stop-motion animation as more than just a special effect. The process of animated film practice also changed with the advent of computers, as much of the

arduous work involved in cel animation – in-betweening, ink and paint etc. – was done through the computer. Post-production in most feature films was also revolutionised by the impact of computer applications and their intrinsic role as a special effect. Digital compositing and motion controlled camera became a norm in feature production comparatively quickly, but it was the work of PIXAR – Luxo Jnr., Red's Dream, Tin Toy and Knick Knack – that led to Toy Story (1995), the groundbreaking CGI film, featuring the now iconic Woody and Buzz.

What is often neglected in this narrative is the presence of Reboot (1993), the first fully computer-generated television animation produced by Ian Pearson, Gavin Blair and Phil Mitchell, which self-reflexively used the computer as its narrative subject, depicting the city of Main Frame where Bob, Enzo and their friend, Dot Matrix battle two viruses, Megabyte and Hexadecimal. Inevitably, with the success →

→ of CGI on the big and small screen, investment in the technology increased and computer-generated images became the dominant aesthetic of animated features and in children's programming. Also inevitably, a variety of approaches to using computer animation have characterised the post-Toy Story era. While Dreamworks SKG has emerged as a serious contender to PIXAR with films like Shrek (2001), PIXAR has continued to innovate in features like Finding Nemo (2002) and The Incredibles (2004). Simultaneously, individual artists like Karl Sims, Yoichiro Kawaguchi, William Latham, Ruth Lingford, James Paterson, Amit Pitaru, Tomioka Satoshi, Johnny Hardstaff and Run Wrake have challenged the dominant look and style of such features, using the available range of computer software packages to create more individual work.

It is clear that as different software packages become more affordable and user friendly, and the use of the computer as a creative tool becomes both a domestic and industrial orthodoxy, the same degree of breadth and variety that has characterised all other approaches and techniques will characterise computer-generated imagery. In many senses, in the same way as the term 'New Media' now seems redundant, it is possible that 'CGI' will also become part of a taken-for-granted lexicon of creative practice in animation.

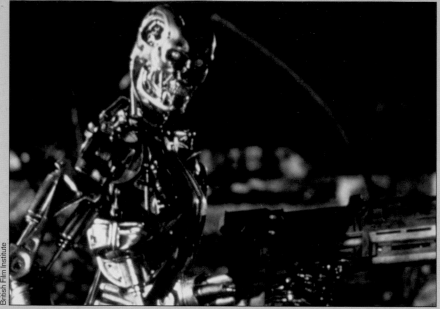
British Film Institute

British Film Institute

Animation and games: Final fantasies

Computer games are phenomenally popular and with each new technological development comes increasingly sophisticated animation. For the most part the animation in games has been in the service of crude movement and action functions, but as narrative and character play more important roles in games, approaches in design and the specificity of the choreography are drawing upon traditional animation. At one level, the relationship between animation and games inspired Hironobu Sakaguchi's Final Fantasy, an attempt to create a feature length adventure with persuasive computer-generated humans, while at another, the emergence of Machinima (see page 186), a web-based fan-cum-creator culture, using games engines to create personal narratives.

↑ **Still from Terminator 2 – James Cameron**
James Cameron uses CGI effectively as a core aspect of the narrative, simultaneously creating the TS cyborg as a character and an effect.

↑ **Still from The Last Starfighter – Nick Castle**
Self-consciously playing on the boom in video games and the popularity of Star Wars, considerable investment was made in computer-generated effects for the first time.

Computer-generated Animation

Computer-generated animation has changed the nature of animation as a form and become the dominant approach in TV and feature work. It has prompted a necessary shift in the definition of animation as a model of film-making made frame by frame, or by more synaesthetic means, to incorporate the idea of the conscious manipulation of pro-filmically constructed synthetic forms in a digital environment. While there is still a fundamental relationship to traditional animation skills and techniques, the software for computer-generated work has changed the nature of the approach.

John Lasseter from PIXAR Animation suggests that there are four key lessons in computer animation:

Lesson One – The computer is just a tool. We don't like the term computer-generated imagery (CGI), because that gives the feeling that it is the computer that generates or makes the images and all through my career it has been assumed that the computer does a lot more than it actually does. We all know the difference between a word processor and a typewriter – the word processor doesn't write the stories or articles; cameras don't take photographs. Artists do.

Lesson Two – You cannot tell what it looks like until it is done. People from the advertising industry always want to come out and 'look down the camera' to see how it is going to look, or go to the set, or something and it was very hard to tell them that with computer animation you always have to visualise it in your head and have a vision of the finished product – it is one of the key jobs of the director to know that throughout the production. Hence, it is also exciting to work with this technology because of that, because you are excited at every stage of production as it starts to come together.

Lesson Three – You get nothing for free. When you watch any aspect of a computer-animated film remember one thing: unlike live action, where you can point a camera at the city and start filming, whenever you see a shot in computer animation, every single item that you see on the screen has to be created in the computer. Typically, computers like to make things that are absolutely perfect and clean and sterile looking, so in our work we are striving to give these worlds a sense of history, a sense of being lived in and that takes a tremendous amount of effort and man hours to be able to do.

Lesson Four – You don't get multiple takes. For those that work in live action, you get to the sound-stage or the location and you get to shoot the scene from a number of different angles, and then get to do a number of different takes of each of those angles. You have coverage. You can take all that film into the editing room and create the film from all these choices. In animation it is so incredibly expensive to produce an animation shot, we get one chance and one chance alone, so we have to plan everything out in advance by using story reels. You have to plan it out in advance.[4]

REFERENCES
4) Quoted in the PIXAR Animation Masterclass, London Film Festival, National Film Theatre, November 2001

Four key lessons in CGI

– The computer is just a tool.
– You cannot tell what it looks like until it is done.
– You get nothing for free.
– You don't get multiple 'takes'.

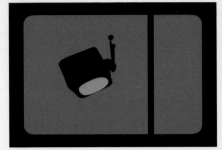

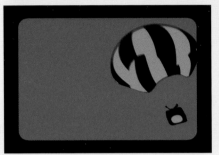
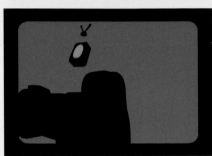

CGI Independent Studio Work

Largely because of artists like John Lasseter at PIXAR and other successful works like Shrek at Dreamworks SKG, computer-generated animation is currently the dominant aesthetic in Hollywood feature animation. This has inspired many prospective animators who want to work in the form and who perceive access to it through the use of comparatively affordable software packages that can be used on a domestic computer, and the proliferation of university and college courses that now teach computer-generated animation as the core approach to the form.

Morgan Powell, a graduate of the University of Teesside, UK and now one of the key figures in Seed Animation, a new company, talks about the process by which he came to engage with animation, how he developed his work, what he learned and how he has set up an independent company. Not PIXAR perhaps, but a more realistic example of how success is possible in the competitive contemporary animation market place.

Beginnings
Powell: 'I had focused on the artistic side of things since I was in primary school and as I

progressed through the years it was the only subject that I continued to get As in. I decided to develop my interests in design and studied graphic design at Leeds Metropolitan University. It was a bizarre time in my life and it felt like I was suffering from illustrator stage fright – I was producing really bad artwork! I decided to leave at the start of the second year – I couldn't pin down why I had failed, so I presumed that some time out would make a difference. I knew that I had an artistic talent and I enjoyed problem-solving and logic, so I searched for an area that would satisfy this.'

From web design to CGI
'Web design was in vogue at the time and this area encompassed design in both the visual and the structural sense, and so I plucked up the courage to try studying again and signed up for the Internet Computing degree at Hull University. The course included computer science, network and software architectures and I became proficient in web-based programming languages. During my spare time I was experimenting with Photoshop and then Flash. Action Scripting became easy because I had actually listened in the programming language theory lectures. By the second year I was creating commercial websites and I had decided to take the Computer Animation Masters degree at Teesside University. The course would hopefully answer a lot of the questions that arose about motion physics and character movement when I was animating in Flash.

The colours chosen for the ident were constants. They were flat colours and chosen on the basis that 3D motion would look impressive on a flat 2D looking character. Having used few 3D objects the animators could use a lot of motion blur, which takes up a great deal of processing power and adds to render time.

The TV was made to bounce in a traditional 'squash 'n' stretch' way, but the motion blur made the motion very smooth and look quite professional. Adding the orange backgrounds and the split screens made the piece very graphical, cartoon-like, sophisticated and humorous.

→ Animating centres of mass

A problem was animating the parachute opening. Online footage was viewed for the motion of the parachute opening, but also camera movement during subject freefall.

It was very difficult to determine where the TV's centre of mass was at a specified point – when the parachute opens. Centre of mass changes from the centre of the body to the mid/top point in the parachute and XSI does not animate centres. Nulls and additional geometry were hidden to resolve the problem.

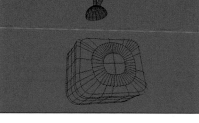
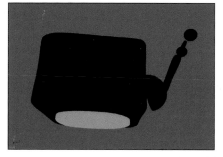

'We were faced with Softimage XSI from day one and it was a struggle to get to grips with the interface and 3D concepts in time for the first hand-in after Christmas. I stuck with it and began to enjoy the virtual realities that I could create. I began to trust my artistic talents again and with the help of my tutors I had suddenly become very focused with all aspects of animation. During my time studying I met a couple of people on the course who used the same sense of humour in their work, who became close friends and we now have an animation studio based in Middlesbrough.'

The choice of CGI animation

This process is not unfamiliar: a sense of what would be good to do; a general idea of personal strengths; pursuing a particular path and not succeeding as well as hoped; trying again and finding things easier to grasp with more experience and practice; trusting core skills to a greater degree; achieving better outcomes and finding the real possibility of progress. This happens to many students, so it remains crucial to know why animation – and particularly computer animation – is attractive, and the ways in which to invest to confirm and corroborate that interest.

Powell (cont.): 'Animation appeals to my artistic, problem-solving and logical mind. A static image can be brought to life and you have full control over the object's motion. It's not just animation though – the process involves modelling, texturing, compositing and editing, and these are all sub processes that equally appeal to me. I enjoy the fact that I can create different worlds and characters – in a way, I can play God! The most rewarding experience is when the job is done and you're watching the audience react to what you have created.'

Influences

'Mark Walsh, a senior animator on Finding Nemo, came to talk at the "Animex" →

Core skill
Approaching 3D CGI

– Taking a course is invaluable, but practising with software in spare time is vital.

– Seek advice from those with more technical experience – it can be a short cut and avoid a great deal of manual reading!

– Engage with the core principles of animation, but embrace the related processes of film-making and graphic design that enable the work to be achieved.

– Remember that this is still an 'artistic' process even when it is at its most technical.

← **2005 Animex sting – Seed Animation**
In the 2005 version of the Animex ident, effects have been added that use particles for rain and splashes that the rain makes on surfaces. Smoke effects were also added for when the TV's jet pack is hit by lightning. Animating lightning required research and like many aspects of the project, were 'firsts' that initially posed problems, but which were resolved and executed by engaging with other animators and seeking out further information.

→ **Stills from JoJo in the Stars – Marc Craste**
Marc Craste's groundbreaking BAFTA Award-winning film JoJo in the Stars readily demonstrated that computer-generated imagery of high quality could be produced outside the major studios and that independent films could be made that explored darker, more complex emotional themes. The design and atmosphere of the piece are influenced by German Expressionism and David Lynch's film Eraserhead, but the film's sense of romantic tragedy also recalls Tod Browning's Freaks and the more sombre of the Universal horror films of the 1930s.

→ International Animation Festival at the University. His talk was inspirational as he discussed the acting involved in bringing his characters to life. He also showed some films that were inspirational to him, which included The Muppets. He explained the genius behind creating believable emotion when there are so many physical restraints on the characters.'

Powell (cont.): 'In terms of decent websites, Keith Largo, another practicing character animator, has a portfolio website that includes quality tutorials. There is an article on his website that takes you through how to animate using "pose to pose". It was written from a Maya standpoint, but the theory translates to any sort of animation program.

'One of the most influential books I have read is Ed Hooks' Acting for Animators in which he explains the art of acting theory for animation including the 11 principles of animation, which is vital reading for any would-be animator.'

The Animex ident
The project included here is Powell's work in creating an ident for the 'Animex' Festival.

Powell: 'The animation involved the "Animex" TV and its short journey to its rightful place on top of the logo. I used Softimage XSI, which I had previously used on my course and during the week I began to use Adobe After Effects to do the post-production, a program that I rely very heavily on now. Aesthetically, my idea was

to go minimal, because I figured that an ident has limited time to get the message across and I wanted my message to be clear. I also chose very bold colours with a limited palette – the black and grey that are the colours of the logo and a bright orange for the background. The reason why I chose this was so that my animation would stand out from the other idents.

'I relied solely on the animation of the character to imply its situation – I didn't see the need to add extra backgrounds, which would remove the audience's focus from the subject. I also used split screen to help the story along and I had always wanted to give it a go.'

The perils of not storyboarding
Inevitably, the working process was not problem free:

Powell: 'The challenge was mainly the screenplay. I had not drawn storyboards for the piece because I didn't need to relay any information to anyone else. I didn't want to stick to a storyboard because I was developing the story as I went and some shots worked and others didn't. I thought the best way was to explore this, rather than plan it out before I had tried. One of the disadvantages of this was that I ended up with a sting that was twice as long as the brief allowed!'

Powell joined his university colleagues to form Seed Animation once they had graduated. They

were invited to make the 2005 'Animex' sting, developing the first concept.

Making the 2005 Animex sting
Powell: 'For the two-minute animation we have gone for a much stronger comic-book feel, with onomatopoeia, split-screen action, manga-style flying shots and strong references to superhero comic art. The premise is the same, the TV's quest to his place on the logo, but the TV is now a superhero, with flight capability and his new journey takes him through Middlesbrough. The colour scheme has been developed to include shades of orange, ranging from yellow ochre to dark red. The playful movement remains and the backgrounds are minimalist, his journey is slightly longer and more deeply explored.'

A Superior
Example of CGI

As in any kind of artistic endeavour, it is usually the more maverick, independent spirits who progress the form beyond its mainstream incarnation. Those artists in animation who explore the codes, conventions, history and preoccupations of the form have a rich vocabulary from which to draw and a language that permits them to originate new work. Like Marc Craste with JoJo in the Stars, Chris Landreth wanted to make a film that while being a personal statement, was nevertheless profoundly related to the animation community and sought to progress the form.

Ryan, directed by Chris Landreth, is one of computer animation's most celebrated short films in that it displays extraordinary technique

in telling a story that is close to the heart of the animation community. Part documentary, part traditional animation, part nightmare, the film is about Ryan Larkin, a Canadian animator, who during the 1960s made Cityscape (1963), Syrinx (1964) and Walking (1969), three celebrated films at the National Film Board of Canada, but who now lives on welfare and begs for change on Montreal streets.

Landreth adopts an approach called 'psychological realism', which uses the fluid language of animation to embrace the concept defined by writer, Anaïs Nin, when she suggested: 'We don't see things as they are. We see things as we are'. Though using Larkin's voice and those of colleagues and friends, the characters on screen are entirely 'subjective'; sometimes fragmented, distorted, or in some way unusual.

Art and technology
Landreth studied Theoretical, Applied and Fluid

Mechanics at Masters and Research level at the University of Illinois before joining Alias | Wavefront in 1994 testing animation software. He made two well received films, The End (1995) and Bingo (1998), the latter being an adaptation of a live theatre performance called Disregard This Play by the Chicago-based theatre company The Neo-Futurists.

Ryan sometimes appears as if it is modified 'live action', but everything was conceived and executed in the computer and all character movement was created by hand and did not use motion capture. The film used Alias's Maya animation software (V 4.0) for modelling, rigging, animation, lighting and rendering of the 3D environment, and Discreet Combustion V2.1 for all compositing and 2D effects. Adobe Photoshop V7.0 was employed for painting and texturing, and Adobe Premiere for creative development and editing.

Stills from Ryan – Chris Landreth

→ Influenced by the confluence of realistic facial and bodily representation, and the sense of the grotesque in works by artists as various as Francis Bacon, Ivan Albright and Andrzej Pagowski, Chris Landreth's Ryan simultaneously depicts interior and exterior states, redefining the parameters of 'documentary' and the relationship between animation and 'live action'.

Digital Effects and 3D Animation

3D digital effects are now the staple ingredient of Hollywood movies, present in every blockbuster and genre film, but an undervalued aspect of contemporary 3D computer-generated animation is the work undertaken for television programmes and graphic inserts. In many ways, this has become a necessary area of research, development and progress in television because the viewing audience has been schooled in the 'state-of-the-art' look of contemporary film. Simply, audiences now expect better effects, even on TV, where budgets, of course, are significantly lower. Invention, therefore, has to be greater.

Andy McNamara and his colleagues in the BBC Digital Effects and 3D Animation unit execute a variety of material from the Cbeebies and BBC 2 idents to more involved work like that undertaken for CBBC Scotland's Shoebox Zoo, a 13-part series written by Brian Ward.

Aesthetic consistency
Paul Kavanagh worked on the character design and graphics for Shoebox Zoo, liaising with Claire Mundell, head of BBC Scotland, production designer, Tom Sayer, and costume designer, Ali Mitchell, to achieve an aesthetic consistency in the work, drawing upon design sources in Celtic mythology. The production was achieved in collaboration with Calibre Digital Pictures in Toronto, Canada, who were responsible for the principal animation.

The story
The story begins with Marnie McBride's eleventh birthday, a low-key affair coming so soon after her mother's death and her displacement from her home in Colorado to Scotland. A passing visit to a junk shop results, however, in Marnie finding a shoebox containing four animal figures – Edwin the Eagle (Rik Mayall), Bruno the Bear (Alan Cumming), Wolfgang the Wolf (Simon Callow) and Ailsa the Adder (Siobhan Redmond) – which eventually come to life and lead her into an unexpected adventure where she must encounter Toledo the shapeshifter, and discover the secrets of the Book of Forbidden Knowledge, written by one Michael Scot. Such stories often rest on the capacity for transformation and metamorphosis, as well as the creation of fantastical forms and contexts, and this is intrinsically related to the vocabulary of animation to facilitate such work.

Plausible reality
This 3D computer-generated imagery is a crucial factor in facilitating the 'fantasy' of the story, but it must also aspire to a plausible reality if the fantasy is to sustain itself as a believable narrative. The animation here, not merely authenticates the narrative, but enables the design sources to reinforce the mythological aspects of the adventure in an accessible and engaging way.

↑ **Progression from original sketch to**
↗ **composited, animated character, from**
→ **Shoebox Zoo – Andy McNamara**
This (above, left) is one of the original sketches for Wolfgang the Wolf, based on the richly decorative animal carvings of the Celtic period. While being 'authentic' in echoing the entwined forms of the relief carving characteristic to these artefacts, this also posed potential problems for the animation of the figures, and the visual appeal of the animals to an audience predominantly made up of children.

The animals' figures had to work both as artefacts in their own right and as manipulatable figures in computer imagery. Consequently, the figures had to work as though they were made out of metal, stone and wood, yet also move in a way that enabled convincing animated action while retaining the

characteristics and properties of these materials. The first CG maquette (facing page, top right) seeks to address this issue and provide the 'frozen' sleeping position of the character before it comes to life. Shoebox Zoo required that each animal figure become an actual prop, so the initial 'rig' of the frozen Wolfgang was sent to Arrk, a stereo lithographic company specialising in creating resin maquettes (above, top left).

Kavanagh worked with Calibre's Jean Jacques Chaboissier on the texturing of the maquettes. The maquette of Wolfgang becomes both a functional prop for the live action sequences and a model for computer-generated extrapolation (above, bottom left). As well as resembling an ancient artefact, the character also had to appeal as a toy. This necessitated research in the now defunct Pollocks' toy

museum in London. Wolfgang is shown as a fully textured computer-generated form (above, top right), now able to move from the 'frozen' initial rig, to a range of 'performance' positions.

All of the CG work in Shoebox Zoo was conducted in Maya, but compositing – the mapping of Wolfgang into the desired physical environment – was achieved using Discreet's Combustion package (above, bottom right). The CG character interacts with the live-action characters and environment; the lighting a key aspect in creating the shadow that enhances the three-dimensional presence of an imaginary, mythic, illusionary figure as a 'real' character in an actual environment.

The three other characters – Bruno the Bear, Ailsa the Adder and Edwin the Eagle – and the series logo for Shoebox Zoo (right).

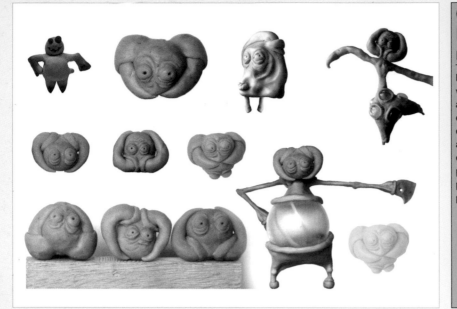

↑ **First draft maquettes and the final**
↗ **monster designs for Oby –**
→ **Anja Perl and Max Stolzenberg**
Students Perl and Stolzenberg worked on various designs for their monster before settling on the final one (left and right). This became the working template for the model sheet. Once the maquette design was decided upon, it was transferred to computer for digital modelling (right).

Rotoscope and Motion Capture

The role of rotoscoping in animated film demonstrates the most self-evident place where live action and animation meet. Mark Langer defines the rotoscope as: A device that allowed the rear projection of a live-action film frame-by-frame on to a translucent surface set into a drawing board. An animator could simply trace each live-action image on to a piece of paper, advance the film by another frame and repeat the process. By these means, the live-action images became a guide to detailed and life-like animation.[5]

The Fleischer Brothers, for example, rotoscoped the distinctive loping 'dance-walk' of singer, Cab Calloway, for their cartoon shorts, Minnie the Moocher (1932), in which he becomes a ghost walrus; and Snow White (1933), where he doubles for Koko the clown, his body at one point changing into a liquor bottle. Disney famously used the process for the human figures in Snow White and the Seven Dwarfs (1937). Ralph Bakshi also employed the technique in his epics, Wizards (1977) and The Lord of the Rings (1978), but for the most part the technique has often been viewed as 'inauthentic' in some way.

Disney veteran, Ollie Johnston, one of the true 'greats' in the development of traditional animation suggests: 'At Disney we used film to study the movement and when we used the rotoscope, we made Photostats of each frame of action so we could trace the movements for an animated sequence. But we noticed something. We saw that film gave us every single movement and tracing it meant that the human body became kind of stiff, and didn't move like a person at all. Film gave us too much information, so we had to emphasise what was important to the animator – the squash 'n' stretch movement of a figure, the anticipation, the overlapping action – and act through the movement, so that you choose what you want to exaggerate to get the right action for the scene and no more.'[6]

From a different perspective, Johnston stresses the limits of live action. The animator must be selective in the choice of what the animated figure needs to do in relation to the requirements of the scene. The movement is not about capturing the physical wholeness of a body, but the specific imperatives that create an action. This is further related to the weight of the figure, the kind of movement through space and time, the sense of rhythm, adaptation to the environment, effort needed and gestural specificity. This is clearly related to aspects of the 'performance' of the animated character as it is determined by the animator as 'actor'. This sense of 'performance' has become intrinsically related to the use of 'motion capture' in more recent work.

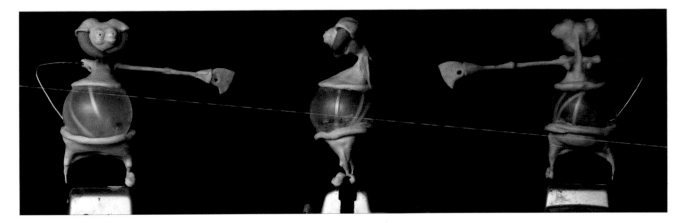

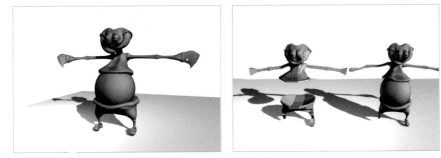

Matt Ferro, visual effects supervisor for The Matrix (1999), while championing the possibilities of 'motion capture' – literally, attaching sensors to a real moving body as reference points for data transferred into the computer to facilitate digitally constructed figures – nevertheless harbours anxiety about the ways in which this supposedly creates 'realism' in the movement of animated characters. He says: 'this stylised naturalism, which is rendered so photo-realistically, and which takes the depiction of violence seriously [in work like Roughnecks: Starship Troopers Chronicles (2000)] and not cartoonally, speaks more directly to games fans', adding 'we need to look at the sub-textual meaning of movement under these circumstances, especially as kids under ten can see this stuff at 8.00am in the morning all over the world'.[7]

Ferro's key point here about the 'sub-textual meaning of movement' in many ways reinforces the point made by Johnston and remains a crucial observation for animators, whatever technology or approach they are using. What remains vital is the authenticity that traditional animation techniques and motion capture can bring to the distinctive 'world' imagined by the animator within the context of the narrative or set of story events.

Motion capture has progressed considerably in recent years, and allied to sophisticated CGI, and the more self-conscious imperatives of actors working through motion capture equipment, this has created work of a progressive nature, most notably in the case of Andy Serkis' truly immersed performance as Gollum in Peter Jackson's The Lord of the Rings: The Two Towers (2002).

Serkis drew on sources as various as Caliban in Shakespeare's The Tempest, Victor Hugo's Hunchback of Notre Dame, Robert Louis Stevenson's Dr Jekyll and Mr Hyde, and works by Otto Dix, Francis Bacon and Brom, in the creation of a character that he had to play as a reference guide for other actors, in real-time motion capture for CGI data, as an 'automated dialogue replacement', creating audio tracks for the character, and as a moving template for the animation process itself.[8]

A combination of processes was used in the construction of Gollum's action: traditional rotoscoping, where fight sequences conducted by Serkis were recorded and his movement drawn over frame by frame to ensure Gollum fought with the high degree of energy and aggression required; key frame animation; on impossible action for humans; and most particularly, the face, and motion capture, where much of Serkis' performance dictated Gollum's onscreen activity.

At the heart of this, once more, was the persuasiveness of Gollum as a character in his own right, where the animation facilitates the character and in this instance, necessarily has to efface the performance of the actor, but must not draw attention to itself as animation, or as an effect. A key point to emerge from all of this is that animation almost intrinsically hides its process, and the 'art' that characterises that process, but it is the final outcome that justifies this necessity.

REFERENCES
5) Langer, M. 'The Fleischer Rotoscope Patent', Animation Journal, Vol 1
6) Interview with the author, April 1999
7) Interview with the author, November 2000
8) All the material here concerning Gollum drawn from Serkis, A. The Lord of the Rings: Gollum, Boston & New York, Houghton Mifflin Company, 2003

Combining Live Action and Animation Using Motion Capture for CGI

Working with motion capture can be helpful for facilitating a particular kind of motion in computer-generated figures, sometimes in a spirit more closely echoing the dynamics of live-action characters that may be in the same environment. Compositing – literally bringing together layers of pictorial elements to create an image – can seamlessly enable live-action characters and environments to co-exist with animated characters and objects in a visual space, informed by the same movement characteristics.

Anja Perl and Max Stolzenberg, students of the Filmakademie, Ludwigsberg, Baden's Institute for Animation, Visual Effects and Digital Post-production, sought in their film Oby to combine live action and animation by creating a 3D CGI monster, Oby and have him have a human encounter with a lady making pancakes.

Oby, while being created with Maya 5.0, also benefited from 'motion capture' using Motionbuilder, which required a human actor to perform so as to generate some of Oby's movements.

Perl: 'The challenge was the motion capture for CGI because we hadn't done that before. A professional dancer and I mimed the dance of the monster, which was quite an experience and later on I was cleaning up the MoCap-data and doing additional animation with a program I had to learn within two weeks, while Max was modelling, lighting, texturing, rendering and compositing the scenes. We had a few fantastic people around us helping, and fortunately we had no major problems in the working process. Maybe we were very lucky, but we had tried to plan a project that is manageable for the two of us and a small crew in a working period of three months. Crucially, Max and I are pretty good in work sharing'.

↙ **Production reference and**
↓ **screengrabs from Oby –**
Anja Perl and Max Stolzenberg
Real world objects were used to give the monster's skin a realistic surface. Images of these objects were scanned and texture-mapped on to the three-dimensionally rendered character using a computer. Layers of texture were carefully built up for a convincing appearance.

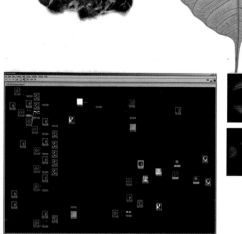

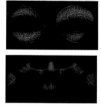

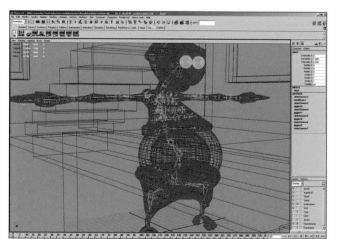

↙ **Production photos and screengrabs**
↓ **from the making of Oby –**
Anja Perl and Max Stolzenberg
The motion capture process involves attaching sensors to human performers as they play out the physical sequences that make up the animation (left), in this case, Oby's dance is enacted.

Using Maya 5.0, the data captured from the performance of Oby's dance is then transferred from the human form on to the fictional monster's form.

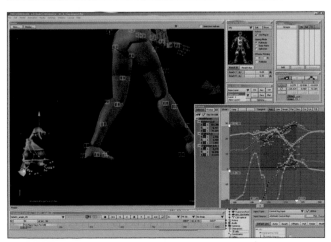

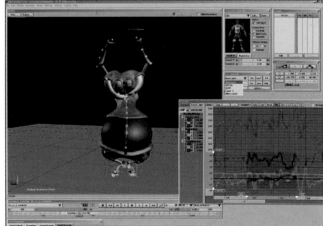

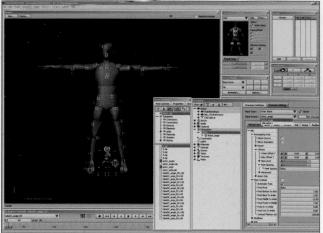
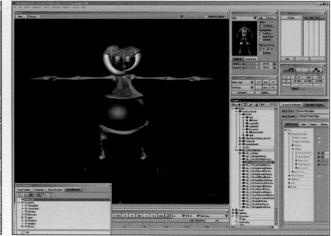

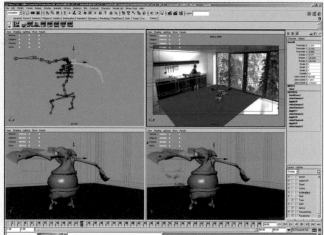

↑ **Screengrabs from the making of Oby –**
← **Anja Perl and Max Stolzenberg**
↓ Once the character has been animated using
the motion capture data in Maya 5.0, the
digitised model is then exported into Motion
Builder software, in order to add
characterisation (left).

→ The final stage in this digital animation was
compositing the character into the intended

context of a kitchen. Lighting was added to the
figure to correspond with the light sources in
the kitchen – the bank of windows – and
helped create the sense of the character really
existing within the space left and below.

Perl and Stolzenberg take the fantasy
creature into the everyday, but simultaneously
into an avant-garde model of narrative and
visual presentation.

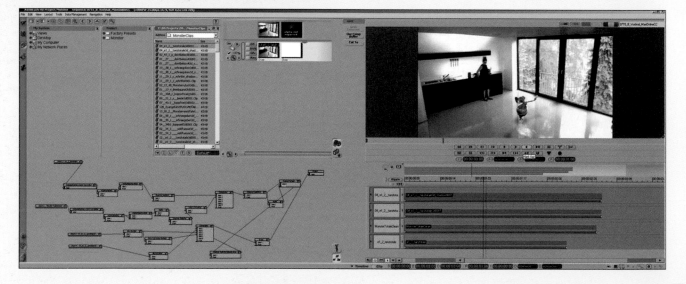

Core skill
Recording project process

There are a variety of reasons for making sure that the process of a project is recorded:

– To preserve its hidden and often invisible 'art'.
– To capture the development of the work in relation to all its changes – preferred, enforced, accidental etc.
– To recognise each aspect of the work as the embodiment of particular specialist and transferable skills and knowledge.
– To observe what is ultimately 'selected' from the developmental process in relation to the final and intended outcomes.
– To collate materials that represent the work in its absence and represent the skills and knowledge that created them.
– To preserve the 'memory' of the work for future consideration, consultation and enjoyment.

The Merits of Flash

In recent years, the arrival and use of Flash animation has provoked considerable debate about its impact, effect and quality. Traditional animators have sometimes dismissed it for legitimising animation of an inferior quality, while new practitioners champion its accessibility and user-friendliness in developing skills in graphic design and animation at comparatively low cost, and with wide availability and ease of distribution on the web.

Simon Downs of Loughborough University and Gareth Howell of Arts and Technologies Partnerships, both users of, and tutors for Flash animation, debate its merits and their experience in using it.

Downs: 'The problem of animation has always been one of scale. The magnitude of the leap from student animator to broadcast professional was large and frequently overwhelming. When I was at art school, animation was an exciting, but exacting activity – not just technically of the skills of the artists working on it, but also demanding of resources. Animation had something of the 'jealous god' about it. It demanded ideas, it demanded equipment, it demanded somewhere to house the equipment, it demanded a group of people sharing a common vision and desiring a common end. Animation was greedy, animation was big.

'Even small animation was big, witness Richard Williams' struggle to raise money, and keep a team together over 30 years in order to complete his The Thief and the Cobbler (1996) film. By its very nature, animation could not be considered a solitary activity. For me, that was a problem.

'I had a sample of this state of affairs in the early '90s, and found it not to my taste. I had been educated as an illustrator (not known for being "The Arts" big team players), and wanted communication that was personal, direct and above all in my control. Technology was about to rescue my interest in animation.

'Technology in the '90s had begun to rewrite these basic assumptions about the nature and scope of animation. There has been much written about the large-scale 3D-driven side of animation. It is big and splashy, and carries the glamour of Hollywood about it, but in many ways continues the studio paradigm – lots of people, working on lots of equipment, at lots of desks. The nomenclature has changed, but the mindset remains – many in service to the ideas of one.

'More important for the future of animation, are the small scale, readily available tools like Flash. These are the tools that will enable the casual visitor to the land of animation to become the full-time resident. Tools that are easy to use, have miniscule demands in terms of equipment, are cheap and above all come with their own means of broadcast built in.

'Flash really is something of a star. How blessed are we to find a tool that not only gives us all the tools we need to create our own mini-masterpieces, but works seamlessly with other graphics tools, on a multitude of computer platforms – nine, the last time I checked – on equipment that many people already own and are familiar with. Never have communications tools of such power been gifted to so many. Flash can create across the entire range of media we use today, from cinema (through its links to other motion graphics tools), to the Web, DVD, TV, and even to a global audience on the move, through Microsoft's Pocket PC software. It gives us control over not just the visual aspects of the animation process, but the sound and the presentation. We have the power to entertain, inform, agitate and reassure a global audience, resting in that box on our desk. We have become auteurs in our own homes and communicators on the world stage.'

Howell: 'I first began using Flash when I was working as a web designer. After years of low-quality GIFS and static html, it seemed an ideal way of getting things moving on screen and also was able to calm down some of my frustrations as an ex-comics artist.

'From Flash 2 onwards, the web became increasingly populated with "web cartoons", and as Flash grew, these became more interactive. The low cost of Flash, however, turned everyone into a Flash animator in much the same way as everyone you met was a DJ, or everyone was

Applications and Outcomes The Fundamentals of Animation

← **Stills from Shoa – Giuliano Parodi**
↙ Parodi's sensitive portrayal of a little boy in the
midst of wartime Nazi atrocities is a
vindication of Flash animation as a technique
that can create work of emotional impact and
dramatic seriousness.

"working on a script" – there wasn't always a guarantee of quality with the work. Nasty splash pages and SWISH text effects were the multimedia equivalent of the Auto Drum Fill on your Casio Keyboard, and Flash enraged as much as it entertained web audiences.

'What Flash did provide was a space for animators to easily publish their work on the web, and create an underground of new ideas and new ways of working that were not vetted or streamlined by producers or the constraints of other distribution methods. New and established animators took advantage of this freedom to develop new work and to get direct feedback from the audience. John Kricfalusi, creator of Ren and Stimpy, and Tim Burton, both used Flash and the web to showcase new work, and attracted new audiences.

'The viral nature of the web also supported a new underground of animators who threw the animation rule book out of the window, creating cartoons that technically were raw (polite), badly made (more like it), but fantastically entertaining, establishing them as cult icons. My first experience of South Park was a Flash animation on the web, hunted out because word was getting round and the "FW: Check this out" emails were coming thick and fast. Of course, it doesn't take the mainstream long to realise when they are on to a good thing, and Joel Veitch's rocking cats and Weebl + Bob are permanent fixtures on everything from MTV to Anchor margarine ads.

'I began using Flash more and more as my main drawing tool, and moving back towards character-based design, which I had begun with my small press comics. I became more interested in Flash as an animation tool and although I was developing interactive work for the web, I was interested in developing single-screen narrative work for video or film. The web forums I visited were not really looking at the use of Flash as another tool for animation production, but increasingly it was becoming visible in animation for TV, pop videos and idents.

'What I liked most about Flash was its drawing tools, I still do. I find them easy to use and I like what they produce. As a fan of simplistic drawing and cartoon work, the block colours and fixed width line were exactly to my taste.

'I decided that rather than use the animation shortcuts in Flash, such as tweening, I wanted to take a fairly traditional approach, drawing each frame, scanning and drawing over in Flash. I wanted to use a limited palette and to simplify the characters as much as possible, so that they looked a little like Playmobils. Flash allowed me to work fairly rapidly, and to experiment as I went; moving characters around, re-scaling objects, even changing the screen ratio back and forth until I was happy. The second stage was to use Toon Boom Studio to create camera moves and depth. I was concerned with creating a cinematic effect, that gave a sense of space and scale, which is

difficult to achieve in Flash, as it has a fixed stage. Much of the first half of the film How it Was We Got to be Angels (see page 142) follows a car on a snowy night through a landscape, and the camera moves gave a sense of the scale of the car in the world and the size of the landscape. The final clips were exported as image sequences, then edited in Premiere. Sound was dubbed and mixed later.

'Whilst Flash may not be the choice for most traditional animators, it has opened the door for a new generation of animators who are up against micro budgets and with little access to resources other than the 10Mbs of free space they got with their dial-up account. The natural home of Flash is the web, but increasingly it finds its way into mainstream animation for video and TV. Happy Tree Friends is now available to rent or buy at your local Blockbusters, and Eminem's videos, White America and Mosh, both make heavy use of Flash.'

Enhancing Flash Techniques

While Flash offered the amateur or the aspirant creative access to animation, it also inevitably prompted concerns about quality among the established animation community. Just as inevitably, though, many practiced animators wanted to bring their skills to a new tool and approach.

Adam Phillips has already received great acclaim for his work on the web, including his films, Bitey of Brackenwood, Bingbong of Brackenwood and Prowlies of the River. Phillips, both an in-betweener and character animator, before becoming head of the effects animation team working at the Disney Studio in Australia, has worked on many of the recent Disney sequels, The Lion King 2, Lady and the Tramp 2 and Peter Pan 2. His true forte, though is as a director and storyteller, using his experience at Disney to enhance his approach to using Flash on the web.

Phillips: 'Working at Disney has definitely influenced my Flash technique. To get a particular movement or acting scene working, I'm always determined to use as many drawings as it takes and refuse to be hamstrung by bandwidth constraints. In these days of spreading broadband, I think it's becoming less of an issue to have a 2 or 3Mb movie →

Core skill
Art direction and effects

All narratives are considerably enhanced by the quality of the art direction – the specific aesthetic style of the piece – and the use of effects – essentially all non-character animation. In relation to art direction, knowledge of landscape, architecture and environmental design may be helpful, as well as a strong sense of the compositional aspects of illustration. In relation to effects, it is still the case that a traditional grounding in animating objects of various weights, sizes and proportion will enable a better engagement with elemental and spectacular execution and effect.

↑ **Stills from How it Was We Got to be Angels – Gareth Howell**
A 'comic style' approach to animated narrative, informed by a range of visual signs and perspectives.

→ Stills from Bitey of Brackenwood, Bingbong of Brackenwood and Prowlies at the River – Adam Phillips

Bingbong of Brackenwood underlines Phillips' ability to create comic ambivalence in his imaginary world. At the outset of the story is a warning that anyone playing with 'faery folk' will be 'trapped forever'. This sense of threat and foreboding is soon undermined, however, when Bingbong flattens the fairy sprites he dances with. The fairy dance in the story exhibits Phillips' use of design as a type of narrative.

↘ The fairy figures have a supernatural quality through their translucency, partly operating as 'figurative' characters, but also as 'abstractions', echoing the traditions of silhouette and cut-out pioneered by Lotte Reiniger and Michel Ocelot.

↘ Here Phillips introduces colour change as an indicator of the sprites' anger as Bingbong joins their dance. It is a simple device, but one that brings an immediacy to the narrative as the dance may become a scene of possible conflict.

↘ Bingbong joins the dance and the scale of his presence is immediately amusing. His lack of fear or threat, and the sheer joy embodied in his spritely spring-heeled movement overcomes all apparent mythic foreboding and enhances the wit of the piece.

↓ Phillips' ninja satyr figure, Bitey, is a more heroic and dynamic figure than the zany Bingbong, but like his fellow character in Brackenwood, he is used as a vehicle to play against mythic and folkloric 'types' in order to create a distinctive 'world', and one infused with wit and humour. It is Phillips' investment in the quality of Bitey and Bingbong's movement, though, which fully defines their characters.

"Bitey"
©1999-2004
Adam Phillips

→ anyway, as it would have been a few years ago when I first started.'

Phillips notes that most animators are predominantly interested in character animation, but offers the view that working in Special Effects can be very enabling in relation to becoming a fully rounded animation practitioner.

Phillips (cont.): 'It really is what appeals to me most. Explosions, water splashes, dust clouds, magic effects, etc. I find special effects exciting and the good thing about it is no other form of animation develops your sense of timing as well as 2D special-effects animation. Effects animation is all about natural forces, physics, gravity, weight and mass. Some study (and preferably experience) in this area makes the timing of character animation come much more naturally, which is why the first things a beginner will animate are not characters, but bouncing balls, floating balloons and flour-sacks. Flash is not only an affordable animation home-studio in itself, but the internet is an instant global audience. What other storytelling medium is so instant? I can upload a new movie to my website and within minutes I'm getting feedback from strangers on the other side of the planet.

'Flash movies can be small enough in file size to be emailed, and much of the challenge in Flash animation lies in keeping the file size down. In cases where file size or playback on someone's computer isn't an issue – for example, animation for television or DVD – you can really go nuts and put in all the detail and special touches that you would otherwise avoid.'

↗ **Bingbong in development – Adam Phillips**
→ Bingbong's urination provides a satisfying punchline to Phillips' Prowlies of the River, and successfully extends the tradition of subversive playfulness of much cartoonal animation.

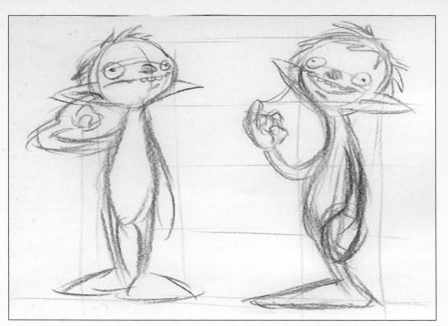

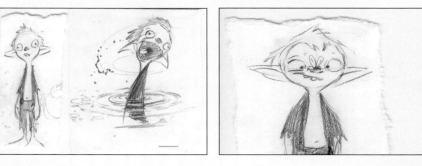

→ Phillips' particular talents in art direction and lighting effects are clearly seen in this landscape, which immediately enhances the distinctiveness of the image and the context in which the characters are placed.

↘ This scene is played out at night and once more highlights Phillips' skill in thinking about the relationship between light and moving water, and the kind of atmosphere he wishes to generate for the mythic aspects of his stories.

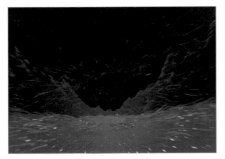

↗ Phillips' wind effects dramatise nature, and the
→ folkloric power of his imaginary Brackenwood world. Bingbong, a naive off-the-wall elfin child is here dwarfed by the nature he inhabits.

Alternative Methods

The term 'alternative methods' merely begs the question – 'alternative to what?'. Within the context of this discussion, the methods that follow essentially operate as an alternative to the trends in industrial production contexts, largely resisting the dominant aesthetics of contemporary CGI in feature work, traditional puppet and model animation, and orthodox cel or drawn material. There is also a resistance to the 'Disney' style, both visually and thematically, and inevitably a more personal or 'auteurist' approach to the work, which often customises a technique to achieve highly specific individualised outcomes.

Previously, this kind of work may have been termed 'experimental animation', and to a certain extent this does embrace the more auteurist sensibility largely present in creating such work, and the strong links it often has with an 'avant-garde' approach or a more specific 'hand-made' connection with fine art. 'Experimental animation' as a term has become more associated with non-objective, non-linear works – which some claim are the purest form of animation – but in other ways it misrepresents a whole range of work that is not necessarily highly progressive in its 'experimentation', but merely of a different order to 'classical' or traditional 2D cartoons or 3D animation. It is essentially 'developmental' animation in the sense that it is often a response to and a resistance of orthodox techniques, in a spirit of creating a personal statement or vision not possible in a big studio context, or within the field of popular entertainment.

The abstract films of Walter Ruttman, Viking Eggeling and Hans Richter in the early 1920s are usually understood as a benchmark for some of the formative ways in which animation was used in the service of an approach to modernist film-making. Richter's Rhythmus 21 (1921), working with Eggeling, sought to use the movement of shape and form as an expression of thought and emotion in its own right. Crucial to these kind of approaches was the combination of the movement of abstract form and sound, in a spirit of creating a kind of 'visual music', a concept progressed by Oskar Fischinger during the 1930s in experimental works like Composition in Blue (1935). It was Lotte Reiniger, though, in her cut-out, silhouette animation – most particularly, her full-length work, The Adventures of Prince Achmed (1926) – who successfully combined abstract work with a visual narrative more accessible to wider audiences. She collaborated with Berthold Bartosch, who later made The Idea (1932), a 30-minute poetic narrative of high technical innovation and achievement.

As the industrial model of animation production emerged at the Disney Studio and elsewhere between 1928 and 1941, experimental work continued. Mary Ellen Bute and Leon Thurmin worked with the idea of drawing with electronically determined codes in The Perimeters of Light and Sound and Their Possible Synchronisation (1932), while Alexander Alexeieff and Claire Parker created the 'pin screen', where raised pins were lit to create particular images in Night on Bald Mountain (1934).

Most particular and influential, though, was the emergence of Len Lye and Norman McLaren, whose work for the GPO Film Unit, under the auspices of John Grierson, significantly progressed experimental forms. In some senses, their films do not seem to sit easily with Grierson's work in documentary and socialist politics, but it is important to remember that Grierson valued these abstract works – made in the guise of commercial films about postal rates – as in the public interest because they were expressions of personal freedom and human feeling; the essence of democratic purpose. Equally, 'art' gave considerable prestige to the sponsor. Lye's Colour Box (1935) was painted directly on film, while Trade Tattoo used stencilling on documentary footage. Norman McLaren, who continued to work with John Grierson at the National Film Board of Canada, experimented with many techniques including direct 'under the camera' animation, pixilation, cut-out and collage animation, and evolving pastel chalk pictures, and made many influential films including Begone Dull Care (1949), Neighbours (1952) and Pas de Deux (1969). Lye and McLaren essentially recognised that animation was a cross-disciplinary and interdisciplinary medium, and had intrinsic relationships to dance, performance, painting, sculpture and engraving. This inspired many to embrace these links and explore different techniques and applications.

This period of high experimentation in the 1930s was arguably the purest expression of what animation could achieve beyond the American cartoonal tradition and the predominantly European 3D stop-motion puppet tradition, and offered animation a credibility as a 'fine art'. Cartoon animation still remained unrecognised as a fully-fledged art form or a high cultural

Applications and Outcomes

The Fundamentals of Animation

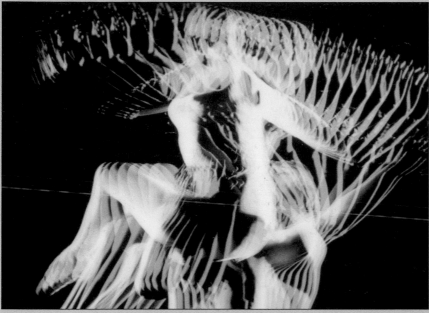

British Film Institute

British Film Institute

practice, so the Disney Studio responded with Fantasia (1941), aspiring to combine classical music with lyrical animation in the same spirit as the abstract artists. The mixed reception to Fantasia in many ways set in train the sense of 'separatism' between different kinds of animation; a trend that continues into the contemporary era. Arguably, all animation is 'experimental' by virtue of its aesthetic, technical and cultural 'difference' as it develops its own art and finds continuing currency in mainstream culture. A figure like the late Jules Engel, though ostensibly an 'experimental' film-maker, worked on Disney features, developed the characters of Gerald McBoing Boing and Mr Magoo at UPA, and worked on individual projects, rejecting the false boundaries within the field.

What is important about 'alternative' animation, though, is its innovation in the use of materials and techniques. Robert Breer used file-cards with different imprints of various kinds for his seminal LMNO (1978); Caroline Leaf deploys sand on glass in The Owl Who Married a Goose (1974) and ink on glass for The Street (1976); Jan Svankmajer uses all manner of materials in Dimensions of Dialogue (1982), which are crushed and pulped, becoming animated matter as well as artefacts; The Quay Brothers 're-animate' detritus and abandoned materials in Street of Crocodiles (1986); while Vera Neubauer creates knitted characters in revisionist fairy tales like Woolly Wolf (2001). In recent years, the rise of 'conceptual art' has enabled the use of all materials and contexts for the suggestion and facilitation of art-making practice. Arguably, animation has always been an art form that has worked in this spirit, defining concepts through the choice, treatment and application of materials in the service of conceptual agendas and abstract meanings. Those who embrace animation from a fine art background and who immediately see a clear relationship between animation and other art forms, work in a way that inevitably progresses the form, and continues the 'alternative' tradition.

Related area of study
The auteur in animation

Live-action cinema has a canon of directors defined by the critical community as 'auteurs' – the presiding authorial voice in a film, or across a number of films, with a recognisable signature style or preoccupying theme. Arguably, though, animation, especially in the context of 'alternative methods' is the most auteurist of media. Often, films are made by one person alone and are expressly dealing with a specific and complex theme; a new technique; or using an experimental approach to a dominant method. Much of the rest of the work in this book has this aspect, either by virtue of extending the parameters of fine art in animation or by using digital technologies and new exhibition opportunities to extend the boundaries of the form.

Here the juxtaposition of the lyricism and innocence associated with the translucency of the watercolour and the irreverent playfulness of the removal of Bonaparte's 'parts' for pickling, effectively reworks anticipated expectations of both the form and the narrative.

Fine Art Practices

The relationship between fine art and animation practice is in some ways an under-explored aspect of animation, while contradictorily, the very method by which it is often understood as an 'art' in its own right. This is partly because the traditional techniques of fine art practice are seen to be applied in a time-based context and may be evidenced not merely through the process work, but in the final film itself.

Elizabeth Hobbs studied Illustration at Edinburgh College of Art. On graduating with a Masters degree in 1991, she started printing limited editions of her own artist's books using stone lithography, screen print and woodcut. In 1998 she studied Electronic Imaging at Duncan of Jordanstone College of Art and Design in Dundee, Scotland. As part of her postgraduate studies, she made an animated film called The

Last Regret of The Grim Reaper in which the Grim Reaper dances everyone on earth to their deaths. She used grey tusche drawing fluid and print-making paper, and sought to capture and animate the image whilst it was still wet, leaving a trail of the animated image on the page. The technique was particularly appropriate to the story in which a trail of destruction was left in the protagonist's path.

From artist's books to animation
Hobbs: 'There is a clear connection between the production of artists' books and animated film, the joy of working in a time-based medium is the drama of screening the film to an audience. I also enjoy animated film, in particular I value the experimental films of Robert Breer, the invention of Caroline Leaf and the legacy of Norman McLaren.' Working out of this tradition, Hobbs sees an intrinsic link between the technique employed and the narrative themes and issues she wishes to explore.

Core skill
Artists' books

Artists' books are the logical extension of sketchbooks and mood-boards in the sense that they accommodate provisional or experimental approaches not merely to free expression and 'content', but to technique. The 'transitional' state of artworks in such books may be viewed as a valuable part of the process orientation of animation, and offer stimulus, continuity and outcome depending on the need of the artist.

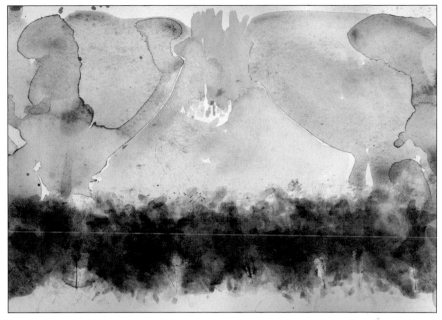

The Emperor Napoleon

'In 2000 I was awarded an Arts Council of England/Channel 4 Animate! commission to make my four-and-a-half-minute film, The Emperor, at Red Kite Productions in Scotland. I had made a series of prints in the late 1990s based on Napoleon Bonaparte's last moments on the island of St Helena and my intention was to use animated film to depict his way of life in exile. During my research, I unearthed the mystery of the sale of his pickled private parts at auction in 1969, which led to my weaving an irreverent narrative between the present day and The Emperor's death, through the eyes of a faithful soldier from Bonaparte's Grand Army.'

Technique

'I used wet watercolour on paper as part of my ongoing exploration into directly bringing a drawing or painting to life. I used a smooth-surfaced print-making paper of 220gsm in weight so that it would endure the multiple application of paint. Using one sheet for each shot, the background was painted in watercolour and left to dry. The animated elements were then painted, filmed whilst still wet, and then lifted off the page and repainted in their next position. The technique is fast to execute, though over the production period, each shot might be filmed many times to get it right.' It is important to note that this deliberate engagement with technique as an expressive methodology should be understood as a model of applied research, and usually comes out of an on-going engagement with a core aesthetic →

↑ **Stills from The Emperor – Elizabeth Hobbs**
Here the imagery works in a quasi-impressionist fashion, representing the ballroom in Paris and its participants, but equally, working as an abstract image privileging colour, fluid shape and form in its own right.

↑ Here Captain Lepissoir arrives on St Helena, the ship and the island purely suggested through the associativeness of object outlines and the perception of physical land forms.

→ principle or thematic concern. Hobbs has been continually preoccupied with the notion of 'fine art in motion', and the ways in which a drawing or painting may be best represented as such through the animated medium.

Technique development

Hobbs (cont.): 'The production of each of my films has brought another development to my practice of direct animation on paper. In the making of The Witches in 2002, I used the wet watercolour technique and augmented it with animated light projection from an overhead projector, in order to create a darker atmosphere. In this way there were two animation surfaces composited directly underneath the camera. In 2005, I made The True Story of Sawney Beane, a co-production between The National Film Board of Canada and Red Kite Productions. I animated with line and tone by drawing and erasing charcoal on paper on to which a watercolour background had been painted and dried.

'The Emperor represents a significant step in capturing the energy and immediacy of painting in its own right, while exhibiting its "motion" as the vehicle for an animated narrative.'

↗ **Stills from The Emperor – Elizabeth Hobbs**
This image – the Emperor in exile – suggests the mutability of the animated form as it catches the shifting perspectives of figures moving through the environment, drawing attention to the representational 'flux' of the body in animation. All the aspects of The Emperor are in motion – everything literally 'flows', vindicating the use and value of the technical and aesthetic styling of the piece.

↗ An impressionistic overview of the Battle of Waterloo, focusing on Napoleon's observation of the scene. Simultaneously, the image suggests individuals, crowds and explosions, but more importantly the chaos of conflict, the darkness of the scene, and the intimation of bloodshed and loss. Animation is capable of embracing 'epic' events and historical concepts.

→ The medium reflects the subject – an effective Turneresque evocation of sea and sky, as a fluid, linked and interchangeable form. The watercolour approach gives a strong sense of the ephemeral and transient condition of the seascape.

→ Stills from Figured Bass –
Suzie Hanna and Hayley Winter

An unusual multimedia approach. 2 x 16mm film
frames were glued to a 35mm spacer with nail
varnish and borders were added made of digital
print, and attached to stickyback plastic. The
animated frame was then rotoscoped on to
35mm film from video via Photoshop, with
additional ink and nail varnish finishes.

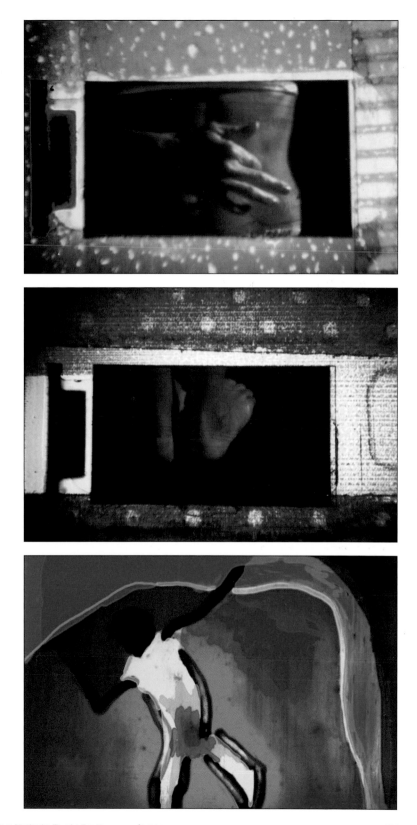

'Hail Mary gave me an opportunity to write and work from a pre-recorded soundtrack. I wanted the images to be in black and white and I deliberately left out an image of a woman. The story was told through the details and the structure was based on the Catholic rosary, which was fun to play with. The voice-over is rather obsessive and the woman uses numbers every time she describes something. It gave the recording a new kind of rhythm especially as the actress added more to the obsessive nature of the details.'

A Philosophical Approach

Animation has long been regarded as a 'metaphysical' practice; one which by virtue of its technique in whatever form, necessitates that the animator is self-conscious about the relationship between the 'idea' and the method of its expression; and for those who teach animation or wish to reach new audiences, how this might be best expressed to students or those with an invested interest. Animation, again especially when played out through 'alternative methods' is very often informed by an exploratory, philosophic sensibility, using the medium to embody a specific view or vision.

Animators like Maureen Selwood and Rachel Bevan Baker, whose views and work appear here, are constantly exploring the relationship between traditional concepts and techniques, and the 'modernity' of the form. This is partly in the desire to extend the artistic parameters of the form, but also to look at the art as a system of ideas. This 'philosophic' approach can then be extended to teaching and alternative forms of exhibition, as well as validating the purpose of the art.

Maureen Selwood is a practising film-maker and tutor at the world renowned California Institute of the Arts (CalArts). She has a particular interest in the relationship between creative work and teaching, and seeks to articulate the approach to her own work as a starting point for facilitating others.

Selwood: 'My work springs from drawing and the ideas that come from the images I create. I feel drawing is a means of expression that is fresh and vital, especially when the line feels active and engaged. In the beginning I studied the work of artists whose images would be interesting to appreciate for their simplicity yet rich subject matter. Jean Cocteau, Miro and Matisse filled my head with the idea that I could draw from an interior place and still find a structure for ideas.'

Influences

'Animation in the beginning was the most exciting form for me to think about these things. My techniques seem to change somewhat with each film, but drawing is always the anchor. I went to film school to study live-action film-making and that period of study has stayed with me in that I still like to marry live footage with animation, but sometimes, too, I like to work with pure drawing. By changing the technique I feel I am in a new place and can move outside myself and have a different take on the place of my story. Writing and drawing share a rather equal relationship. I remember reading about Miro and how he described his process of writing about the drawings and paintings he was going to make. I understood this and found it like animation.'

Experimentation

Again, it is important to recognise that this kind of film-making likes to draw upon the 'theorisation' of creative practice as it has been addressed by artists of all kinds. Reading about the ways in which artists think about their work and seek to execute it is fundamental to both establishing a technique and a set of skills, but it also prompts ideas for renewing or extending experimentation in a different form. In the following examples, Selwood stresses her continuing interest in technique, but also the place that her work finds in the active experience of living her life. 'Creativity is fundamentally inspired by remaining conscious of the relationship between methods of expression, knowledge of a range of fine art and popular forms, and the articulation of personal thoughts and feelings at any one period of living.' Selwood has clearly engaged with the animation medium, and in bringing her knowledge of art and personal experience to the work, has been able to make distinctive films. She recognises, however, that the student starting out may not have the confidence to fully embrace the possibilities.

Selwood: 'I think when students first start to draw for animation they aren't sure if they possess their own work yet. Animation can take a long time to feel identified with it. There are many famous names with distinct styles that at first confront the student of animation. It is important to study the form, but it is also important to allow that new voices are crucial in developing it. It can take a→

Applications and Outcomes   The Fundamentals of Animation

↗ **Stills from Flying Circus –**
→ **Maureen Selwood**

'Flying Circus: An Imagined Memoir was made at a time when I wanted to play with colour and how it affects mood. I adapted the opera Parade by Cocteau, Satie and Picasso and used it to instil a memory from childhood that shows the rich healing power of the imagination of a child. I worked with many different colouring methods and time-lapsed painted still photographs. I thought of the animation as showing the tensions of balance and imbalance for the sense of mood and place inside a circus tent. I loved animating this film. It was liberating, but quite difficult to animate. I worked with other animators for the first time on my own work and found collaboration exciting.'

→ unique approach to help students claim this territory. I think it is most helpful for students of animation to give images to the mental processes that move their imagination fairly early on. I believe drawing is the first step towards that. But of course, collage, photography and puppetry are starting points too. Drawing can become a kind of handwriting to realise ideas and narratives.'

Approaches to teaching

Selwood has some approaches to her teaching that seek to liberate them from the constraints that can sometimes be very inhibiting. Students can often not progress their work effectively if their benchmark is the 'full animation' of Disney or PIXAR, or the virtuousity of McLaren, Svankmajer, or Norstein.

Selwood (cont.): 'There are also metaphorical concepts that can help a student illustrate an important way to tell a story. The labyrinth, for example, can be an excellent way to open a film

about a struggle where a protagonist is fleeing an unsafe place. In this case I will bring to the class a myth associated with the metaphor. I love live-action films where the photography is especially meaningful to me. I find it inspiring and it often will segue into my own dream life of images and stories. Dreams are always a most interesting place not for a fully realised story, but for moments to let one's imagination picture a scene or idea. I teach drawing workshops for students on surrealism. We study the period of surrealism and appreciate how a painting may be limited, while the time-based aspect of film allows for an arrangement of images over time and thus a more restrained telling, but with a surprising outcome. It can be one that allows the viewer a process to enter into the complexity of the world of the artist. Students love this method. The mix of images they create and how quickly they are able to conceptualise often surprises them. I too find this a rather marvellous method. These same images sometimes gather in a different

arrangement allowing for a freedom with
storyboarding previously thought to be a difficult
process.'

An alternative approach

This use of established myths, metaphors,
dream imagery and surrealist painting liberates
the student from a 'literal' interpretation of the
world, a 'realist' approach to representation,
and the structural demands of classical narrative.
This 'alternative' approach enables students to
work creatively in a different way from the
methodologies outlined earlier in this book.
Crucially, it is enabling in getting students started
and points them quickly to the ways in which they
would prefer to work, and the type of work they
would like to engage in.

Selwood: 'CalArts is a place with many diverse
schools of thought throughout, whether it is
critical thinking, dance, theatre, music, art or
animation. There are always influences. In the
Experimental Animation Programme where I teach
drawn animation, I fuse experimental techniques
with classical skills. But for me the ideas come
first. I think if a student has the passion to say
something, that will drive the discipline to do it the
best way possible. I try to help students warm up
to the process of animation. I try to teach about
how to make things move in an inspired and

engaged way. The old UPA cartoons are just as
viable as any current films by important animation
artists working today'.

Working process

'Computer technology now has a presence not
previously thinkable in the beginning of teaching
animation. I try to get students as quickly as
possible to use the computer so the process of
conceptualising isn't foreign to how they will make
their projects. I am amazed at what students are
able to accomplish and how quickly the learning
curve is learned'.

Selwood, like many animation practitioners, seeks
to illuminate her own working process by making
films about it.

Selwood: 'At the moment I am working on two
films, Drawing Lessons and As You Desire Me.
In Drawing Lessons I am hoping to make a truly
humorous film about the obsessive nature of
trying to learn to draw by doing the same
exercise over and over again. The mind gets
distracted, but the process of drawing continues.
I will use an awkward drawing style, but one that
is easier to animate to tell the story of a woman
obsessed with learning to draw. By shifting the
style of the drawing, the process of animating
reveals the humour in this struggle'.

Alternative Methods: A Philosophical Approach

Stills from Beaches – Rachel Bevan Baker
These images from Beaches represent the variety of preparatory 'artworks' that might be produced for a project, which may find a range of exhibition contexts.

Very much in the spirit of Maureen Selwood, Rachel Bevan Baker seeks to explore through drawing and to find new contexts and audiences for animation. Her work Beaches has found a place in a traditional gallery and as live work on the web. This embrace of tradition and modernity is fundamental to many working in an 'alternative' and more auteurist fashion, but often starts from some basic principles.

Baker: 'I love drawing and always had a very lively free style to my line, so it felt very natural to make my drawings move. It seemed an easy step to take. I like the freedom animation gives – no rules of the real world. I increasingly like the aspect of working with sound – at first I didn't spend much time on soundtracks (limited by knowledge and technology), but now that side of film-making excites me almost more than the drawing. I like the fact that animation can be such a complex process because it forces simplification – it is similar to poetry in that respect, that a short, apparently simple film can

be full of ideas and meaning – they can be intense experiences to watch'.

On location

Baker's Beaches project was funded by a Creative Scotland Award from the Scottish Arts Council, and came as a response to working in a studio context making The Green Man of Knowledge at Red Kite with the animation team for the best part of a year, and feeling the need to work with greater personal freedom again, released from the restraints of studio production and delivering to broadcasters.

Baker: 'I wanted drawing to return to the heart of my work again and to work intuitively, away from studio trappings of dope sheets/animatics, etc. I wanted to work on location as much as possible – not a tradition of animation!

'I worked around the theme of beaches, to create a series of animated pieces of work, linked by theme, but very varied in approach,

Core skill
Tradition and modernity

Aspirant animators should always embrace 'tradition' – the knowledge and skills learned from past achievements and experience in the field – and 'modernity' – the most up-to-date approaches, technologies of expression, and means to creativity. Some obvious ways in which this might be done:

– Watch and critically engage with as many animated films of whatever style or era as possible.
– Read as much historical, critical and technical material about animation from a range of disciplines.
– Use trade publishing and the world wide web to glean up-to-date information about the field.
– Attend animation lectures, events and festivals.

subject and technology used. The project also gave me a chance to learn some new software, and use it in a non-commercial way. Some of the films were abstract, some more documentary in style, some worked with soundtracks forming first (collaborating with composer John Harris for two of the 11 films). Some were created completely on location with a digital camera mounted on a tripod; I animated on paper, sand, paint, and on acetate, directly under the camera. I wanted to create very immediate, impressionistic animation, inspired by surroundings and weather, and events taking place around me. I also created animated sketchbooks – all drawn on-site, working in a layout pad from back to front, drawing as quick as possible, creating animation of people, surroundings and events as they happened.'

Technology
'I used very immediate technology for some of the films (e.g. Achmelvich, Portmahomack) to

work as spontaneously as possible. I wanted as little technology or studio processes to get between the inspiration and the animation.

'For others (e.g. Chanonry Point, Picking up Stones) I used Flash. They involved ideas gathered over a longer time and repeated visits to the beaches. The films took a little longer to "form". I also wanted to learn new animation software. As a result these were created a little more "traditionally", working with storyboards, all "back at base" in the Red Kite studio.

'Both Waiting for Dolphins: Chanonry Point and Picking up Stones are excellent examples of translating directly observed activity, through sketching, into an animated form. The former is entirely composed of watching people at the seashore, looking out at passing boats, skimming stones, picking up shells, taking photos, walking with different gaits and purpose, and reacting to the oncoming waves. The "narrative" here is an act of "capture" – recording the small narratives of people by the sea. Woman in the Zone, again using Flash, distils this into a meaningful incident as a woman gazing at her reflection in the sea recalls her childhood games at the sea edge, and picks up a shell as a further 'souvenir' of the memory.'

Refining technique
'After McLaren, I used the technique of charcoal on paper (using it in the same way as paint on glass, working on one sheet of paper and moving, smudging and removing the charcoal frame by frame), because I'd always wanted to try the technique and these short experimental films gave me the opportunity. As in all creative work, some degree of learning takes place and necessitates doing different things than might have otherwise been anticipated. This can have beneficial rewards, too.

'I was working mostly alone and with no producer – my own choice. It was great to have this freedom, but it was also a bit lonely. So I found I enjoyed the films that did bring me back to the studio and allowed me to gain feedback from colleagues. It was refreshing for Red Kite too, to have me in and out of the studio, creating new work and trying new techniques. I ended up taking the role of producer myself, creating schedules of work, budgeting, setting some "rules" to the structure of the work (how many films, how connected, etc.), and organising post-production. This was a learning curve, but very rewarding.'

↑ **Stills from Life in Norway – Hee Holmen**
A teacher is also presented as a sheep, but most challengingly, as one who propagates racist attitudes and bullies a class who, ironically, are made up of overseas students. The word 'neger' or 'nigger' is used in everyday exchange without recognition of its potentially highly charged meanings or political intent.

Animated Documentary

I have written elsewhere about 'animated documentary'[9] and suggested that it operates in four modes – 'imitative' (borrowing from established conventions in newsreel, TV documentary, travelogue etc.); 'subjective' (concentrating on individual perspectives that offer alternative 'histories' or social narratives); 'fantastical' (repositioning social or historical subjects or events in a newly fabricated context to suggest different interpretations or models of critique); and 'post-modern' (where all social and cultural narrative may be subject to no proven or evidential 'authority' or 'actuality', but may offer a relevant 'truth').

Hee Holmen was trained as a painter and print-maker in the classical tradition at Hongik University and took her Masters degree in Experimental Animation at CalArts, under Jules Engel, Bill Moritz and Christine Panushka. Holmen particularly enjoyed exploring the music and theatre departments at the same time, and saw animation as a cross-disciplinary form that could work in many contexts.

Holmen's Life in Norway, 'an interactive animated documentary CD-ROM', is particularly interesting in this respect in the sense that like Baker, Holmen was seeking new contexts to present animated works and wanted to progress the form by exploring 'genre' and technology.

Animated documentary

Life in Norway chronicles Holmen's experience studying in Norway and provides a satirical 'take' on what became a difficult year for her in which she constantly encountered racism and the casual and unconscious rejection of non-Norwegians by the indigenous communities she was part of. The CD-ROM contains short animations that draw attention to particular issues, but these are part of a range of materials, including texts, graphs, photographs and interactive activities, which the viewer/reader can choose from.

Digital technology

Holmen: 'I come from a traditional "experimental" animation film-making background. Because I choose the method according to the story, I don't have a signature style. I have worked in drawing, cut-out, photography and 3D CGI. This time around, I was investigating non-linear storytelling, and the possibilities of digital media in presentation. I wish more animators would explore what digital technology can offer and not focus only on 3D computer animation. I was experimenting in small Director-based games and thought this could be a good medium for documentary. For Life in Norway, I made small humorous animation segments, as well as an interactive game, slide show and texts. The design is straightforward and simple to use, with just one level to investigate. I prefer a quick access to a long navigation. I used the most prominent contemporary software: Director, Maya, Photoshop, After Effects and Painter.'

Future projects

Having created her work as a CD-ROM, but without a ready market for such work, Holmen is looking to present her documentary on the web. Her experience has made her grow as an artist.

Holmen: 'I consider digital media as a new tool for presentation, meaning that content will always be most important, not the fancy technology. This is my first try at animation documentary and it was great fun. It breaks many digital documentary conventions, such as not having any authentic interviewed voice. I would like to experiment more to find what can be the best rhetoric for animation documentary. Technique-wise, I am quite happy to try something new and make it work. The design structure was quite satisfying for me. The possibilities of digital presentation are countless and I hope others would experiment more with different narrative structure. For future projects, I want to research different ways to navigate; for example, with simulation technology and voice recognition. My other collaborated project in progress, SMAALL, is about multilingual learning for small kids, using voice recognition.'

REFERENCES
9) See Wells, P. 'The Beautiful Village and the True Village: A Consideration of Animation and the Documentary Aesthetic' in Wells, P. (ed) Art and Animation, Art & Design profile No 53, John Wiley / Academy Group, 1997, pp 40–45

→ Stills from Life in Norway – Hee Holmen

In a very witty example of a short silent film, Holmen effectively uses inter-titles to demonstrate the relationship between a 'foreign' boy and a Norwegian girl, implying that the Norwegians suspect that black people are merely seeking to marry to gain entry to the country and citizen status. The simple graphics point out the racist agenda directly and effectively.

→ Stills from Sparky – Hee Holmen

In a short CG piece, Sparky the dog, looking forward to his daily walk is thwarted by a phone call home, which threatens to be a long 'this is what I am doing in Norway' conversation between a mother and her daughter. Inventively, he pulls out the phone connection and gets to have his walk!

↓ Stills from Life in Norway – Hee Holmen

Holmen's student companions are presented as 'soap' fixated bores who alienate her, but crucial here is the soundtrack as the conformist 'baa' of sheep is replaced with an aggressive growl.

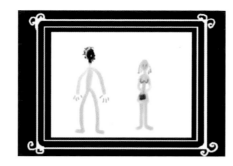

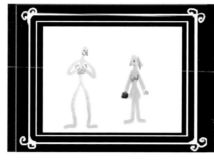

Contexts
Introduction

The first two sections of this book have been concerned with the pre-production and production processes of making an animated film, of whatever technique, principle or approach. This final section looks at the latter stages of completing a production and some of the ways in which a piece of work might be a vehicle towards finding future employment or training opportunities; the target audience a piece of work might be appropriate for; and the contexts in which an animator might seek to develop a career. This section also provides information for further reading and study. Investment in the field is absolutely vital and consistently thinking about what can be achieved intellectually, creatively and technically is essential. Constantly pursuing resources to facilitate that process is fundamental to development and eventual success.

Post-production

Post-production is essentially defined by the technique employed, but two factors that are key aspects of all post-production processes are the use of special effects and the final soundtrack.

Special Effects

Post-production is essentially defined by the technique employed. Special effects, sound mixing and compositing etc. are usually 'final' aspects of a production process, but in the digital era they are increasingly absorbed within the production process itself. Consequently, students and practitioners need to take special care over the specificity and quality of each element – special effects, for example, offering a particular challenge.

Thomas Walsh, an ex-Don Bluth and Disney Effects animator and post-graduate researcher addresses special effects as 'the zen of animation'.

Walsh: 'Norman M. Klein, in his essay "Hybrid Cinema: The Mask, Masques and Tex Avery", contemplates the phenomena of special effects

cinema, particularly in relation to the film The Mask and the work of animator Tex Avery. Klein seeks to establish a tension between the functions of the "effect" and the "character" in animation, stating that:

"Animation has always been fundamentally an interactive, not a dramatic, form of story; the characters are dominated by, or at war with, the effects. It is more like an epic form, about rising and falling, characters as types within the whole, or as elements like machine parts designed to move the spectacle along. The spectacles are narratives about environments, not characters, at risk; about folklore, carnival, the caricature of community in commedia dell'arte."[1]

'Klein collapses together character and effect as parts of a greater "spectacular" machine, and it seems that the tension existing between these two elements gives the spectacle its dynamic force. This tension is an important factor in any effort to define the essence of special effects practice.

← **Production shot of post-production work on Hide and Seek – Aaron Wood and Kerry Drumm**

→ **Stills from haircare advertisement – Studio AKA (Marc Craste, Philip Hunt and Nic Greaves)**
Studio AKA here plays out the relationship between character animation and environmental effects, essentially linking the 'organic' nature of hair with the natural environment, all created through the demanding 'artifice' of CGI.

Through its constant oscillation between "abstraction" and "representation", the special effect simultaneously binds character to environment, but sometimes overwhelms character and environment to become mere spectacle in itself.

'During Disney's production of Tarzan (1999), producer Roy Conli once described special effects practice as "the zen of animation". The use of the word "zen", with its connotations of metaphysical meditation on one hand, and heightened awareness of the natural world on the other, does help to illustrate some of the tensions in the effects process. As esoteric as it might seem, this explanation goes towards asking a very straightforward question: in character animation, the animator always has his own bodily presence as a reference for his work, but what about the special effects animator? How can one act like fire or behave like water? How can one dissipate like smoke or tumble down a mountainside like an avalanche?

'Technically speaking, special effects perform certain important functions in a classically animated feature film.

– They can serve to heighten the dramatic tension of a scene or exemplify the characters' mood by an effective use of lighting, or detailing other climatic conditions.
– They can also perform a climactic event, which releases the dramatic tension of a sequence, usually in the form of an explosion or a cataclysmic natural disaster.
– They can assist in establishing a sense of environment and give the characters a greater sense of presence in that environment.
– The effects layer also bridges the gap between character and background, and as the final layer of drawing produced for the scene, it helps to homogenise the different elements into a final cohesive image.

'Commercial narrative conventions demand a number of effects-heavy sequences to punctuate the dramatic development of a story. A good effect is always one that supports the character action and serves its purpose in the development of the narrative. This means that a good effect does not necessarily reside in the largest, most dramatic on-screen moment, but is more often in the subtle detail that is taken for granted and goes unnoticed. For example, in Disney's Tarzan, the dapples of light on the characters' bodies were the result of a painstaking job performed by the effects department. Despite the long hours it took to accomplish, it goes almost unnoticed. But because of its very innocuousness, it succeeds in placing the characters more firmly in their environment, giving a greater illusion of a lived-in space. It bridges the gap between character and layout, and homogenises the final image. And dramatically, in a plot that concerns itself with ideas of family and home, it gives a more intense sense of the encompassing womb-like space of the jungle, which curves its leaves and branches around the bodies in its midst.

'For an effects-driven narrative, which demonstrates the sometimes-volatile tensions between effects and character animation, there are few sequences better suited than 'The Sorcerer's Apprentice' from Fantasia (1940). In his essay 'The Animation of Sound', Philip Brophy examines the use of sound synchronisation in Disney and Warner Bros. animations, and pays particular attention to sequences from Disney's Fantasia.[2]

'He notes how fluid substances represent the dynamic flow of the music. By extension, it is possible to consider the water effect in 'The Sorcerer's Apprentice' as moving towards actually representing the ethereal and abstract form of the music it strives to signify. The over-production of water in the narrative, working both literally and metaphorically as a special effects layer, threatens to overcome its character animation counterpart. It thereby illustrates the tensions between character and effects as suggested by Klein earlier. In this sequence,→

→ the employment of warped glass and the mix of dry brush with traditional cel painting, the evocative use of shadow and the excellent realisation of water's substance, all help to display the multifaceted discipline of an effects artist.

Walsh (cont.): 'Even though there may be some aesthetic tensions between effects and character artwork, to achieve the complex spectacle of an animated feature film, close coordination between departments is absolutely necessary. Since the effects level is usually the final level of drawing to be produced on any given scene, the effects artist must pay close attention to the other levels on the x-sheet and liaise with other departments whenever necessary. Placing the scene in the context of its sequence is also important to preserve continuity in design and action. Developing a strong design sense and a good vocabulary of abstract shapes is also important. Although the effects artist is usually supplied with a design workbook – which is similar to a character animator's model sheet – especially on such design-heavy productions like Hercules (1997) and Mulan (1998), they are still required to invent new forms in the process of keying the animation, whilst also maintaining the overall aesthetic style of the film.

'Observation of physical phenomena is the most important activity for an effects artist. To a certain degree, this brings us back to the concept of effects practice as "the zen of animation", where the artist is immersed in contemplation of the natural world. Therefore, observation of physical phenomena is of utmost importance if an effective sense of timing is to be developed. This is particularly important if the production is engaged in a hyper-realist aesthetic.'

REFERENCES
1) Klein, N. 'Hybrid Cinema: The Mask, Masques and Tex Avery', in Sandler, K. (ed.) Reading the Rabbit: Explorations in Warner Bros. Animation, New Brunswick, New Jersey and London: Rutgers University Press, 1998, p214
2) Brophy, P. 'The Animation of Sound', in Cholodenko, A. (ed.) The Illusion of Life, Sydney: Power Publications, 1991

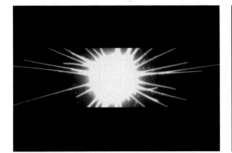

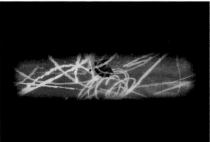

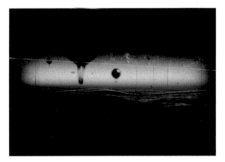

Sound in Post-production

Sound in the post-production phase is usually concerned with adding emphasis to or correcting balance within an already developed soundtrack during the production process, or post-synching and scoring after animation is complete.

Here are some examples of sound strategies and techniques that are based in post-production as described by Tom Simmons:

Simmons: 1) 'Foley and sound effects; sound which is used to emphasise objects, characters and environments: Aardman's Chicken Run (2000) employs a range of sound effects to emphasise the realism of models and objects. Though guide sounds were used in the animating process, the majority of sounds that can be heard in the final soundtrack were added later. These were either pre-recorded at a sound props studio and edited into the mix or performed by Foley artists in direct relation to the animated sequences. The God by Konstantin Bronzit (Pilot Studios, Moscow, 2003) and How to Cope with Death by Ignacio Ferreras (2002) also make extensive use of sound effects to emphasise character attributes.'

2) 'Speech that is over-dubbed or recorded after the animating process: Hayao Miyazaki's Spirited Away (2003) is an animated film produced collaboratively between Miyazaki's studio in Japan and Disney in the USA. Two language versions of the film were distributed on its release; an original Japanese version and an American English version. A significant amount of energy was dedicated to achieving similar characters in each version of the film. For the team involved in the production of the English language version, this meant many hours recording different actors in voice-over recordings before mixing in the sound effects and music tracks from the original Japanese version.

'The final compilation of soundtrack and animation – and any opening and closing credits – will inevitably require considerable skill and sensitivity. Compositing, final cut, and mix down, played out through the appropriate software and system – Shake, Final Cut Pro etc. – is the final act in making a piece of work. Look back at the earlier advice about editing and crucially, plan the final phase of the work carefully allowing enough time to complete the work to the standard required.'

Critical Evaluation

Throughout the process of creating any animated film there needs to be a degree of objectivity in monitoring progress and evaluating each aspect of the work as it unfolds.

Critical evaluation may be achieved in a number of ways at both a 'pragmatic' and 'artistic' level. For example, it remains crucial to constantly check budget and resources as the film is being executed. Similarly, all the technical aspects that may include equipment checking through to file saving must be addressed as the core facilitation aspects of the project.

Crucially, the developmental creative elements of the project need constant assessment and attention. The creation of an animated film in many senses relies on its pre-production process to ensure the success of the project. It is no accident that PIXAR takes so long on the script stage of its films before embarking on the animation itself. Preparation is vital and should be informed by a critically engaged set of choices about design and execution. Facilitating the inciting idea, the key narrative elements, and the thematic and conceptual premises of the work are constant preoccupations throughout the creative process. While technical errors sometimes have some points of redress, it is very hard to recover a piece of work that is narratively, aesthetically or conceptually flawed. Care and attention in the pre-production phase should ensure intended and hopefully successful outcomes.

Contexts

The Fundamentals of Animation

God on Our Side is a superb example of the way in which a personal film can engage with a research process thematically, artistically and technically, and succeed as emotionally profound and politically invested work. The film stands up to extensive critical evaluation by its makers, its viewers and those who seek to learn from the practices of others.

Evaluation Guidelines

Here are some key questions to pose when looking back on a project and some sample answers from an imaginary film, which might be critically helpful in improving practice when embarking on a new project:

What aspects of the process – artistically or technically – prompted the greatest degree of satisfaction and why ?

The designs for the soldiers were historically accurate and came out of research at a Military Museum. The uniforms were adjusted to make sure that there were not too many elements that would be difficult to animate. Using Photoshop proved really helpful at that stage.

What aspects of the process – artistically or technically – posed problems or difficulties, and how were they resolved?

The main issue was time management. Everything took longer than expected and that meant corners had to be cut. Problems were resolved by improvising ways in which action could be suggested without actually being seen, or through minimal imagery. Also, a sequence was mislaid and took an age to recover. This caused tensions between the collaborators that had to be resolved. The answer was having clearer roles and responsibilities, and better organisation. Also, the 3D bits in Maya were a bit beyond our expertise. These were mostly replaced by 2D sequences.

As a consequence of thinking about these former questions, what can be identified as the core strengths and weaknesses of the approach to and execution of, the project?

The strengths were in the quality and detail of the script, which enabled the pre-production process to go relatively smoothly. There was a realisation, too, that the work should be mainly in 2D as we could draw well, but were less able using the 3D software. The weaknesses were in the ways in which disorganisation and not using time effectively disrupted the team.

Having identified the strengths and weaknesses of the process, how does this translate into an evaluation of core skills and knowledge – what are the key skills that have been gained and what are the main things that have been learned?

Key skills would be the technical quality of the script designs and full drawn 2D animation, including persuasive lip-synch. The project clearly shows the capacity to 'animate'. The main thing learned would be the necessity to make sure that the script is completely right before starting.

In retrospect, what are the key strengths and weaknesses of the final outcome of the project? What aspects have been most successful, and why? If it were possible to change something, what should be changed and why?

The opening of the film was successful because it was achieved purely visually and used the soundtrack to evoke concern for the main character. The battle scene was also effective because instead of making it look epic through showing thousands of soldiers ready to fight, it showed the battle from within, with close ups of injured bodies and falling horses. The 'love interest' aspect of the narrative should be changed – it slows down the story and doesn't add much in relation to the main character.

What set of 'recommendations' or 'conclusions' can be drawn from evaluating the project, which will be useful on another occasion?

The key recommendations would be to have a better planned schedule and to stick to it. To be more clear about roles and responsibilities. To make sure that the right technique is chosen and there is competence in using the equipment and software. Finally, to look at the script again – it seemed just right – but the problem about the 'love interest' was in there all along, with fairly pointless scenes.

This response is honest and enabling. It stresses the importance and usefulness of research; the necessity to keep re-drafting the script, constantly asking hard questions of its narrative strength and its suitability for animation; the need to be clear and honest about technical competences and the techniques required for the project; the significance of project management and effective collaboration at all levels and finally, the fundamental belief in the idea and what can be achieved.

Portfolio

One of the key aspects of becoming a professional animator and working in the creative industries in general is the ability to present a portfolio to a potential employer. This is usually a CV (or résumé), a show reel and the materials that may be presented for interview. In the contemporary era, there is also the possibility of showcasing work on personal websites and in a range of formats for cross-platform presentation.

If applying for a specific position it is important to find out the exact requirements of the role, and most importantly, what is required by the company at the point of application. It is also important to know what the company does and its expectations of the people who work for it. This can often be obtained on company websites or in informal phone or email exchanges with recruitment personnel at the company.

Chris Bowden, Senior Producer at Cosgrove Hall Films manages the recruitment of new animators and other personnel for Cosgrove Hall's productions. Bowden emphasises three aspects of a great portfolio:

– The pertinence of the show reel.
– The relevance of the CV.
– The discipline of the work itself.

Bowden: 'A CV and a show reel should be indicators of seriousness and commitment to the serious demands of the art and craft of animation. Only by demonstrating a professional investment in the form will the possibility of a professional opportunity become available.

'When attending an interview, it is important to be articulate about any work previously undertaken, and to show pertinent examples of pre-production work and production work that has been realised. In answering questions it is useful to signal knowledge of the company's work; the pertinence of, and evidence for, relevant skills; and most importantly, a level of critical and →

168   **Contexts**   The Fundamentals of Animation

Best Advice
Senior Producer at
Cosgrove Hall Films,
Chris Bowden

– The thing we look for most in an animation
show reel, is (not surprisingly) an ability to
animate. We look for examples of animation
where there has been some thought and
sensitivity applied to the movement.

– Most companies are inundated with reels so
make a concise collection of your best shots
or sequences at the beginning. Add full-
length films after. Whilst pop video editing is
certainly clever and flashy, it rarely gives the
viewer a chance to actually see the
animation clearly. Remember what you're
trying to achieve.

– Try to keep your CV to a page in length, two
at most. Avoid using smaller type just to fit
more on, it makes the reader's eyes hurt.

– It may sound obvious, but at an interview or
on work experience be enthusiastic. It's a
quality that can't be trained into an individual
and counts a lot. Animation is a painstaking
process and invariably involves a lot of hours
spent standing up under hot lights. You have
to want to do it more than (almost) anything.

– Be prepared to work as part of a team.
Broadly speaking television series animation
is a collaborative effort. Your shots will be
most effective when they enhance the telling
of the story and work with all the other shots
from all the other animators. Every shot can't
be a splashy show reel number.

– Television series animation will provide a well
of experience for animators, but requires a
certain discipline. Typical series demand
10–15 seconds a day on average, so be
prepared that you cannot always spend the
amount of time you'd like to on a shot.

– Try to find the creative challenge in what
you're doing – think 'How can I make my
shot great in the time I have?', rather than
sweeping your hand across your brow and
screaming 'How can I perform under these
conditions?'!

↓ **Guidelines for show reels**
↘ Aardman Animation's show reel requirements
are very similar to those listed in the text, but
have additional and very helpful detail.

→ creative understanding that shows autonomy, independence and initiative, while being committed to a collaborative and industrious ethos. As in any job, a good sense of humour is a standard requirement.'

Show reel

The standard requirements for show reel are simple and straightforward:
– Reels should be on DVD or VHS (NTSC or PAL) – NO Beta, 3/4" or CDs.
– Include a detailed credit list/reel breakdown explaining what you did on each shot (including techniques) and what software (if applicable) was used to achieve the effects.
– The length of your reel should be limited to five minutes and consist of work that you're most proud of, starting with your best, most recent work.
– Music isn't necessary.

This takes into account format, supporting technical information, the 'best at the front' rule (it is likely only two minutes, at most, will be watched of any reel), and the subtle guidance that a hip-hop groove or high-end guitar riff in support of a rapid edit may not best show work to the most impressive advantage.

A number of colleges and universities, particularly in regard to the presentation of CGI skills, recommend a two-minute show reel demonstrating the process of construction (rigging, rendering etc.), before the revelation of the final character/environment in a short narrative situation. Also, in such a sequence – for any animation discipline – showing lip-synch (using pertinent vocal delivery and sound mixing, not merely an engaging piece of music) and a particular movement, which demonstrates a knowledge of the core skills of animating, are also helpful in showing particular and necessary abilities.

The show reel must ultimately impress first, by demonstrating core skills executed to a high level

Aardman

SUBMISSION GUIDELINES FOR SHOW REELS

Creating your show reel

Your show reel is your one chance to shine without necessarily being present. It needs to demonstrate, in a couple of minutes, the genius of many years of hard work. It's not just a compilation; it's the unique you and your life ambitions condensed into a few minutes. It's also the ticket to your future. Here are some tips for creating a show reel that will potentially stand out from the crowd.

— NEVER SEND THE ORIGINAL!
— Utilise College facilities — while you can.
— Accept your own strengths and weaknesses - Assume that your show reel will be compared to those of other candidates and that you are therefore pitching yourself against them. A six-minute show reel with 30 seconds of exceptional work can be completely diluted by five and a half minutes of average work. Focus on what you do better than anybody else. Don't spend time chasing positions that play to your weaknesses. It is better to spend more time aiming at fewer ideal positions.
— Be creative - It sounds obvious, but remember that you are trying to differentiate yourself from the crowd. Try to think of innovative ways of presenting your work e.g. if you can't send a copy portfolio, film your life drawings and title card them.
— Know your audience - You've just finished the course, you're all fired up and want to unleash your brilliance on the whole world. Your instinct will be to blanket drop show reels to all and sundry, but it's not an effective use of time or resources. Research the companies that interest you so that you have a better understanding of what they are looking for e.g. check that a 3D specialist will accept 2D show reels.
— Running time should ideally be 4-6 mins - It can be longer, but remember it's in a queue of show reels that all need to be viewed.
— Assume that only the first 2 mins will get watched - This will ensure that you grab your audience from the start with a compilation of the best bits of everything. You can always show longer versions after that.
— Best work first - after your amazing compilation, order the remaining work with the best first to give it a better chance of being seen.
— Get the format right — For stop-frame animation we accept: VHS and DVDs. For CGI animation: VHS or DVDs. Please do not send us CDs, links to your website or email attachments.
— Include a running order and related information - preferably on the tape or sleeve. This will save potential employers from spending time trying to work out what they are watching and you don't want them trying to adjust the sound if it's a mute project.
— Describe your contribution - particularly when it is group work. An audience focused on the character on the left when you animated the one on the right doesn't help anybody.
— Label it - It's easy for paperwork to get detached. Put your contact details on the show reel.
— Don't send it by itself - When recruiting, companies need to know specifically what sort of position you are interested in and will always want to see a CV (See 'Supporting Documentation' opposite).
— Attention to detail - Double-check everything before you send it. Try to imagine that you are receiving and assessing your show reel. Watch it all the way through a few times. Make sure it doesn't cut to Eastenders part way through.

of achievement and second, by individual flare and talent in choices and presentation.

CV/Résumé

It is often the case that individuals create a CV for themselves and send it to any potential employer or for any available post, unrevised. In a highly competitive field, CVs need to be made relevant to each application and be revised if necessary. The 'relevance' of a CV to a particular post or role is crucial because it is likely that such a post will have highly specific tasks and required outcomes.

CVs, of course, also have to evolve and become 'working' documents because different levels of achievement and ability will necessarily have to be presented in different ways as a career unfolds. A student, for example, will have to present what they have achieved as a student in relation to the course undertaken, any work experience and some measure of the standard and achievement in what has been done. A slightly more experienced professional might have gained other skills and done more work, so needs to present that accordingly. An even more experienced person may have a list of credits, but it is crucial that a CV does not merely turn into a list and remains an accurate, but appealing and impressive document about a specific individual – you.

The presentation of a CV is very important, but there is a fine line between over-elaborating the design and creating an engaging, easy-to-read document. The information in a CV is the most important aspect of it, but clearly that can be ordered and presented in a number of different ways. This is closely related to the need to revise a CV to make it relevant to a particular employer, if necessary. Indeed, many employers now provide a CV cover sheet indicating the core information required and this may make a personal CV almost redundant. In such an instance, a CV must offer more detail and place greater emphasis on personality, skills and achievements.

Supporting Documentation

The following documentation should be included in all show reel submissions:

- Personalised cover letter - It's tempting to run a generic mail shot, but taking the time to personalise your letters makes a big difference. If you really want to work for a company, tell them why. What is it that you like about their work?
- What type of position do you want - be specific about either the advertised vacancy that you are applying for or about the type of position you would like e.g. Storyboard Artist, Art Director, Character Design, Stop Motion, CGI Animator, Administrator, if it is a speculative enquiry.
- A full CV - list all your relevant skills and experience, a credit list alone will not suffice.
- Hard copy examples of art work where appropriate - in an accepted format and not originals.

Labelling and presentation of all submissions

The presentation of the materials you submit and adequate labelling of them has a big impact. Please bear in mind that yours could be one in a pile of many mixed format submissions. In addition, any show reel that we keep is filed in a tape library. For these reasons and to give yourself the best chance:

- Be viewer friendly - make everything as easy as possible to handle and view.
- Label everything - show reels, work samples and paperwork can get separated while waiting to be viewed and any show reel we keep is separated from unattached paperwork before going into the library. A show reel that stands out on the shelf will get noticed. An excellent show reel with no contact information is of little use.

Where to send submissions

- Advertised job vacancies will contain the relevant contact details.
- Speculative submissions: Stop-frame animation to Show reels, Aardman Animations Ltd., Gas Ferry Road, Bristol BS1 6UN. CGI animation to CGI Department, Aardman Animations Ltd., Gas Ferry Road, Bristol, BS1 6UN.

Waiting for a response after submission

- Your work will be reviewed by one or more members of a panel made up of Aardman staff with years of experience in multiple disciplines.
- We receive a high volume of material so please don't think that no contact means that we are not interested. We do look at all submissions that meet the above guidelines, but it can take up to eight weeks for them to be assessed.
- We are not able to return all the materials we receive so please don't send us originals.
- Speculative submissions may be kept on file for future recruitment. Submissions for specific vacancies will be kept on file for six months and if no other suitable vacancy arises during that period, they will be destroyed in accordance with the Data Protection Act. If you would prefer that we did not keep your details on file as described above, please let us know so that we can remove them.

Blue Sky Résumés addresses these issues, and advises on the presentational aspects of CVs, predominantly in the American marketplace, and across disciplines and institutions. The following 'before' and 'after' comparison shows how material can be better presented to enhance the credentials of any one individual.

Though this is only one example, notice the difference between presenting a 'bare bones', phone contact, listed career history and basic education, compared to a statement with an understated design motif, full contact details, a personal summary with an endorsement from a senior figure, a focus on professional highlights before a more detailed career history informed by its key roles and achievements, additional but relevant work, like teaching and public speaking, and education and core technical skills. Self-evidently this will vary from person to person and it may be that 'education' and 'technical' skills come much higher in the document, but more than anything else the CV offers a more comprehensive and appealing statement about the person, and with care and thought, something similarly impressive can be constructed at whatever stage of a career. Many people 'naturalise' the things they do and don't think of them as 'skills' and 'achievements'. This is particularly important in the early stages of a career when there will inevitably be less experience and external achievement. It is vital, therefore, to think through the production process undertaken in any educational context to state if there has been strength in preparation and organisation, script development, technical skills, collaboration and teamwork, research etc. The role of work experience, other courses, festivals and events attended, and extra-curricular activities, may also be very significant indicators of additional skills, knowledge and investment in an area.

A CV is a statement about you. Make it informative and attractive, but most importantly relevant to the employment sought.

Mona Vinar
555.555.5555 home
555.555.5555 cell

Career History:

2000 – Present	**Director**, DVD Highlights: *"A Lion's Story"* ForKids Animations, San Francisco, CA
1999 – 2000	**Director**, feature film Highlights: *"The Moose and the Bluebird"* ForKids Animations, San Francisco, CA
1997 – 1999	**Animation Director**, Direct-to-Home Video/DVDs Highlights: *The Spider Makes a Friend* *Six Cats and a Mouse* ForKids Animations, San Francisco, CA
1995 – 1997	**Senior Animator**, Various Highlights: *The Boy Who Loved Christmas* ForKids Animations
1996 – Present	Instructor, Animation Department New York University
1992 – 1995	**3D Artist/Animator**, Various TV Productions Highlights: *Two Small Pigs* Pixen, Inc.
1990 – 1995	**Contract Artist/ Proprietor** Movin' Graphic Design

Studies:

BA, Graphic Design, NYU
MA, Computer Graphics and Animation, UCLA

← **A dummy CV demonstrating the value of**
→ **presentation – Blue Sky Résumés**
Though considerable emphasis is placed on the show reel in a practice context, an impressive CV page can be a strong indicator of the person, the profile and the appropriateness of a candidate to a role. A good deal of thought and attention should go into its preparation and presentation.

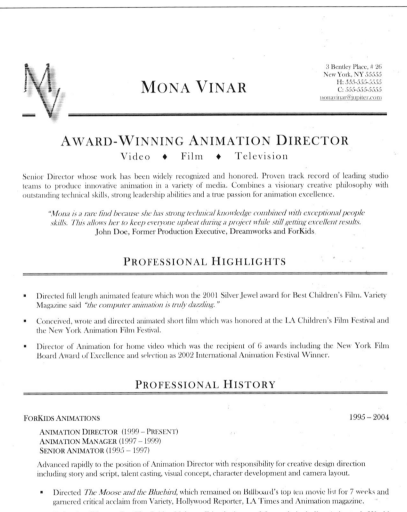

3 Bentley Place, # 26
New York, NY 55555
H: 555-555-5555
C: 555-555-5555
monavinar@jupiter.com

MONA VINAR

AWARD-WINNING ANIMATION DIRECTOR
Video ◆ Film ◆ Television

Senior Director whose work has been widely recognized and honored. Proven track record of leading studio teams to produce innovative animation in a variety of media. Combines a visionary creative philosophy with outstanding technical skills, strong leadership abilities and a true passion for animation excellence.

"Mona is a rare find because she has strong technical knowledge combined with exceptional people skills. This allows her to keep everyone upbeat during a project while still getting excellent results.
John Doe, Former Production Executive, Dreamworks and ForKids.

PROFESSIONAL HIGHLIGHTS

- Directed full length animated feature which won the 2001 Silver Jewel award for Best Children's Film. Variety Magazine said *"the computer animation is truly dazzling."*

- Conceived, wrote and directed animated short film which was honored at the LA Children's Film Festival and the New York Animation Film Festival.

- Director of Animation for home video which was the recipient of 6 awards including the New York Film Board Award of Excellence and selection as 2002 International Animation Festival Winner.

PROFESSIONAL HISTORY

FORKIDS ANIMATIONS   1995 – 2004

ANIMATION DIRECTOR (1999 – PRESENT)
ANIMATION MANAGER (1997 – 1999)
SENIOR ANIMATOR (1995 – 1997)

Advanced rapidly to the position of Animation Director with responsibility for creative design direction including story and script, talent casting, visual concept, character development and camera layout.

- Directed *The Moose and the Bluebird*, which remained on Billboard's top ten movie list for 7 weeks and garnered critical acclaim from Variety, Hollywood Reporter, LA Times and Animation magazine.

- Animation Director for *The Spider Makes a Friend*, winner of 6 awards including Animator's World Award of Excellence and 1999 Silver Telly award for exceptional children's entertainment.

- Animation Supervisor for 1995 television special *The Boy Who Loved Christmas* which has aired annually for the last nine years.

Collaboration

Due to current funding strategies most contemporary animation production involves collaboration. There are often tax incentives for international projects, or other economic drivers such as comparative wages that may be paid to animators inside and outside Europe or the USA. This results in feature films and series that are designed in one country and realised in several others through partnerships between the originators of the idea, animation companies, production houses, merchandisers and distributors.

↓ **Sketches and still from Faisal and Friends**
The series follows the adventures of Faisal, a young frog and his friends, grasshopper Saleem, butterfly Laila, snail Professor Aamir and fish Mrs Jamila who all live in or next to a pond. The set of characters represents family figures and they have different skin colours, reflecting the diversity of Islamic origin.
The scripts promote ideas about responsible world citizenship and are not exclusive to a Muslim audience.

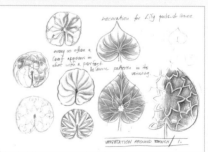

Animation series are often created with the intention to broadcast them in many languages and there can be a 'dumbing down' of strong cultural identities in order for these films to be regarded as commercially viable in the international media market. This can affect any aspect of the production from background design (homogenised environments rather than localised landscapes), to actual behaviour of characters (more likely to be seen eating burgers than noodles or fish and chips).

But new markets for animated series, films and commercials are developing across the world. Recent research into Middle Eastern animation broadcasting content suggests that currently it does not include any distinctive children's animation series containing aspects of language, culture and heritage that Arab parents and children may identify with. The majority of children's programmes aired on Arab networks are supplied by entertainment providers from the West and the Far East, which are unlikely to

satisfy the growing demand for animation productions made with cultural sensitivity, as media influence in the Muslim world grows.

Faisal and Friends (see Character Development pages 46–49) is a series in development that is targeted at this new audience and is being created through cross-cultural collaboration between companies in Egypt and the UK.

Faisal and Friends is a new series being created by Aladdin Media Limited (London), Ugly Studios UK and Imprint Studios in Egypt. Characters and environmental designs have been developed by animators at Ugly in close collaboration with Aladdin, every step in the process being vetted for Muslim sensibilities. Islamic designs are incorporated into the whole fabric of the production, from the plants in the animated world, to textures on the characters' skin and clothing.

As with most CGI animation, the original visuals are all hand drawn and in this case are emailed to

Contexts

The Fundamentals of Animation

← **Stills from Pampa Juice commercials –
Brown Bag Films**
International collaboration on advertisements is
common, but requires a particular sensitivity to
'local' audiences in relation to humour,
recognisable characters and events, and the
nature of the product.

↓ **Stills from Saudi Arabian State Television
news program identities –
Brown Bag Films**
Brown Bag Films create an 'international'
identity to the introductory idents by using
iconography common to station branding and
news coverage elsewhere, while privileging the
key identifying imagery of the station and its
delivery.

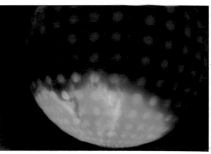

Imprint Studios for 3D realisation. A strong
dialogue and mutual respect has developed
between the animators in both countries, daily
image swops and critiques helping to ensure a
common vision of the project.

Cathal Gaffney of Brown Bag Films, Dublin, has
been engaged with international collaboration,
animating commercials for the Middle Eastern
market since 1997.

Gaffney: 'We have a good system of approval
that is done over the internet either
by email or by downloading larger files from our
FTP site. We are in the process of installing a
Telestream system that will allow us to send
completed files directly to the broadcasters'.

In 2004, Brown Bag won the prestigious
'Phoenix' award for work on a series of
commercials for Pampa Juice featuring Jean
Luc. This involved a live-action shoot of Jean
Luc against a green screen background in
Beirut. Then taking the footage back to Ireland
and producing a locked off edit from which they
created a series of 3D animated characters and
3D background elements.

Brown Bag Films also re-branded Saudi
Arabian State Television, which involved
creating over eighty motion graphic identities.

Gaffney: 'When doing business with the Middle
East it is normal to haggle over quotes for any
job and that you must not be surprised by
passionate positive and negative reactions to
the work in progress. Creative directors in the
Middle East have a great knowledge of visual
language, so once the animation is underway,
there is no discernable difference between
working for a client there than anywhere else.
Details such as the phonetic break down of
Arabic to get lip-synch working correctly can
be difficult but most people we deal with
speak perfect English so it's not too much
of a problem'

Faisal and Friends is based on characters
created by Aladdin Media, but Ugly Studios
redesigned them with the audience in mind,
then Imprint Studios took the drawings into
CGI. This is not design by committee,
each part of the process is clearly owned,
although consultation continues throughout.
All scripts and designs are approved by
Aladdin Media before the next stage is
undertaken, ensuring that the right tone and
message is maintained.

Working as an Independent

'Employability' in the animation and creative industries can be understood in a number of ways.

The 'portfolio' discussed earlier is largely constructed with studio/independent companies in mind, and is concerned with applying for particular posts or work experience opportunities. Employment can be gained in other ways, but requires a different approach if it is to be achieved either through forming an independent company, or seeking grants or other kinds of funding to make an independent film, both of which may be intrinsically related.

Morgan Powell of Seed Animation has been highly instrumental in creating a company that has achieved a great deal in its first formative period of development and growth. Here he describes his experience of setting up Seed Animation.

Powell: 'Setting up a company was at first very exciting and then it hit us that none of us knew much about business. We have just finished our first year and everything seems to be going very smoothly, although it has been a very fast learning curve! The University of Teesside has helped us in giving us quality advice and subsidised rates. To tackle our lack of business acumen we sought the advice of Business Link, The Prince's Trust and Digital City, which is an organisation up here in Middlesbrough. We decided that we should stay around Middlesbrough because it's cost effective and there are a lot of practicing animation tutors with good contacts in the business. I must stress that the university has been extremely supportive, as Digital City intends to populate the area with media companies to

TROUBLE STIRS IN THE CITY...

rival Soho's creative cluster. Middlesbrough is also the home of Animex and this is where we are going to showcase our year's work this year.

'A year on from forming Seed Animation Studio and we came third in a regional business plan competition, we are now incorporated, we have a strong show reel and we are rushed off our feet! Much like any new company, we have had to take on work from clients that don't have large budgets and so carrots are dangled, so that we

do the work for cheap. We decided that we would choose the projects that would give the higher profile, so that we can do the work cheaply.

'I have just finished a sting for an E4 competition and am hoping for it to be aired early next year. I previously animated an e-flyer for Universal Pictures and as a company we have completed among other projects, two trailers for paying clients and we are currently working with Curtis Jobling

← **Stills from E4 television stings –**
↙ **Seed Animation**
Entering competitions in the hope of winning or being spotted is a vital part of finding both a market and an audience for new work.

← **Stills from new projects – Steve May**
↙ Like many animators working in the commercial sector, Steve May, while contributing work to Monkey Dust (BBC) (see page 76), also makes his own personal films on an independent basis.

(Bob the Builder's designer) on five interstitials for festival broadcast.

'We have also been successful in pitching an in-house idea called Freerange Farm, which features four groups of trigger-happy sweet looking farmyard animals. We will be making a trailer in the hope of securing further funding for its development.

'Our first year aim was to develop our show reel to a standard that the advertising agencies consider to be good enough. We also wanted to learn more about the business side and we wanted to buy decent computers to cope with our workload. We have succeeded and this next year's aim is to get at least a piece of work on to television, raise our profile and look into employing a seedling!'

Working as an Independent

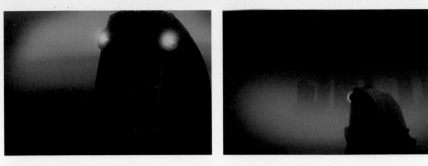

↑ **Stills from Loetzinn – Aaron Bradbury and**
↗ **Chris Gooch**
→ Bradbury and Gooch's Loetzinn is set in a
barren and hostile landscape. The two main
characters are two old mechanical toy boats
that happen to cross each other's path as
they travel endlessly across the vast ocean.
Their un-oiled joints squeak and creek as they
struggle towards each other. Their pathetic
efforts to destroy each other are more than

futile. The film operates in a 'tragi-comic'
style in the sense that the amusement arises
from the ludicrous and inept nature of their
struggle. Animation for the motion of the
boats was achieved by using a mix of
dynamics solutions and keyframing. By
animating in this way there is in some ways a
relationship to puppetry, again giving a sense
of the traditional even when using digital
applications.

↓ **Stills from Freerange Farm –**
Seed Animation
Seed Animation plays with the 'cute'
associations with animals in animation by
making its characters arbitrarily and
comically violent.

The Pitfalls

**Brown Bag's Cathal Gaffney had a
different and in some senses more
problematic experience.**

Gaffney: 'At that time there was another
incubation scheme called ICE (Irish Creative
Enterprise), which helped start up small
businesses. I didn't want to start a business really.
All I wanted to do was to make my own little art
films. I had made another short film and that won
first prize at the Galway Film Fleah – it was called
Rush and was a rendered fine art animation piece,
and I did another called Expressive Dimensions. I
was working on an idea about an old woman from
the West of Ireland called Peig Sayers, who did
nothing with her life except write a book about her
hardship and misery, and it was inflicted on
students for decades in Ireland, and everybody
hated it, and people would not speak a word of
Irish after studying it, all their school lives. I, and the
guys I was working with, wanted to take the living
piss out of Peig, and absolutely get our own back
for all the hassle she had inflicted on us! So we
approached RTE and they said, go ahead and
make the series.

'We didn't have a clue about budgets and
contracts, and I did not know about VAT
numbers, and we did not know what we were
doing. This TV series was worth 50 grand; we'd
go down to the bank and take out £1500, and
give it out, without receipts or invoices, or
anything. We were the best example of how not

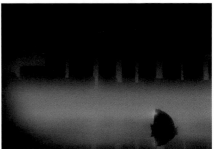

to do a business. It was sink or swim, but we made the series in 1994 and it was very popular and is still remembered today. The nation was talking about it. We thought we were going to be media moguls and be loaded. But nothing happened. That was the end of it. Later, we went to the bank with another business plan, and they said "No". Our parents became our guarantors on a loan, though, and we moved to Gardner Place. We had an electric typewriter, a photocopier, two months' rent, and a whole lot of drawing desks!

'This was in 1995 and for about two years we did subcontracted service animation for other studios – King Rollo, Honeycomb – episodes of Wolves, Witches and Giants and the like, so we all did drawing animation on it. We learned a lot about production procedures. We moved again and got a computer! We wanted to develop our own ideas again. We did inserts for a TV programme called Barstool and sold it to BBC Choice and the Paramount Comedy Channel. Very slowly we were building things up organically. We never got any big investors. We did another TV series called Taxi about Dublin taxi drivers and that was very popular too. At that stage, we set up a company called Brown Bag Development, so we could keep all the intellectual property rights separate from all the bread-and-butter leases and loans, staffing costs etc. of the production company.

'All the time it was not easy. We got a few ads and some CD-ROM work, and work for other companies, but we wanted to develop our own ideas. We developed a 13-part, half-hour animation series in children's cartoon style, which bombed. More than anything, the ultimate aim was still to pay yourself, and your staff, so we had to get critical mass to do that, and only after that was it about the kind of work you want to do. You subsidise personal work through commercial business. For a while you have to recognise that you have more in common with the local shopkeeper than the artist. It has to be about commerciality and profit first.'

Points to consider in forming an independent company

– Seek advice from a number of sources about setting up a business. Consult with established small businesses, banks, business support organisations and anyone who might offer relevant professional acumen.
– Look to Business Enterprise and Incubation schemes as possible ways of establishing a company. Equally, seek out an established company to mentor the development of a new enterprise.
– Try to associate your company with a network of geographically or professionally close businesses and organisations. Sometimes being in a 'business park' can be helpful in sharing information, resource and custom.
– Get as much information and support as possible from regional arts and media organisations, and constantly look for funding opportunities.
– Create the best show reel possible to signal the ethos, potential and talent of the company. Constantly update the reel as work is completed.
– Seek out small-scale, low-level, cost-effective work in the first instance to build the show reel and portfolio of the company. Potential clients need evidence of quality and achievement related to economic sense. Trailers, advertisements, interstitials, CD-ROM inserts etc. are required in a number of broadcast and exhibition outlets. Make enquiries in a number of contexts to seek out possible contracts for comparatively small-scale work.
– Enter competitions, festivals, exhibitions etc. and use any context to promote the identity, quality and distinctiveness of the company's work.
– Seek out subcontracted work with more established companies.
– Try and establish a 'core idea' for an investment project, which may be pitched to larger organisations and broadcast outlets. This may be a more 'personal' project or one that seeks to compete in the established professional arena, but hopefully, it will be a 'breakthrough' project that succeeds in gaining the company more work and other creative opportunities.
– Keep the artistic, technical and commercial principles of the company under constant review in order to make strategic and operational decisions to develop the organisation.
– Try to establish a supportive network of parents, friends and professional colleagues to endure difficult times or unsuccessful periods.
– Try to sustain confidence, the courage of conviction, enthusiasm and the commitment to hard work, sometimes with little reward, as the company grows.
– Remember that all success is hard earned, should be enjoyed and used to sustain 'a career' – this is not a hobby anymore!

Postgraduate Opportunities

In what is now a hugely competitive area of work, success at undergraduate level or other training initiatives may not be sufficient. If having read the demands of a portfolio or CV, or the requirements in setting up an independent company, it is clear that more training or experience may be required, then postgraduate courses may be beneficial.

↑ A still from I Married a Strange Person – Bill Plympton
Many postgraduate courses have a number of visiting professionals who help and advise on working practices and careers in animation. Independent Bill Plympton, for example, has conducted many workshops and offered pertinent advice about entering the sector.

If you embark on a degree it is likely that the first year will be an uphill climb, where learning the basics necessitates a lot of diagnostic and advisory support. The second year tends to be much more consolidatory and many students properly engage with the tasks and assessments with much more acumen and insight for the first time. Only in the third or possibly fourth year on some deliveries, does work feel potentially autonomous and independent. This can be the springboard for seeking work immediately, but for many it is a place to take stock and sustain achievement in a postgraduate context. Many of the young animators in this book have undertaken a postgraduate course because it has been an opportunity for them to fully understand what stage they are at in their development and to make work that more fully represents their ability, outlook and potential. It is often such work that can be confidently sent to festivals, potential employers, or funding councils to enhance the possibility of more opportunities.

The choice of a postgraduate course is important and requires a lot of research – information is freely available on the web, but requesting prospectuses and making visits to the places of study is crucial. Each course will have its own ethos and agenda. Take for example the following cases:

The Animation course offers a supportive environment for all approaches to frame-by-frame methods of moving-image production.

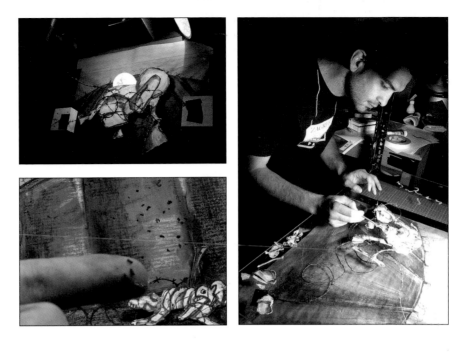

The aim of the course is to provide the opportunity for students to extend their ideas and abilities and to gather the confidence and powers of self-criticism, which will help them to continue developing as artists. An exciting range of screenings, lectures and discussions on contemporary and outstanding historical films is offered to students during the course. The course aims to develop and extend students' existing skills and to produce innovative practitioners in animation. The course offers the opportunity to combine new and traditional forms to create exciting and original methods of image-making. Sound is given particular emphasis with workshops and specialist seminars developing an aural awareness enabling new skill levels to be developed. The course builds communication skills and an intelligent use of animation as a fine, applied or commercial art. **Royal College of Art**

All degree courses provide a unique cross between the science and art of computer graphics, ensuring that the students understand the technology upon which their artwork is implemented. This allows them to use and modify the technology to meet their own creative needs. **Bournemouth University National Centre for Computer Animation**

The program, with its strong focus on character animation techniques, examines both contemporary and traditional approaches to animation. Animation affords students the opportunity to master their drawing skills and sense of acting and motion, and to apply them to the art of human and animal dramatisation, and animation storytelling. Sheridan's experienced instructors build upon their professional and teaching insights to provide an education that covers many aspects and eras of animation. **Sheridan College**

Wholly dedicated to creation, resolutely professional, a great place on the artistic side. A place where students can take classes, make films and meet key industry professionals. Two principal aims: to train and nurture creative talent to develop the art of animation; to contribute to the creative evolution of a quality cinema. **La Poudriere, Ecole du Film d'Animation**

These are not merely statements about the courses, they are statements of principle about approaches to animation as an art, a craft, a technique, a means of expression, a mode of employment and an attitude to life. Careful attention is required to choose the right course for an individual's personal development and needs. Make contact with the key personnel on courses and visit institutions before and after application. Make choices on fully-informed grounds and in relation to career aspirations.

Making an Independent Film

In 1967, UBU Films in Australia created a manifesto that insisted upon the idea that an independent abstract film could be made under any circumstances. It was designed to reject the 'studio' ethos and to encourage the disempowered creative person or experimental artist to make their work and not be inhibited by financial or contextual constraints. While the manifesto is of its 'counter-cultural' time – the ideas still apply and have some currency, nearly 40 years later (see Manifesto opposite).

← Production sketch and still from God on
↓ Our Side – Michal Pfeffer and Uri Kranot
Pfeffer and Kranot drew upon Picasso's 'Guernica' thematically and aesthetically in their design work, which readily contextualised the artistic and political agenda of the piece. Allying form and content is fundamental to the emotional and philosophical immediacy of the final film.

you can keep your costs down to a low level then it is much easier getting your money back.

'The third rule is the most important part for me: to make it funny. I don't make the rules; I don't dictate what the make up of the audience anywhere is, but in general the audience likes to laugh and for some reason expects to laugh at animation. Now there are a lot of film-makers who make beautiful, sensitive films, or political films, or more artistic films – like Michael Dudok de Wit, for example, who makes serious films and is very successful – but in general, that's a rarity and funny animation finds an audience quicker. That's great for me, because I grew up trying to draw funny cartoons and I like hearing people laugh. I like telling jokes and for me that is easy and luckily that's the main market. Visual humour can be universal – whether it is China, South America, Australia, or England, a visual joke plays almost exactly the same in every screening. I could be in a theatre in China or England and the laugh will come at the same time and with the same volume.'

A less avant-garde, radical perspective is offered by independent animator, Bill Plympton, who by a range of strategies – making shorts as parts of features or as vehicles by which to fund longer work, working on the web etc. – seeks to create independent work in a contemporary commercial context.

Plympton: 'The first rule is to keep the film short – about two or three minutes – because it is much easier for a festival or for a TV station to programme it and for a compilation programmer to include it. My films are about five minutes, although I have done an eight/nine-minute short.

'The second rule is to make the film cheaply. The audience doesn't really care that much if it is loaded with special effects or loaded with orchestral music or fancy digital imagery – they want to see the characters; they want to see a simple story told by engaging characters. I tried to keep the cost down to $1000–$2000 a minute. If

UBU Films manifesto

01–Let no one say anymore that they can't raise enough money to make a film – any film scrap can be turned into a hand-made film at no cost.

02–Let photography be no longer essential to film-making – hand-made films are made without a camera.

03–Let literary considerations of plot and story no longer be essential to film-making – hand-made films are abstract.

04–Let no more consideration be given to direction and editing – hand-made films are created spontaneously.

05–Let no media be denied to hand-made films – they can be scratched, scraped, drawn, inked, coloured, dyed, painted, pissed-on, black and white or coloured, bitten, chewed, filed, rasped, punctured, ripped, burned, blurred, bloodied, with any technique imaginable.

06–Let written and performed music be rejected by makers of hand-made films – let hand-made music be created directly on to the film by any technique of scratching or drawing etc., imaginable.

07–Let no orthodoxy of hand-made films be established – they may be projected alone, in groups, on top of each other, forward, backwards, slowly, quickly, in every possible way.

08–Let no standard of hand-made films be created by critics – a film scratched inadvertently by a projector is equal to a film drawn explicitly by a genius.

09–Let hand-made films not be projected in cinemas, but as environments, not to be absorbed intellectually, but by all senses.

10–Most of all, let hand-made film-making be open to everyone, for hand-made films must be popular art.

→ **Stills from Westerkerk – Holly Rumble**
↓ These images are from Holly Rumble's film Westerkerk and are rotoscoped from video, through tiny prints from the timeline, with crayon drawn over to emphasise selective aspects. These images were then re-filmed. The effect is one of enhancement, but the hand-drawn element gives an organic, analogue impression of what is otherwise a digital process. Holly Rumble undertook the MA in Animation and Sound Design at the Norwich School of Art and Design, UK.

Screening Opportunities

The most important part about being a creative person is not merely being creative in relation to the art form itself, but in the ways in which you can remain inventive and find an audience for the work and in turn, stimulate more opportunities for the animator to gain work or present elsewhere.

Markets

In any walk of life, 'networking' is important. Getting to know people within the creative industries might lead to the possibility of work, exhibition or profile activity. Taking any opportunity and making the best of it, even if it is not the absolutely desired task or role, may facilitate other contacts and access to other projects and possibilities.

Independent animator, Bill Plympton has had not merely to be 'an artist', but also an entrepreneur and an agent to promote his work. His short films ultimately funded longer films; his website has presented his work and sustained a profile; and his constant presence at festivals has enabled him to make contacts to facilitate more projects.

Plympton: 'After I did Boomtown I did get a reputation, as it was quite successful and I was approached at a party at a festival by a Russian émigré who said "I want to give you $2000 to make your next film". At first I thought this was great, but I was lying in bed thinking that that would mean he would own the film and would get to dictate the content of that film. I suddenly realised that I had $2000 from my illustration work, and I thought if I don't believe in myself, why would I expect someone else to believe in me, so I invested my own money in Your Face, which cost $3000 and went on to make $30,000. I learned it is better to invest in your own film than have someone else invest in it, because whoever has the money has the power; that is the way it is in Hollywood and that is the way it is in life. I realised that

I needed to have that film be a success, artistically and commercially, so I really pushed myself to make sure it would work and the audience would like it. A lot of 'arty' film-makers are alien to that concept, but I always believe the audience should like the film. If you don't want them to like it, why show it and if you don't want to show it, why make it? If they like it, you get your money back.'

Plympton recognised that he needed to market and promote his own films and learned about negotiation and the specific sales of 'rights' to his work in different markets.

Plympton: 'Guys would come up to me and say we would like to offer you $1000 to show your film on our TV station and I would say, great, not knowing if I should ask for $5000 or $10,000 or whatever. I was just grateful for the money. So I hooked up with a distributor called Eteltoons, based in New York. They marketed short animated films throughout the world and had great success with Allegro Non Tropo and other Bruno Bozzetto and Guido Manuli films. I started getting regular quarterly cheques of $15,000 strictly from foreign rights, then I would get domestic rights from MTV, Tourneé of Animation, Spike and Mike shows, and individual TV stations, and I only knew about these people from the festival circuit because they would approach me. There are always new markets, someone says "Cartoon Network" is buying shorts now, or the BBC, or someone like Atom Films comes along, which distributes on the internet, which gave me a flat fee, and helped me fund Mutant Aliens and they have the rights to sell in certain territories.'

Contexts   The Fundamentals of Animation

Popular animation festivals worldwide

Anima Mundi,
São Paulo/Rio De Janeiro, Brazil
Animac,
Lleida, Spain
Animated Encounters Festival,
Bristol, UK
Animerte Dager,
Fredrikstad, Norway
Animex International Festival of Animation,
University of Teesside, UK
Annecy: Centre International du Cinèma d'Animation,
Annecy, France
Bradford Animation Festival,
'BAF' Bradford, UK
Brisbane International Animation Festival,
Griffith University, Brisbane, Australia
Cartoons on the Bay: International Festival of TV Animation,
Positiano, Italy
Cineme International Animation Festival,
Chicago, USA
Fantoche International Animation Festival,
Baden, Switzerland
Hiroshima International Animation Festival,
Hiroshima, Japan
Holland Animation Festival: 'HAFF',
Utrecht, Holland
New York Animation Festival,
New York, USA
Norwich International Animation Festival,
'FAN' Norwich, UK
Ottawa International Animation Festival,
Ottawa, Canada
Spike and Mike's (Sick and Twisted) Festival of Animation,
Touring, USA
Zagreb World Festival of Animated Films,
Zagreb, Croatia

Festivals

Animation festivals are in many senses the life-blood of independent animation and the animation community. It is important to remember though that different festivals have different identities, some more specifically embracing individual 'auteurist' work, others prioritising commercial work in television and feature films. One need only to note Annecy's 2004 Festival in figures (see page 184) for example, to see the possible scale of international business negotiation and commercial outlets.

RAI Trade organises Cartoons on the Bay in Italy, also as a commercial platform, 'in order to sustain, in the spirit of public service that characterises RAI Italian TV and Radio Broadcasting Company, the effort of authors and producers worldwide [to] unite art to entertainment and to help buyers, TV distributors and executives, offering them a wide choice of successful and innovative products.' This then is more about economic issues and trade than it is about art and culture, although these issues can never be wholly marginalised in the consideration of appropriate, appealing and quality work in the field, whether it is for a popular audience or not.

The Fredrikstad Animerte Dager festival in Norway, however, has a much more educational, artistic and geographically sensitive stance to its operation. Practitioner, writer and historian, Gunnar Strøm shares his thoughts.

Strøm: 'Fredrikstad could offer Animerte Dager a very attractive environment. That the city's own film and media industries are in rapid growth, also gives the festival a valuable role to play beyond the festival weeks. The festival has now also been incorporated into the official arts programme for local schools. This local identity is an important and necessary building block as the festival looks towards its next ten years as the most important meeting point for animators from the Baltic and Nordic countries'.

One of the most anticipated festivals is the Ottawa International Animation Festival, whose Artistic Director, Chris Robinson, offers the following reasons why festivals are crucial to the budding professional animator.

Robinson: 'Despite the phenomenal growth of animation over the last two decades, animation festivals still remain one of the few places where independent animators can get their work shown to their peers and to a general audience.

'As such, this is an essential place for any aspiring animator to be. Not only will they see like-minded animation from all over the world, they will have an opportunity to meet their peers and share stories, ideas, develop friendships, partnerships etc. Festivals are an essential meeting place for animators – whether you want to go the indie or industry route.

'Awards are not so important in my view, but still, festivals are a place where your films are judged →

→ by your peers. It gives you some sense of where you stand, and heck, awards can help you get work/funding in the future. But even without awards, it's so hard to get accepted into festival competitions that you should be pretty pleased just to get your film shown (even if it's a non-competitive showcase). As a comparison, consider the Oscars. You need money and friends to get your film entered for consideration. In the end, the Oscar for Short Animation has maybe 300 entries. That's a far cry from the 1500 or so entries that festivals like Annecy and Ottawa receive annually. Point? Animation festivals may not get you a trip to Hollywood or TV appearance, but they are a significantly better gauge of short animation production than the Oscars.

'Festivals have this communal quality about them. It's a really special, unique opportunity (in this internet age) to sit across a table from a person from another country and talk to them.

'If you want work, festivals like Annecy and Ottawa attract industry recruiters, buyers, producers. They're good places to network and you get to travel to places you might never venture (Hiroshima, Ottawa, Annecy, Zagreb, Utrecht, Stuttgart, Brazil).

'You spend a year working alone in a darkened room, probably wondering what the hell you're doing with your life making a "cartoon" that no one will see. Well, the animation community is relatively small and intimate, and there's a dysfunctional family quality to it. Attending festivals (with or without a film) is like going to a family reunion. It can be painful and tiring, but you're with your clan, your blood, your people. You belong to something and isn't that what we all want at the end of the day? To connect with people with similar tastes and experiences?

'If you're still drooling to get an Oscar, here's the thing. If you win first prize in a category at Ottawa, Zagreb, Hiroshima or Annecy, you can skip the usual qualifications and have your film considered instantly for Oscar consideration. So there it is. What's not to like?'

Annecy 2004
Festival in figures

5300 badge holders
900 companies registered
More than **200** exhibitors
Over **100** buyers including the main purchasers for children's programmes
50 countries represented
300 journalists
500 films screened
263 films in the official selection
Screenings from **10** am to **11** pm in **6** theatres
An open-air giant screen
100,000 admissions during the week

↑ **Production shots of the set and**
→ **equipment and stills placed in sequence**
↓ **from I Woz 'Ere – Richard Coldicott**
Coldicott's avant-garde chase cartoon recalls traditional cartoon figures and gags while using the contemporary notions of installation and performance art by setting his work in an empty exhibition space.

Contexts

Sometimes it is important to think 'out of the box' in relation to where work might be placed or indeed, take place. Employment, postgraduate training, and festivals are in many senses orthodox contexts where animation can be created and find a context for broadcast or exhibition, but there are further ways to think about using animation:

– Creating animation in a non-traditional context and relating to other disciplines or performance arenas.
– Using the materials created in the process of making animation and images from the final film, as 'artworks' in their own right for display, dissemination (i.e. in educational contexts) and exhibition.
– Engaging with 'fan' cultures in the production, dissemination and appreciation of non-professional work, which gains its own 'artistic' or 'cultural' currency.

Richard Coldicott, a student animator at the Norwich School of Art and Design, UK created a film called I Woz 'Ere, ostensibly a simple chase cartoon between an enveloping black cloud and a small figure. The distinctive feature of the work was executing the film by using a large empty room and painting and affixing materials to the wall. The space itself, the images produced and the final film have a strong sense of a mix between animated film, installation and performance art.

Following on from this, art critic, Jonathan Jones' claim that 'the most radical new idea has been of video and film installation as a genre in itself, independent of cinema, while seeming to fill the absence of an alternative culture of the moving image'[3] is especially extraordinary for two reasons. Animation has always provided an alternative culture of the moving image since its inception and it is strange to think that just because avant-garde 'film' projects have been placed in a gallery by named 'artists', this somehow invalidates all the experimental works played out in animation, which have not insisted upon their cross-disciplinary credentials and their status as 'art'. Crucially, then, Coldicott's work embraces this principle, at one and the same time drawing upon the cartoon tradition, but also the conceptual idea of installation and performance art.

REFERENCES
3) Jones, J. 'The Moving Image', Turner Prize Supplement, The Guardian, November 2003, p7

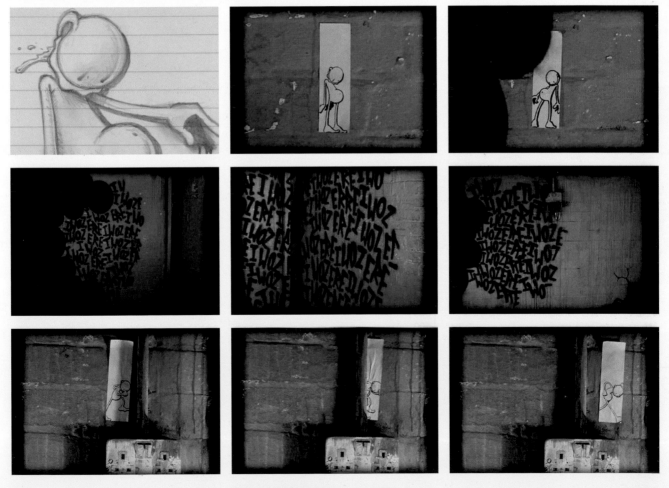

An innovative animator, again reconciling traditional practice with new exhibition opportunities, Rachel Bevan Baker has taken Coldicott's intentions further by actually placing her work in a gallery space, but even this is not of a traditional order. Her project Beaches was already different in rejecting the often highly controlled studio-bound activity of much animation practice, by animating outdoors. This 'on-site' location work produced 11 short films, funded by a Creative Scotland Award from the Scottish Arts Council. Her work was presented in a travelling gallery that toured Scotland.

While Baker has exploited the web to productive effect and the web in general has become a comparatively new professional exhibition space (see earlier examples), another way it can be used for less aspiring, but nevertheless committed animators is in its 'fan' culture, and the activities emerging from 'amateur' or 'hobbyist' practices.

One of the most notable of these is the phenomenon of Legofilms. Karin Wehn, an academic at the University of Leipzig, Germany, has been engaged in research about this aspect of animation, suggesting:

Wehn: 'This movement emerged independently in the mid-1980s and was not encouraged by Lego, but the company responded in 2000 by creating a Lego Steven Spielberg "Movie-maker" set, though it was not popular. It is a male dominated community and it has embraced the easy principles of stop-motion to create work out of materials that are resilient, limited but accessible, and iconic. At a professional level, artists such as Michel Gondry have picked up on the phenomenon; he made a pixillated Lego pop promo for The White Stripes. There are now over 312 film-makers and 600+ films on the Lego website, and it is clear that from its small beginnings with film-makers like Dave Lennie and Andy Boyer, it is growing from an amateur practice into an art form in animation'.

All progress in any art form starts with someone saying 'what if?', and then seeking to play out an idea in the most practical and efficient way possible. Experience brings growth, and investment in research more understanding and improvement. It is hoped that this book has helped encourage and support animation practice in a number of ways and that students of all ages will benefit from it, and progress the art further still.

↓ **Machinima Poster and still from Quixote's**
← **Last Dream – Ricard Gras**

Ricard Gras is both a champion of, and an artist participating in the web-based 'Machinima' movement, in which practitioners are seeking to make their own animated films by re-editing and modifying animation from games engines. He argues: 'In a time where audiences are becoming more sophisticated, Machinimators are a proof that hybrid authorship is the way to go. The days of the creative dictatorship of (linear) film and TV might be over. Audiences increasingly want to be involved actively in the creative process.'

↑ **Shots of 'The Drawing Room' travelling gallery – Rachel Bevan Baker**
The artworks were valuable in their own right and could be viewed as such, but the gallery also promoted the works exhibition on the web. Under these auspices Beaches could be seen by a wholly different audience, and one that might not have been reached under other circumstances.

↓ **Stills from a Lego walk cycle – Legofilms**
Legofilms successfully illustrates how a fan culture can create a work that is both simple and sophisticated, offering an opportunity for the beginner and the advanced practitioner to make an accessible stop-motion animation. Every technique, however, has its walk cycle!

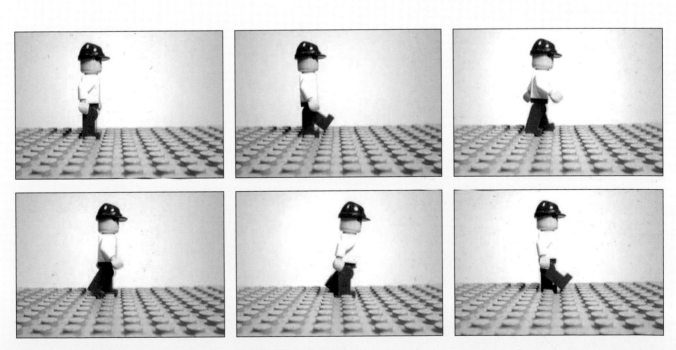

Appendix

Bibliography and Webography

Animation History

Adams T. R. (1991)
Tom and Jerry : 50 Years of Cat and Mouse
(New York : Crescent Books)
Adamson J. (1974)
Tex Avery : King of Cartoons
(New York : Da Capo)
Barrier. M (1999)
**Hollywood Cartoons: American Animation in the
Golden Age**
(New York & Oxford : OUP)
Beck J. (1994)
The 50 Greatest Cartoons
(Atlanta : Turner Publishing Co)
Beck J. (2004)
Animation Art
(London : Flame Tree Publishing)
Bendazzi G. (1994)
Cartoons: 100 Years of Cartoon Animation
(London : John Libbey)
Brion P. (1990)
**Tom and Jerry: The Definitive Guide to their Animated
Adventures**
(New York : Crown)
Bruce Holman L. (1975)
Puppet Animation in the Cinema: History and Technique
(Cranberry : New Jersey)
Cabarga L. (1988)
The Fleischer Story
(New York : Da Capo)
Crafton D. (1993)
Before Mickey: The Animated Film 1898–1928
(Chicago : University of Chicago Press)
Eliot M. (1994)
Walt Disney: Hollywood's Dark Prince
(London : Andre Deutch)
Frierson M. (1993)
Clay Animation: American Highlights 1908–Present
(New York : Twayne)
Holliss R. & Sibley B. (1988)
The Disney Studio Story
(New York : Crown)
Kenner H. (1994)
Chuck Jones: A Flurry Of Drawings
(Berkeley : Univ. of California Press)
Maltin L. (1987)
**Of Mice and Magic: A History of American Animated
Cartoons**
(New York : New American Library)
Manvell R. (1980)
**Art and Animation: The Story of Halas and Batchelor
Animation Studio 1940–1980**
(Keynsham : Clive Farrow)
Merritt R. & Kaufman J.B. (1993)
Walt in Wonderland: The Silent Films of Walt Disney
(Baltimore & Maryland : John Hopkins University Press)

Sandler K. (ed) (1998)
**Reading the Rabbit: Explorations in Warner Bros.
Animation**
(New Brunswick : Rutgers University Press)

Art and Animation

Allan R. (1999)
Walt Disney and Europe,
(London : John Libbey)
Faber L & Walters H. (2004)
Animation Unlimited; Innovative Short Films Since 1940
(London : Laurence King Publishing)
Finch C. (1988)
**The Art of Walt Disney: From Mickey Mouse to Magic
Kingdoms**
(New York : Portland House)
Gravett P. (2004)
Manga: Sixty Years of Japanese Comics
(London : Laurence King Publishing)
Jones C. (1990)
Chuck Amuck
(London : Simon & Schuster)
Jones C. (1996)
Chuck Reducks
(New York : Time Warner)
McCarthy H. (2002)
Hayao Miyazaki: Master of Japanese Animation
(Berkeley, California : Stone Bridge Press)
Pointon M. (ed) (1995)
**Art History [Cartoon: Caricature: Animation], Vol 18 No 1,
March 1995**
Russett R & Starr C. (1988)
Experimental Animation: Origins of a New Art
(New York : Da Capo)
Wells P. (1997) (ed)
Art and Animation
(London : Academy Group/John Wiley)
Wiedemann J. (ed) (2005)
Animation Now!
(London & Los Angeles:Taschen)
Withrow S. (2003)
Toon Art
(Lewes : Ilex)

Animation Studies

Bell E. et al (Eds) (1995)
**From Mouse to Mermaid: The Politics of Film, Gender
and Culture**
(Bloomington & Indianapolis : Indiana University Press)
Brophy P. (Ed) (1994)
Kaboom!: Explosive Animation from Japan and America
(Sydney : Museum of Contemporary Art)
Bryman A. (1995)
Disney and His Worlds
(London & New York : Routledge)

Byrne E. & McQuillan M. (1999)
Deconstructing Disney
(London & Sterling : Pluto Press)
Canemaker J. (Ed) (1988)
Storytelling in Animation
(Los Angeles : AFI)
Cholodenko A. (Ed) (1991)
The Illusion of Life
(Sydney : Power/AFC)
Cohen K. (1997)
Forbidden Animation
(Jefferson, North Carolina & London : McFarland & Co)
Furniss M. (1998)
Art in Motion: Animation Aesthetics
(London & Montrouge : John Libbey)
Hames P. (Ed) (1995)
Dark Alchemy: The Films of Jan Svankmajer
(Trowbridge : Flicks Books)
Kanfer S. (1997)
**Serious Business: The Art and Commerce of Animation
in America from Betty Boop to Toy Story**
(New York : Scribner)
Klein N. (1993)
**Seven Minutes: The Life and Death of the American
Cartoon**
(New York : Verso)
Lent J. (Ed) (2001)
Animation in Asia and the Pacific
(London & Paris : John Libbey)
Leslie E. (2002)
**Hollywood Flatlands: Animation, Critical Theory and the
Avant Garde**
(London & New York : Verso)
Levi A. (1996)
**Samurai from Outer Space: Understanding Japanese
Animation**
(Chicago & La Salle : Open Court/Carus)
Leyda J. (Ed) (1988)
Eisenstein on Disney
(London : Methuen)
Midhat A. (2004)
Animation and Realism
(Zagreb : Croatian Film Club Association)
Napier S. (2001)
Animé : From Akira to Princess Mononoke
(New York : Palgrave)
Peary G. & Peary D. (Eds) (1980)
The American Animated Cartoon
(New York : Dutton)
Pilling J. (Ed) (1984)
**That's Not All Folks: A Primer in Cartoonal
Knowledge**
(London : BFI).
Pilling J. (Ed) (1997)
A Reader In Animation Studies
(London : John Libbey)
Pilling J. (Ed) (1992)
Women and Animation: A Compendium
(London : BFI)

Sandler K. (ed) (1998)
Reading the Rabbit: Explorations in Warner Bros. Animation
(New Brunswick : Rutgers University Press)
Smoodin E. (1993)
Animating Culture: Hollywood Cartoons from the Sound Era
(Oxford : Roundhouse Publishing)
Smoodin E. (Ed) (1994)
Disney Discourse: Producing the Magic Kingdom
(London & New York : Routledge/AFI)
Stabile C & Harrison M. (eds) (2003)
Prime Time Animation
(London & New York : Routledge)
Wasko J. (2001)
Understanding Disney
(Cambridge & Malden : Polity Press)
Watts S. (1997)
The Magic Kingdom: Walt Disney and the American Way of Life
(New York : Houghton Mifflin)
Wells P. (1996)
Around the World in Animation
(London : BFI/MOMI Education)
Wells P. (1998)
Understanding Animation
(London & New York : Routledge)
Wells P. (2001)
'Art of the Impossible' from G. Andrew, 'Film: The Critics' Choice'
(London : Aurum Books)
Wells P (2002)
Animation : Genre and Authorship
(London : Wallflower Press)
Wells P. (2002)
Animation and America,
(Edinburgh : Edinburgh University Press)

Animation Practice

Blair P. (1995),
Cartoon Animation,
(Laguna Hills, Ca : Walter Foster Publishing)
Beckerman H. (2004)
Animation; The Whole Story
(New York : Allworth Press)
Birn J. (2000),
Digital Lighting and Rendering
(Berkeley, Ca : New Riders Press)
Corsaro S & Parrott C. J. (2004)
Hollywood 2D Digital Animation
(New York : Thompson Delmar Learning)
Culhane S. (1988)
Animation: From Script to Screen
(London : Columbus Books)
Demers O. (2001)
Digital Texturing and Painting
(Berkeley, Ca : New Riders Press)
Gardner G. (2001)
Gardner's Storyboard Sketchbook
(Washington, New York & London : GGC Publishing)
Gardner G. (2002)
Computer Graphics and Animation: History, Careers, Expert Advice
(Washington, New York & London : GGC Publishing)
Hart C. (1997)
How to Draw Animation
(New York : Watson-Guptill Publications)
Hooks E. (2000)
Acting for Animators
(Portsmouth, NH : Heinemann)
Horton A. (1998)
Laughing Out Loud : Writing the Comedy Centred Screenplay (Los Angeles : University of California Press)

Johnson O & Thomas F. (1981)
The Illusion of Life
(New York : Abbeville Press)
Kerlow, I.V. (2003)
The Art of 3D Computer Animation and Effects
(New York : John Wiley & Sons)
Kuperberg M. (2001)
Guide to Computer Animation
(Boston & Oxford : Focal Press)
Laybourne K. (1998)
The Animation Book
(Three Rivers MI : Three Rivers Press)
Lord P & Sibley B. (1999)
Cracking Animation: The Aardman Book of 3D Animation
(London : Thames & Hudson)
McKee R. (1999),
Story: Substance, Structure, Style and the Principles of Screenwriting
(London : Methuen)
Meglin N. (2001)
Humorous Illustration
(New York : Watson-Guptill Publications)
Missal S. (2004)
Exploring Drawing For Animation
(New York : Thomson Delmar Learning)
Neuwirth A. (2003)
Makin' Toons: Inside the Most Popular Animated TV Shows & Movies
(New York : Allworth Press)
Patmore C. (2003)
The Complete Animation Course
(London : Thames & Hudson)
Pilling J. (2001)
2D and Beyond
(Hove & Crans Pes-Celigny : RotoVision)
Ratner P. (2004)
Mastering 3D Animation
(New York : Allworth Press)
Ratner P. (2003)
3D Human Modeling and Animation
(New York : John Wiley & Sons)
Roberts S. (2004)
Character Animation in 3D
(Boston & Oxford : Focal Press)
Scott J. (2003)
How to Write for Animation
(Woodstock & New York : Overlook Press)
Segar L. (1990),
Creating Unforgettable Characters
(New York : Henry Holt & Co)
Shaw S. (2003)
Stop Motion: Crafts for Model Animation
(Boston & Oxford : Focal Press)
Simon M. (2000)
Storyboards
(Boston & Oxford : Focal Press)
Simon M. (2003)
Producing Independent 2D Character Animation
(Boston & Oxford : Focal Press)
Subotnick S. (2003)
Animation in the Home Digital Studio
(Boston & Oxford : Focal Press)
Taylor R. (1996)
The Encyclopaedia of Animation Techniques
(Boston & Oxford : Focal Press)
Tumminello W. (2003)
Exploring Storyboarding
(Boston &Oxford : Focal Press)
Webber M. (2000)
Gardner's Guide to Animation Scriptwriting
(Washington, New York & London : GGC Publishing)
Webber M. (2002)
Gardner's Guide to Feature Animation Writing
(Washington, New York & London : GGC Publishing)

White T. (1999)
The Animator's Workbook
(New York : Watson-Guptill Publications)
Whitaker H & Halas J. (2002)
Timing for Animation
(Boston & Oxford : Focal Press)
Williams .R (2001)
The Animator's Survival Kit
(London & Boston : Faber & Faber)
Winder C & Dowlatabadi Z. (2001)
Producing Animation
(Boston & Oxford : Focal Press)

Animation Reference

Clements J & McCarthy H. (2001)
The Animé Encyclopaedia
(Berkeley, California : Stone Bridge Press)
Edera B. (1977)
Full Length Animated Feature Films
(London & New York : Focal Press)
Grant J. (2001)
Masters of Animation
(London : Batsford)
Halas J. (1987)
Masters of Animation
(London : BBC Books)
Hoffer T. (1981)
Animation : A Reference Guide
(Westport : Greenwood)
McCarthy H. (1993)
Animé!: A Beginner's Guide to Japanese Animation
(London : Titan)
McCarthy H. (1996)
The Animé Movie Guide
(London : Titan)
McCarthy H. & Clements J. (1998)
The Erotic Animé Movie Guide
(London : Titan)

Students can also consult the Animation Journal, Animator, Animation, American Cinematographer, Sight and Sound, Screen and Film History for relevant articles. There are also other titles purely dedicated to feature films, studio output etc., which may also prove useful. Don't forget that books on comedy often have some information on cartoons etc. Similarly 'readers' of essays about television etc. often have animation-related discussions.

Recommended Websites

Animation World Network : www.awn.com
Animation Resources: www.toonhub.com
Animation Links: www.public.iastate.edu/~rllew/animelinks.html
Origins of American Animation:
http://memory.loc.gov/ammem/oahtml/oahome.html
National Film Board of Canada: www.nfb.ca
US Animated Cartoons Reference: www.toonarific.com
UK Animated Cartoons Reference: www.toonhound.com
Cartoon News and Discussion: http://forum.bcdb.com/

Many of the suggested texts also have lists of links for all aspects of animation from practice tutorials to festivals to archives to research and study.

Index

Index

Credits and Acknowledgements

I would like to thank the following people for their help in the creation of this book:

Brian Morris, Natalia Price-Cabrera and Renee Last at AVA Publishing SA, without whom this book would never have existed. Dan Moscrop at Them Design for all his hard work and beautiful design solution. Suzie Hanna, for work over and beyond the call of duty – many thanks! Andy 'Harry Tuttle' Chong and Ben Dolman, for unfailing technical and moral support – always appreciated. All my colleagues at Loughborough University School of Art and Design, Kerry Drumm, for helping out quickly at the start, Simone Potter (BFI), Jackie Leonard (Brownbag Films), AJ Read (Cosgrove Hall), Richard Barnett (Slinky Pictures), Tina Ohnmacht (FilmAkademie), Avrim Katzman (Sheridan College), Chris Williams (University of Teesside), Mark Walsh (PIXAR), Helen Cohen (SilverFox), Graham Ralph (SilverFox), Sarah Woolway (BBC), Andy McNamara (BBC), Siddiqa Juma (Aladdin Media), Dick Arnall (Animate!), Hélène Tanguay (NFBC), Shelley Page (DreamworksSKG), Louise Fletcher (Blue Sky Resumes), Mette Peters (Netherlands Institute of Animated Film), and of course, all the talented named contributors within the text.

Courtesy of the British Film Institute: p6–7 **The Incredibles** Disney/PIXAR; p19 **Jurassic Park** Amblin Entertainment; p31 **Cow on the Frontier; The Fly;** p36–37 **Monsters Inc.;** p43 **Creature Comforts;** p44 **The Hand;** p77 **Creature Comforts;** p78 **The Lord of the Rings;** p79 **The Iron Giant;** p88 **Humourous Phases of Funny Faces; Gertie the Dinosaur;** p90 **Steamboat Willie; Fritz the Cat;** p91 **Akira;** p100 **Tale of the Fox;** p101 **King Kong;** p102 **Jason and the Argonauts;** p103 **Chicken Run;** p122–123 **Tron;** p124 **Terminator 2; The Last Starfighter;** p147 **Pas de Deux; Colour Box.**

p8, 125, 126–127, 128, 176–9 Images courtesy of Seed Animation; p9 Images courtesy of Paul Wollenzien; p10–11 Images courtesy of Martin Pullen; p15–17 Images courtesy of Paul Driessen; p19, 31, 32, 184 Images courtesy of Peter Parr; p20–23 Images courtesy of Minoru Maeda; p24–25 Images courtesy of Joanna Quinn; p28–29 Images courtesy of Mario Minichiello; p28–30 Images courtesy of Gerald Scarfe; p33, 104, 105 Images courtesy of Barry Purves; p34–35 Images courtesy of Sennep/Williams Murray Hamm; p38–39, 40, 41, 42, 44 Images courtesy of Hibbert Ralph; p45, 180 Images courtesy of Bill Plympton; p46–49, 174 Images © Aladdin Media 2004; p50–52 Images courtesy of Brian Larkins; p53–55 Images courtesy of Cathal Gaffney; p56–59 Images © Shynola/Interscope Records; p60–63, 92–95 Images courtesy of Aril Johnson; p64–65 Images courtesy of Suzie Hanna; p67–69 Images courtesy of Chris Shepherd and Maria Manton; p69 Image courtesy of DFGW/COI/Maria Manton/Chris Shepherd; p70–71, 77 Images courtesy of John Grace and An Vrombaut; p72–73, 140–141 Images courtesy of Giuliano Parodi; p74–75 Images courtesy of Christa Moesker; p76 Images © BBC Photo Library; p80–81, 96 Images courtesy of Animation Workshop (John Grace, Andy Chong and Brian Larkins); p82–85 Images courtesy of Martin Pullen; p89, 147 Images courtesy of the Halas and Batchelor Collection Ltd.; p96 Images courtesy of Eadweard Muybridge; p97 Image courtesy of the Department of Transport/COI/Darcy/Maria Manton/Chris Shepherd; p98–99 Images courtesy of Koji Yamamura; p106 Images courtesy of Timon Dowdeswell; p108–109 Images courtesy of George Pal; p110–113, 162 Images courtesy of Aaron Wood and Kerry Drumm; p114–115 Images courtesy of Dave Johnson; p116 Images © Cosgrove Hall Films Ltd. 2003; p117, 118–119, 121 Images courtesy of Michael Frierson; p129 Images courtesy of Marc Craste; p130–131 Images courtesy of Chris Landreth; p132–133 Images courtesy of Andy McNamara; p134–139 Images courtesy of Anja Perl and Max Stolzenberg; p142 Images courtesy of Gareth Howell; p143–145 Images courtesy of Adam Phillips; p148–150 Images courtesy of Elizabeth Hobbs; p151 Images courtesy of Suzie Hanna and Hayley Winter; p152–155 Images courtesy of Maureen Selwood; p156–157, 189 Images courtesy of Rachel Bevan Baker; p158–159 Images courtesy of Hee Holmen; p163–165 Images courtesy of Studio AKA (Marc Craste, Philip Hunt and Nic Greaves); p166–167, 179, 180 Images courtesy of Michal Pfeffer and Uri Kranot; p168 Image © Create TV & Film Ltd. 2004; p169 Image courtesy of Cosgrove Hall. DangerMouse is a registered trademark of FremantleMedia Ltd. Based on the FremantleMedia television programme DangerMouse © 1981 Cosgrove Hall Productions Ltd. Licensed by FremantleMedia Licensing Worldwide www.fremantlemedia.com; p170–171 Images courtesy of Aardman Animation; p172–173 Images courtesy of Blue Sky Resumes; p175 Images courtesy of Brown Bag Films; p177 Images courtesy of Steve May; p178–179 Images courtesy of Aaron Bradbury and Chris Gooch; p183 Images courtesy of Holly Rumble; p186–187 Images courtesy of Richard Coldicott; p188 Images courtesy of Ricard Gras; p189 Images courtesy of Legofilms.